M000305503

Praise for
transformative

"This book is both powerful and practical. It's a masterclass in how to turn your company into a market leader."

Josh Linkner, five-time tech entrepreneur, *New York Times* bestselling author, and venture capital investor

"William Kilmer has distilled his successful track record as an investor, founder, and executive into powerful lessons for operating in today's economy that every leader will benefit from. This is a must-read book."

John "JG" Chirapurath, Chief Marketing and Solutions Officer of SAP

"Creating a transformative company is hard work, but how to do it shouldn't be a mystery. Kilmer helps leaders think through their opportunities and key challenges, and develop a plan for success in a straightforward, practical way."

Matt Desch, CEO of Iridium Communications

"To disrupt an industry and become a market leader requires transformation, not just of your business, but of your culture. In this book, technologist, operator, strategist, and venture investor William Kilmer shows you how to create an organization capable of game-changing success."

Whitney Johnson, CEO of Disruption Advisors and *Wall Street Journal* bestselling author of *Smart Growth: How to Grow Your People to Grow Your Company*

"Organizations need new strategies to navigate the ever-accelerating pace of innovation. The concepts in this book will challenge you to rethink your market and change the way you lead your organization."

Timothy Chou, Chairman of the Alchemist Accelerator, Stanford lecturer, and former President of Oracle on Demand

"Weaving innovation principles and strategies, William Kilmer provides an innovative framework for transformative change to create a customer-centered, capabilities-driven organization. *Transformative* is a must-read for today's business leaders, CEOs, and boards."

Saleema Vellani, Founder and CEO of Ripple Impact and author of *Innovation Starts With I*

"The ultimate outcome of innovation is value. It's easy to get wide-eyed over sexy products and big promises, but unless organizations focus on the outcomes they deliver to customers, their efforts will always fall short. In *Transformative*, William outlines the blueprint every leader yearns for to rethink their business, transform their industry, and build a strategy based on an innovator's mindset."

Carla Johnson, Innovation Architect, speaker, and bestselling author of *RE:Think Innovation*

"*Transformative* should be in every executive's e-reader or sitting on their desk as a dog-eared playbook. This is a must-read roadmap for driving business success as we approach the technical and political disruptions of the next decade."

Mark Testoni, former CEO of SAP NS2

transformative

www.amplifypublishing.com

Transformative: Build a Game-changing Strategy,
Retool Your Organization, Innovate to Win

©2023 William Kilmer. All Rights Reserved. No part of this publication may be reproduced, stored in a retrieval system or transmitted in any form by any means electronic, mechanical, or photocopying, recording or otherwise without the permission of the author.

For more information, please contact:
Amplify Publishing, an imprint of Amplify Publishing Group
620 Herndon Parkway, Suite 320
Herndon, VA 20170
info@amplifypublishing.com

Library of Congress Control Number: 2022901176

CPSIA Code: PRV0622A

ISBN-13: 978-1-63755-033-5

Printed in the United States

To my wife, whose encouragement, sacrifice, and guidance made this possible.

transformative

Build a game-changing strategy
Retool your organization
Innovate to win

william kilmer

amplify
an Imprint of Amplify Publishing Group

Contents

Section I

The Challenge
to Be Transformative

Chapter 1

Walking Back through the Door

Why shouldn't you and I walk out the door, come back, and do it ourselves?

Andy Grove, former CEO, Intel Corporation

By 1985, the writing on the wall was undeniably clear for Intel: the company was in trouble. Intel Corporation—founded just seventeen years before by industry legends and former Fairchild Semiconductor employees Robert Noyce, Gordon Moore, and Andy Grove—was fighting for its life in the memory chip market.

For nearly two decades, Intel rode the wave of Moore's law, Gordon Moore's famous 1965 prediction that the number of transistors in a given area of a semiconductor would double every eighteen to twenty-four months.[1] This growth in transistor density led to cheaper and more powerful integrated circuits, creating more ways for electronics companies to use Intel's semiconductor technology. One of the promising initial markets was in dynamic random-access memory (DRAM), and the company had built that business for nearly two decades. In the 1970s, Intel became the dominant supplier of DRAM chips to electronics manufacturers around the world. However, by the early 1980s, Japanese competitors had gained significant ground.

At first, companies such as Hitachi, Fujitsu, and Nippon Electric filled excess demand as secondary suppliers. However, these competitors, funded with low-cost debt backed by the Japanese government, increased memory density and quality while building the manufacturing capacity to significantly drive down memory costs. Soon they attained a 40 percent share of the memory chip market and had the momentum behind them to unseat Intel and dominate the market.

Intel tried to protect its market position by creating niche memory products and developing more differentiated features. But it was impossible to differentiate themselves in a market that was focused squarely on price competition. They also looked for other markets for their transistor technology, and one, microprocessors for computers like the early IBM personal computers (PCs), had started to show potential. Intel saw such microprocessors as an emerging market, but because it represented a low-volume business, the company continued to focus on its core business of selling memory chips.

In 1984, Intel's DRAM business took a dramatic downward turn. A sharp decrease in demand for memory exposed just how badly Intel was losing market share and margin to its high-volume, high-quality, and low-cost Japanese competitors. Intel's management team created multiple proposals to solve its dilemma. Using an established and rigorous debating practice the company had cultivated called "constructive confrontation," the group evaluated various options to regain Intel's low-cost position by building scale—a costly approach—or to further differentiate their products in niche applications, a strategy that had so far proven unsuccessful. The management team also considered a third radical proposal to leave the memory business altogether, but that proposal failed to generate consensus.

After seemingly endless discussions and reviews of options, the ever-insightful Andy Grove approached the issue from a different perspective. Looking out from the windows of the Intel headquarters building in Santa Clara to the California's Great America theme park a few blocks away in the distance, Grove turned to CEO Gordon Moore and asked, "If we got kicked out and the board brought in a new CEO, what do you think he would do?"

Moore straightforwardly acknowledged the obvious. "He would get us out of memories," was his reply. This confirmed Grove's perspective. "Why shouldn't you and I walk out the door," he responded, "come back, and do it ourselves?"[2]

As was typical in the action-oriented Intel culture, senior executives Moore, Noyce, and Grove drafted an ambitious plan to exit the memory market and immediately put it into motion. The next few years were painful as the company lost revenue, laid off thousands of employees, and endured several uncertain and unprofitable years. Intel remained dedicated to developing a significant microprocessor business for the personal computer (PC) market. In 1982, it launched the Intel 80286, or 286 processor, a sixteen-bit CPU (central processing unit) used in IBM's new PC/AT personal computers. Soon after, other manufacturers launched PCs that copied the IBM PC architecture and used the same Intel chip. This accelerated Intel's microprocessor business.

Learning from their experience in the memory market, Intel's leaders set out to create an ambitious strategy that would change the nature of competition in this new market. Betting on the new market opportunity in computer microprocessors, they designed a standard computer architecture featuring Intel's processors at the very center. They provided this new architecture to any interested computer manufacturer as the blueprint for building PCs. They also cultivated a hardware and software ecosystem of other companies that optimized their products for Intel-based processors. This instantly made any design lacking the Intel chip inferior. Further, they created world-leading manufacturing plants with the capacity and processes to maintain the highest performance and lowest cost. No one would ever again undercut Intel's standard of performance to cost.

Then, to ensure that they would compete on their own terms, the company took the unprecedented step of licensing its designs to competitors, setting them up as secondary suppliers. This had two effects. First, it gave computer manufacturers like IBM an assurance that there would always be a backup supply of CPUs if Intel ever had manufacturing problems. Just as critical, it put the competition in the back seat, always dependent on Intel's designs for their innovation and limiting their manufacturing scale.

Finally, they did what no other semiconductor vendor had ever done by investing in branding. Intel started marketed directly to end users and paid the PC manufacturers to advertise the Intel brand. This gave customers confidence that buying a PC branded with the Intel logo was a safe bet and, in the process, created one the world's best-known companies. This move forever changed the way businesses and consumers evaluated and purchased computers. The customer outcome went from buying new technology with uncertainty to buying with confidence so long as "Intel Inside" was stamped on the outside. By owning the computer design, encouraging software vendors to support their processors, and advertising to get end users to ask for Intel by name, the company had transformed the semiconductor market around themselves and ensured lasting advantages.

As a result, Intel became one of the most successful technology companies of all time, dominating the microprocessor market with as much as an 80 percent market share over the ensuing years while growing revenue from $1.6 billion in 1984 to over $60 billion today.

As a former manager at Intel who joined the company nearly fifteen years later, I have always admired Intel's transformative success. The company had faced an existential threat that most companies wouldn't have survived. Nevertheless, the management team successfully backed the company out of its existing market and pivoted to another before it was too late. The result was a much stronger and more competitive company that dominated its industry.

What always impressed me more about Intel's success story is its deliberate and intentional focus on recasting its position in the emerging PC microprocessor market, a move that would change the industry forever. Intel's story is not just about a successful company turnaround, as impressive as that may be. The most compelling feature of its transformation is how the company's leadership learned from their experience in the memory market to alter their new market so they would hold a long-term advantage. This started by creating unique value for their customers, both PC manufacturers and the end computer consumer, and was enhanced by building new capabilities for the organization and rethinking the industry structure to put themselves at its center. Intel succeeded by transforming an emerging semiconductor industry to play by their rules that resulted in more than 35 years of market-leading success.

As a technology company executive, venture capital investor, board director, consultant, and adviser, I have long been fascinated with the intersection of innovation and strategy. I have a particular interest in organizations like Intel that have been able to create innovation strategies that completely transform the markets they enter.

In addition to running two companies as CEO, I have been a venture investor and board member on many others and twice stepped into an interim CEO role to manage an organization's transition to a new strategy and new leadership. This book combines my personal experiences from the hundreds of organizations I have reviewed, advised, or led, with years of personal research into some of the world's most successful and transformative companies.

As I have had the privilege of meeting with and working with management teams from hundreds of organizations, I have come to see that leadership teams almost universally struggle with three fundamental elements of their business. Specifically, how to:

1. Create a product or service that is uniquely differentiated and valuable to the customer.
2. Define and execute a strategy to reach a market leadership position, including the right goals and actions to achieve it.
3. Cultivate an agile organization that can thrive through a constantly shifting business environment.

Despite the importance of these foundational elements, the leaders at many organizations don't put in the effort to answer them. When they try, they often focus on product innovation as the primary source of differentiation and competitive advantage, essentially mistaking product innovation for strategy. This is understandable at the early stages of the company when an organization seeks product-market fit. However, it often results in a continuous focus on innovating features and function without a clear strategy. The result is a product that is different without being differentiated and a failure to create real long-term advantage.

The type of transformative change that organizations seek isn't accomplished with great innovative technology alone. While product or technical innovation is essential, focusing on it exclusively will not produce the type of change that shakes up market leadership and rebalances the odds in a company's favor.

In fact, great technological innovation often leads to complacency in strategy. This is particularly true when companies enter an existing market with a new product or service. For example, a few years ago, I met with a CEO seeking venture investment in his company. Despite entering an existing market, he believed he would succeed because his software platform was a generation better than the competition, providing new features that others didn't. Undoubtedly, his company had a very good product and had already shown some signs of success with growing revenue and a few high-profile customers. When I asked him about his innovation strategy and what would be different for customers who considered his solution, he continually referenced the differentiating features, which, although good, were unlikely to persuade large numbers of customers his solution was that much better.

Likewise, when I asked about his go-to-market strategy, he responded that his competition had already written the playbook for him. All he needed to do was to raise the investment capital to copy what they were doing, hiring the same profile of salespeople and building the same marketing campaigns to catch up. His attitude was that with his better technology, he would be successful while following a playbook written largely by his competition.

By insisting on playing by the existing rules, this CEO accepted that the only variable he had to work with was new and better product features. Doing so failed to give him many options.

Many organizations fall into this same trap. To me, it is often the difference between seeking product innovation and business innovation. Business innovation starts with a new result for the customer but goes much further. It requires rewriting the rules, enabling the organization to generate something that is both unique and defensible in a way that others find hard to copy. Bain and Company calls this a "full-potential transformation," defined as "a cross-functional effort to alter the financial, operational, and *strategic trajectory* of the business, with a stated goal of *producing game-changing results* [emphasis mine]."[3] This is the essence of how companies innovate to win. Yet, despite its success, practice shows that leaders rarely consider this approach.

Organizations are led by people, and people are constrained by their biases. Particularly detrimental are cognitive biases—errors in thinking that affect our judgment and decisions. They include overconfidence in our capabilities and a common misbelief that any new technology that a company creates is "disruptive" and, therefore, will be successful. Perhaps most damaging of all is an anchoring bias, simply an everyday acceptance of the industry status quo, which negatively impacts an organization's strategic decision-making.[4] We don't create the opportunity as Intel did, to walk out the door and think about how we would re-enter our industry.

There are significant advantages in a more comprehensive view of where and how to innovate, which can help overcome these biases and increase the potential for a successful outcome. One of the best ways to do this is to look for patterns of how other companies have successfully produced industry-changing results and distill what has made them successful. My aim is to analyze and illuminate these patterns so that organizations can build their own innovation strategy from the ground up.

Objective

This book aims to provide organizational leaders with the tools and structure they need to create their own game-changing innovation strategy, that is, to be transformative. It reaches beyond technological innovation to focus on how organizations innovate customer outcomes, create larger market opportunities, and build a more innovative organization. Because these techniques are applicable to both startups and large organizations aiming to reshape markets, I hope to do more than help readers understand how transformative companies operate. My goal is to help you break out of existing biases to rethink and reconstruct a broad-based innovation strategy no matter your market and industry.

This book originates from my personal experience as an investor, advisor, and CEO. Moreover, it stems from years of research into companies that have successfully entered and transformed existing markets by developing category-creating solutions that expanded market opportunities, and toppled industry leaders by changing the nature of how to compete.

In this book, we will focus on the methods they use to accomplish it, emphasizing three key areas for a new approach to innovation that will help you to:

Build a game-changing innovation strategy for success. We will start by understanding the steps needed to create truly game-changing innovation, starting with shifting focus to innovating customer outcomes. Then we will discuss the best ways to align and invest in the right core capabilities and rethink and reframe your industry structure to create a lasting advantage.

Innovate to win. Finally, we'll discuss how to create a market that you can win by attracting new customers, creating more profitable business models, and leveraging scale accelerators to shift and expand current markets.

Retool your organization for success. To increase your chance of success, I will present ways you can retool your organization to become more engaged, innovative, and agile. This includes developing a sense of intentionality that defines upfront what winning looks like and engages your team in the process. Then, I'll explain how to build a strong organizational culture that feeds your strategy and increases innovation and adaptation. We'll also discuss how to use a challenge-setting loop to accelerate your competitive clock speed.

From a broad perspective, the concept of innovating to win means taking a broader perspective that includes not just building innovative products but game-changers and becoming an organization that engages in true business innovation. To reinforce this concept, I focus on research into nearly two dozen transformative companies that have succeeded in either changing well-established markets with dominant competitors or consolidating highly fragmented market opportunities. Although you already may be familiar with many of these companies, including Amazon, Apple, Dell, Ford, IKEA, Lyft, Uber, and Walmart, my analysis will show them to you in a different light. I will reveal how these companies have followed key transformative principles so you can see how to apply them.

While this book focuses on a framework of principles that have led to winning innovation for other organizations, it doesn't hand you a generic formula for success in which you plug in the variables. Although it demonstrates the patterns in how these companies have been successful, I have taken pains to avoid being formulaic or prescriptive. There is no strategic absolute, no single way to win in a particular industry, and no checklist that will guarantee an organization's success. Success comes from orienting yourself in your industry, creating a vision, setting objectives, defining and executing a strategy, and then going about a continual process of investment, experimentation, and adjustment to achieve it. The intent of this book is to provide you with the tools to think differently about the possibilities of change and highlight questions to help leaders focus on how they can creatively incorporate the lessons from these companies into their own organizations.

This book is divided into four sections and twelve chapters as follows:

Section I sets the groundwork with a discussion of how to create an innovation strategy, one that will establish the pattern of transformative innovation that companies can pursue to change markets and create long-term advantages. Chapter 2 explains the dangers of overreliance on technical innovation alone, the concept of creating a strategy for innovating to win, and the need for pursuing broader courses of innovation. Chapter 3 focuses on the first two principles of the transformative framework, explaining how to create a transformative advantage by focusing on developing category-creating solutions and identifying opportunities for game-changing structural innovation.

Section II begins a detailed exploration of the transformative framework by focusing on outcome and structural innovation. Chapter 4 dives into how companies change their focus to improving customer outcomes to enable category-creating solutions that shift markets and attract new customers. Chapters 5 and 6 review the critical elements of structural innovation: aligning and investing in distinct company capabilities and rethinking and reframing industry structure.

Section III spotlights how to innovate to win by introducing six scale accelerators that help organizations create a path to market leadership. Chapter 7 details the capabilities of democratizing and simplifying. Chapter 8 covers the approach of new customers first and how to build new business models. Chapter 9 highlights the power of the practices of recombining and rule breaking.

Section IV focuses on how transformative leaders can retool their organizations to maintain innovation and ongoing advantage. Chapter 10 examines how organizations can use intentionality to create engagement and pursue innovation that is both unique and valuable. Chapter 11 describes using organizational culture to feed strategy and sustain ongoing advantage. Finally, chapter 12 concludes by highlighting how to become a challenge-setting organization, explaining how to set a clock speed of defining new challenges to deliver results.

Walking Back through the Door

I started this book with Intel's transformative story because even though the choice to leave the memory market now seems so obviously right, it was difficult for the Intel leadership team to make at the time. I joined Intel through an acquisition 15 years after its decisive move into the PC semiconductor market. The company was successfully riding its upward momentum of growth that came from that decision. During that time, I saw the strength of Intel's senior leadership team firsthand. I had worked on several projects that I presented to Andy Grove and quickly learned that he was as decisive as he was intelligent and perceptive. Robert Noyce and Gordon Moore were similarly brilliant and bold. Yet, at the time, even with the facts before them, the three had difficulty making that rational decision to make change happen. When they finally took the decisive step, it so irreversibly transformed the dynamics of how the semiconductor industry worked to their sustained advantage that it's hard to imagine it any other way.

I believe that many organizations today face an even more significant leadership challenge than Intel faced: developing the momentum and the strategy for change, even when the need for change isn't immediately apparent. This is the greatest challenge all organizations face: to walk out the door and come back through again with a fresh perspective on how to create something better and the determination to achieve it.

Fortunately, most organizational leaders already recognize that change is necessary. A survey found that 94 percent of Fortune 500 CEOs agreed with the statement "My company will change more in the next five years than it has in the last five years."[5] The question for most organizations is how to develop the momentum to walk back in the front door with a viable and winning innovation plan.

I designed this book to help readers understand how to build that momentum and take advantage of the opportunity to do something truly transformative. It includes time-tested and industry-proven actions that have successfully helped both incumbents and new market entrants rethink customer outcomes, align their organization's capabilities, and use change to their advantage.

In many ways, business leaders are accepting that the very foundations of their industry are changing in the coming years. They now need to decide if those changes will occur because of what they do or happen *to* them based on the actions of competitors and new entrants. I will teach you the tools to walk back through that door and create something transformative.

Chapter 2

A Framework for Transformative Change

Transformation is perhaps the most overused term in business. Often, companies apply it loosely—too loosely—to any form of change, however minor or routine.

McKinsey Report

Organizational leaders are more confident than ever in their ability to create technology to disrupt markets and lead their company to success. Belief in technological innovation as the primary reason why companies succeed or fail creates a confidence bubble that limits organizations' ability to execute a broad-based innovation strategy. Transformative companies create category-redefining solutions that open new market opportunities and enable distinct company advantages. The transformative framework defined in this book helps organizations understand how they can more broadly think about enabling their organization to innovate to win.

A Lesson from GE

In the fall of 2017, General Electric CEO Jeffrey Immelt had a message to deliver, and he couldn't have chosen a more prestigious platform through which to tell it. *Harvard Business Review* allowed the outgoing CEO to write his own swan song on how he had transformed GE into a digital powerhouse. But behind the scenes, the story was already unraveling.

Immelt had just announced his retirement after 16 years as CEO of the conglomerate. Now the magazine's front cover featured a lead article from the outgoing CEO and Harvard alumnus, promising to take readers "Inside GE's Transformation." Immelt told his own story of how he had remade GE, leading the multinational conglomerate of 300,000 employees through a digital transformation and sharing what he had learned about how "to lead a giant organization through massive changes."[1]

Immelt led readers through six lessons of change management at GE. Under his leadership in 2013, the venerable 125-year-old company embarked on a companywide transformation effort. Focused on redeveloping itself as a technology company, it invested billions shifting the organization, its products, and employees into the digital future. GE Digital, an internal group with the mandate of running as a profit center, had even started selling its services as transformation consultants to outside businesses.

Formerly the epitome of a big industrial company, GE moved quickly to reposition itself as a new "digital industrial company." In 2013, the company promoted Predix, its analytics software platform, as the new operating system for the digital industrial market, a core element of its strategy. By 2014, after its first in a series of acquisitions, the company announced it would achieve more than $1 billion in revenue from 40 different industrial Internet of Things (IoT) projects, claiming that Predix now powered the industrial Internet. The next year, GE Digital became a separate business unit with Predix App Factory positioned as the platform that would allow companies to create digital industrial applications in just weeks. Jeff Immelt claimed that GE was on track to become a "top 10 software company" and that it would reach $10 billion in software revenue by 2020.

GE had invested more than $4 billion in digital transformation over six years, including doubling its research and development budget. It spent billions more on an acquisition strategy to build out its technology profile.[2] The results of GE's transformation efforts, however, failed to live up to expectations or achieve its technology portfolio's overhyped and overpromised goals. In 2020, GE's software business, while laudable, is barely one-tenth of the size it had previously projected.

The problems went far beyond the state of GE Digital. During that same period, the company's revenue fell from $147 billion in 2013 to $120 billion in 2019. Both earnings per share and dividends dropped, and the company's debt burden swelled by almost $80 billion. It fell from number eight on the Fortune 500 list in 2013 to twenty-first in 2019.

This rapid decline led to widespread fallout; for the company fallout, CEO Immelt, the CFO, the head of the largest business unit, and half of the board exited within 10 months. In late 2017, the company announced a layoff of more than 12,000 employees. *Fortune* magazine published an article in 2018 entitled, "What the Hell Happened at GE?" in which it stated, "Few corporate meltdowns have been as swift and dramatic as General Electric's over the past eighteen months."[3]

The GE Digital group has now reported a year-over-year revenue decline. The outlook for Predix, once heralded as the analytics software that would power the industrial Internet, became less ambitious. While it achieved over $500 million in revenue, the company scaled back dramatically into a set of software tools for developing new applications. General Electric cut GE Digital's budget by more than $400 million, and in 2019, the company considered selling it off. Then GE chose the low-key path of spinning Predix off into a separate company as a subsidiary of GE. Overall, underperformance resulted in tens of thousands of layoffs and a share price drop from $27 per share at the start of its digital transformation to just above $6 per share at the time of this writing.

The issues with General Electric's transformation efforts are complex, including organizational reporting structure, the conflicting requirement for the GE Digital business to focus on both growth and short-term profits, product delays, and technical challenges. However, one of the most critical stumbling blocks was corporate leadership's attitude that by simply mixing in some technology, it could reinvent the company. As Alex Moazed wrote in *Inc. Magazine*: "GE Software and GE Digital were set up for failure... True digital transformation is about rethinking your current business model for the 21st century. The process is not just about adding technology to the existing model. Most companies do the latter, because doing the former is extremely difficult."[4]

GE's assumption that blending in new technology would lead it to ride the digital transformation wave obscured the more significant innovation opportunities that could have ultimately led to success. But it's not that GE is a poorly run organization. In fact, the point is that GE failed *despite* being a well-run organization. But like many companies, large and small, GE made the mistake of thinking it could rely on investments in technology alone to drive real innovation.

Aren't technology and innovation the same thing? Not quite. New technology is part of innovation, but it is only one part. True, we have never had more significant opportunities to use technology to innovate the way we run businesses, reach customers, and create solutions that produce new market opportunities. But technology is only one part of the bigger equation of innovation.

Most companies achieve less-than-desirable results from their innovation efforts. A 2019 study by McKinsey found that an astounding 94 percent of executives are dissatisfied with their company's innovation performance.[5]

Missing real innovation opportunities is costly at best and catastrophic at worst. And if GE, one of the world's best-managed companies, could fail at creating real innovation, you can imagine how easy it is for other organizations to do the same.

In this book, we'll identify how to unlock the full potential of transformative innovation. But first, let's explore some common traps organizations face today that block them from their real innovative potential.

The Rise of Technological Optimism

Innovation has always offered both promise and frustration. It's difficult, and results are inconsistent. Despite that, organizations are focusing on technological innovation more than ever, and leaders are more optimistic about the prospect of technology changing their businesses to an even greater extent. For proof, you just need to peer into the executive suites of large organizations around the world.

A KPMG study of CEOs revealed that 60 percent of those in the corner office reported that "disruptive technology," a term that has described the number one existential threat to their business for the last 25 years, is now seen as their company's number one opportunity.[6]

To understand the significance of this change, you only need to look back at how quickly attitudes have changed. In 2017, top CEOs were asked about what concerns they had for their businesses' growth prospects. Some 70 percent expressed angst over the *negative* impact of the pace and speed of technical change—a concern that had been steadily rising year after year. Then, in 2018, the number of concerned CEOs suddenly plummeted to just 38 percent. It fell again in 2019 with only 28 percent of CEOs expressing the same concern about disruptive technology, a decrease of 60 percent in just two years.[7] It seems leaders everywhere began to feel that technology was now, finally, on their side.

Disruption Is Dead. Long Live Disruption.

The recent about-face to optimism is a dramatic one for organizational leaders who have long perceived disruptive innovation as a threat. For more than two decades, since Harvard Business School professor Clayton Christensen introduced the concept in his book, *The Innovator's Dilemma*, disruptive innovation has been a major corporate cause for concern.

Disruption, as Dr. Christensen outlined, involves a unique set of circumstances by which companies can use inferior and less expensive technology to find a foothold with unserved and underserved customers and then improve that technology to eventually dominate the market. With Christensen's compelling examples from the steel, disk drive, and construction equipment industries, it was evident that this pattern of disruption was more than theory. Disruption became an overnight buzzword with headlines and news stories carrying the concept everywhere, portending the imminent doom of every incumbent company in nearly every industry. Journalists, authors, and consultants began to find real examples of disruption every day, compounding the concerns that disruption was the new existential threat. Highlighting its profound influence, the *Economist* dubbed the theory of disruptive innovation "the most influential business idea of the early 21st century."[8]

Worldwide, leaders became convinced that disruptive innovation was happening everywhere. Observers overgeneralized the term, using it to describe *any* technology that was novel or new, whether it fit Christensen's definition or not.

At the same time, two other trends fueled the fires of corporate concern. The first was the unprecedented growth of both the rate of innovation and the acceleration of technological adoption. In particular, the last twenty years has seen multiple obvious and impactful technological advancements, including mass adoption of the personal computer, the Internet, mobile phones, smartphones, cloud computing and applications, location-based services, improvements in data analytics, and artificial intelligence.

Not only has the pace of new technology accelerated, but we have also adopted those technologies at a faster pace. As MIT's Michael DeGusta pointed out, it took 39 years for telephones to be adopted by 40 percent of households in the US, but just four years for smartphones to achieve that same level of adoption.[9]

Along with technology innovation and adoption, the second trend was the dramatic increase in the rate that companies were falling from industry leadership positions, notably those rapidly dropping from the ranks of the Fortune 500. In their 2001 book *Creative Destruction,* McKinsey consultants Sarah Kaplan and Richard Foster showed that while the average tenure of a company on the Fortune 500 had previously been thirty years, it had subsequently decreased by 40 percent to a mere eighteen years.[10]

To even casual observers, the conclusion was clear: as new technology rose dramatically and was adopted quickly, upstarts used it to topple incumbents from their market leadership positions faster than ever before, resulting in massive disruption of large corporations by technology-fueled startups. This convergence of these two trends drove the fear of disruption into the corner offices and boardrooms of nearly every major corporation, spreading concern that technological change would overtake them and the next new tech upstart would upend their industry. Large companies responded by investigating any new company for the scent of disruptive technology while venture capital firms invested billions in startups, looking for the next disruptive opportunity.

Over time, the panic over disruption has changed to optimism. Armed with the knowledge that disruption happens less often than expected and that companies have more time to anticipate and defend against it than expected, companies are more confident than ever about the prospects of technical innovation.[11] Driven by the hope of digital transformation, nearly two-thirds of CEOs feel that they have harnessed innovation and their company is leading in actively disrupting their industry rather than waiting to be disrupted.[12] According to International Data Corp., companies are now spending at record levels to adopt new digital technologies and hire those with technical skills to implement them. IDC estimates that in 2018 alone, corporations spent $1.3 trillion on digital transformation and predicts that number will rise to $2.1 trillion by 2021, a 60 percent increase in just three years.[13]

Digital transformation leverages a broad range of technologies to improve process automation and customer solutions. It includes data analytics, machine learning, artificial intelligence, the Internet of Things, drones, robotics, blockchain, and virtual and augmented reality, which collectively could unlock more than $100 trillion in new market value over the next decade.[14] These digital catalysts intersect with existing products and services, creating the potential for new levels of profitability while creating new market opportunities in traditionally nontechnical industries.

The Technology Effect

These digital catalyst technologies are now typically available as on-demand services sold in standard "off-the-shelf" packaging. As a result, organizations adopt and scale them as needed. Experts at IDC predicted that 60 percent of organizations worldwide would be in the process of implementing an organization-wide digital transformation by 2020.[15] Enthusiastic about the impact on their business, some 80 percent of organizations say that digital transformation is at or near the top of their boardroom agendas.[16] Furthermore, 25 percent of CEOs say that they are actively and personally engaged in their organization's digital transformation.[17]

As a result of this focus on acquiring new digital technology and disrupting their industry, most leaders feeling confident about their new-found technology position. According to Gartner, 41 percent of CEOs now think of themselves as "innovation pioneers," a self-assessment that has increased by half since 2013. Tellingly, another 37 percent see themselves as "fast followers" who are quick to adopt innovation. Only 22 percent classify their organization as anything other than at or near the bleeding edge of technical innovation.[18]

It's understandable why organizational leaders focus on technical leadership. For more than 25 years, they have become attuned to disruptive innovation, accustomed to rapid technological change, and witnessed the constantly changing ascent and descent of organizations from the pinnacle of industry leadership. Preoccupation with disruptive technology's impact on an organization's fate has produced a curious and verifiable result: these leaders assign technological innovation the central role in determining a company's success or failure.

Researchers including Brent Clark call this "the technology effect." It comes from our "constant exposure to advances in technology [that] has resulted in an implicit association between technology and success that has conditioned decision-makers to be overly optimistic about the potential for technology to drive successful outcomes."[19]

A result of the technology effect is associating technology as the primary predictor of a company's success. The technology effect stems from our own personal interactions with technology and our positive association with successful technology companies. The largest five companies in the world by market capitalization are now tech companies, and we frequently use their products. Because of survivor bias, we tend to forget company failures and only become aware of successful organizations when they emerge as rapidly growing or dominant companies in a market (e.g., Uber, Airbnb, Facebook). Using this small data set of successful technology companies, we form a positive bias toward them, forgetting about the thousands of companies that failed before them or ascribing their failures to "bad technology."

The danger of the technology effect is that it produces an overly simplistic, one-dimensional view of how companies succeed and fail. It encourages overinvestment in technological innovation and underinvestment in other improvements and strategies, limiting possible paths to success. Academic research by Brent Clark et al. on the technology effect shows that given a choice between investing in technology or nontechnology options, our bias is toward investing in technology. Interestingly, this research shows that the less familiar we are with the technology, the more powerful is our positive bias. We actually believe *more* in the ability of technology to lead to success when we understand it *less.*

As a venture investor, advisor, and former executive in the technology industry, I have seen this technology effect in action. Executives at nearly every company I meet with believe they will succeed because their company offers "next-generation technology." This bias is understandable, at least partly because technology is so tangible and identifiable and because startups spend so much time and capital on technological innovation. Most of the companies I work with start off by spending between 50–90 percent of their budgets on research and development early on, so of course they are certain that technology must be a determining factor of success. This belief is often fueled by investors who encourage companies to "go deep" on the technology to build value.

A recent example of the consequence of the technology effect is the former tech giant Yahoo. While Yahoo was once a darling of the dot-com era, attempts to revive it under CEO Marissa Meyer from 2012 to 2017 focused on bringing new technology into the company as quickly as possible. During that time, Meyer and Yahoo's board proceeded to spend an estimated $2.3 billion acquiring 53 companies to build a portfolio of products to bring the company out of its market slump. They attempted to create a "MaVeNS" (mobile, video, native advertising, and social) portfolio of technology that covered nearly every major tech trend in the market. This was heralded as the tech turnaround effort of the decade. But, in the end, their aggressive acquisition strategy only steepened Yahoo's decline. Yahoo had difficulty piecing together various pieces of technology into a viable solution. The acquired companies often withered under Yahoo management. Despite efforts to create a new tech conglomerate, the company shrunk until it fell from the S&P 500 in 2017, and its core business was sold to Verizon for $4.5 billion, or just 4 percent of its peak historical market cap.

Trapped in a Confidence Bubble

Despite the optimism for, and record spending on, digital transformation, the results have not been incredibly encouraging. Digital transformation success has been elusive for most companies. According to separate estimates by both McKinsey and the Harvard Business School professor and change-management guru John Kotter, 70 percent of organizational transformations either fail to be completed or do not reach their intended goals.[20] The impact of digital transformation efforts on the company's profitability is even worse. Bain Consulting found that digital transformation efforts fully reach or exceed their expected results only 5 percent of the time. In 75 percent of cases, their actions actually diluted company performance and resulted in sub-optimal results.[21]

Regrettably, the enthusiasm surrounding technological innovation often produces less innovative outcomes and poorer results, creating a confidence bubble for many organizations. Life in the confidence bubble leads organizations to ignore new sources of competition and dismiss forward-thinking opportunities for innovation that are not steeped in technology while over-estimating the value of new technology.[22]

Although incumbent organizations embrace technological innovation faster than ever to thwart the efforts of their competitors, the confidence bubble presents a barrier to achieving lasting results because of three critical errors. Each precludes companies from identifying more broad-based opportunities to create truly transformative change. They are a failure to create better customer outcomes, the innovation paradox, and the error of self-limitation.

The Failure to Create Better Customer Outcomes

The first error is leaders' failure to focus their innovation effort on defining and creating new and better customer outcomes. Customer outcome is defined as the extent to which the customer reaches their objectives or solve their problems. As we'll see in the next chapter, successfully changing customer outcomes is what initiates market change.

Failure to focus on outcomes is nothing new. For decades, the most significant error in pursuing "disruptive technology" was the failure to recognize the very reason why disruption worked. Where disruptive innovation has been successful, it has always created new customer outcomes, serving those that were unserved or underserved by existing solutions. Disruptive innovation provided a different and better result to those for whom the previous outcome wasn't satisfactory, and then improved over time to produce a universally better outcome accepted by the larger market.

The current digital transformation wave brings even more challenges for many organizations as it presents them with two possible paths to pursue: maximizing company operational efficiencies or improving customer outcomes. They are not two mutually exclusive paths, but regrettably, the latter option isn't a priority for most companies, which are generally focused on the near-term returns of using digital transformation technologies to achieve efficiencies instead.

When IDC asked business leaders what "digital business" meant to their organizations, the top two responses were enabling worker productivity and managing business performance, reflecting a corporate focus on increasing operational efficiencies. Not even half included improving their solutions for the customer as an objective.[23]

Even more troubling is that companies may not know enough about their customers to prioritize improving customer outcomes. In a study by British Telecom (BT), over a third of CEOs identified that the single biggest issue impeding their digital transformation strategy was a "lack of insight into what customers want and need."[24]

It's easy to see why organizations look at operational improvements as a priority. Efforts to improve productivity, operational efficiencies, and processes are effective because they bring profitable, near-term, tangible returns. These types of returns involve all the existing known qualities of current customers and markets. They are easier to envision, manage, and measure and are more palatable for boards of directors and shareholders who want improved profitability and higher returns on assets. They are a safer bet.

Whenever an organization fails to use innovation to change the customer outcome, it leaves the door open for others to "out-innovate" them with a new and better result. It's noteworthy that none of the long list of companies that have been unseated from their leadership position, such as Eastman Kodak, Blockbuster Video, Borders, Nokia, Blackberry (Research in Motion), Kmart, and Sun Microsystems, were "out-innovated" by a competitor who just did the same thing better and more efficiently. In each of these cases, as in hundreds of others, the incumbent was replaced by a competitor that produced a new and more compelling customer outcome.

The Innovation Paradox

The second fatal error of the confidence bubble is an innovation paradox: presuming that technology innovation improves a company's differentiated advantage when it may often actually lower it. Real differentiation, as I describe later, is a result of producing something that is valuable, unique, and difficult for others to copy.

In the case of digital transformation, the adoption of digital catalyst technologies is leading companies to believe they are creating uniqueness when, in fact, they are often losing it. This innovation paradox occurs as companies increasingly emphasize technological innovation as the basis of their company's success. However, because of the global scarcity of tech talent and the easy availability of "off the shelf" digital technology, organizations often turn toward the same sources of innovation as everyone else. This decreases the likelihood that their technological innovation will be unique.

Exacerbated by today's global dearth in technical talent, organizations' pursuit of digital transformation has created a booming industry of consultants, outsourcing firms, cloud services, and software code repositories. The big consulting firms McKinsey, Bain, and Boston Consulting Group are experiencing double-digit growth driven by thriving digital transformation practices. GitHub—the leading repository of sharable, reusable software code driving software development—has grown to over 100 million repositories of code as companies share software for their digital projects. In 2018, Microsoft acquired GitHub for $7.5 billion to fuel further distribution of shared software.

This shared pool of technical talent, cloud resources, and software has helped facilitate many digital transformation efforts. But organizations now utilize the same strategy and business transformation consultants; tap identical consulting firms to design, develop, and test web and mobile applications; use the same cloud computing partners; leverage code from the same open-source repositories; develop algorithms on standard machine learning platforms; and so on. In doing so, they accelerate digital transformation but dilute the value of technological innovation as a differentiator.

Strategies that can be copied, internal processes that are developed by consultants, and new technology that can come from code repositories or banks of contract software developers create, at best, a transitory advantage. Ultimately, unless companies can achieve unique and sustainable outcomes provided in their own unique way, digital transformation and other "disruptive" innovations will not offer real and lasting advantages.

The Error of Self-Limitation

Finally, the third and most damaging critical error of the confidence bubble is how companies limit themselves in finding and acquiring other ways to innovate and create value in a unique and sustainable way.

Distraction and enchantment with technological innovation is a factor. A 2017 survey by Innosight found that 81 percent of leaders believe that the top management in their organization sometimes or often doesn't pay attention to new growth products and ideas.[25]

As shocking as it is that over eight in ten businesses deliberately or inadvertently limit their innovation potential and ignore real opportunities, the foundation of this error is in all of us. It stems from an anchoring bias, which occurs when our decisions become "anchored" to information that we have previously received or observed, limiting us to a predetermined conclusion. While anchoring bias is often associated with purchasing decisions based on an initial price, it also occurs when we accept norms based on our initial receipt of information.

Organizational leaders are subject to anchoring bias when they take the norms, rules, practices, and structure of their industry as a given, placing limitations on their ability to consider broader approaches to innovation that break down industry norms.

The pursuit of innovative business models is a perfect example. There is ample evidence that truly transformative innovation is nearly always accompanied by the introduction of a uniquely new business model. Almost every instance of substantive industry change, from the Apple iPhone to Netflix and from Airbnb to Walmart, has involved a shift away from a traditional business model to a new one.

Today, while nearly half of CEOs believe that their own business model is under threat of change, most do not consider making changes themselves to their models.[26] An Innosight study of top leaders, 72 percent responded that they were investing only moderately, not investing at all, or were unsure of their own company's investment and efforts to innovate their business model.[27]

Business model innovation is a powerful tool for change, as I describe in chapter 8, but it is only one example of how organizations miss an opportunity to innovate. Business leaders do not consider many other behaviors and norms of industry structure as innovation options because organizations are anchored in what they currently see as standard practice in the market.

The Path to a Game-Changing Innovation Strategy

An article in MIT's *Sloan Management Review* summed up the current state of innovation for most organizations today: "Few companies are responding appropriately to digital disruption, according to our findings. While 90 percent of companies indicated that they are engaged in some form of digitization, only 16 percent said their companies have responded with a bold strategy and at scale."[28] Another article published in *Harvard Business Review* reported that fewer than 50 percent of organizations had formed any strategy at all around innovation when looking at digital transformation.[29]

It's no surprise then that 85 percent of CEOs are dissatisfied with how effective their organization is at achieving new innovation in the first place.[30] Like many others, they believe they could be producing better results but don't know where to start on fixing the situation.

This book proposes that the solution to delivering better innovation is for organizations to move beyond the outdated concept of innovation as a technological end result and develop a broader-based and more dynamic innovation strategy that incorporates innovative thinking at all levels, from solution and company to market and even industry structure.

Strategy, as John Lewis Gaddis describes, is the way an organization aligns "potentially unlimited aspirations with necessarily limited capabilities."[31] Applying the perspective of strategy to innovation means focusing the organization on creating a set of shared and unifying goals, such as new or better customer outcomes. That, in turn, is supported by a defined set of required actions, capabilities, and resources to reach your goals. This book will help you understand how to stretch and think more broadly about what those outcomes can be and the tactics to achieve them that define innovating to win.

Such a strategy focuses companies and becomes an antidote to the free-for-all innovation efforts typically spread across research and development departments, innovation labs, digital transformation teams, corporate venturing groups, external alliances, outsourced development organizations, and other groups. It aligns the entire organization behind its customer-focused objectives.

Despite these benefits, organizations rarely take the time to articulate a strategy for innovation, instead of relying on product roadmaps and lists of new features and performance requirements to be their guide. Such roadmaps generate limited, linear innovation that can't generate game-changing results.

By contrast, an innovation strategy should lead an organization to ask the critical question of "Where can we want to take the customer?" It should then empower leaders to put all options on the table to examine new approaches to reach the desired outcome, including products and company capabilities, and how they fit within or change industry structure. The goal is to break out of conventional thinking about products and the structure of their industry to create something that is both unique and valuable to the customer, and achieve something game-changing as a result.

An innovation strategy approach serves as a check to competing objectives and activities and weeds out those that burn up valuable resources without achieving value. Further, it should invite the organization to continually think about how to maintain innovation momentum and evaluate what is working and adapt when needed.

As this book examines how organizations achieve transformative outcomes and the tools they used to achieve it, we will analyze a cross-section of companies that have achieved game-changing innovation while looking at the patterns and principles to understand how they became successful. The intention is to help you understand how you can incorporate these principles into your own innovation strategy.

Transformative Organizations: A Model for Innovating to Win

The companies reviewed in this book create bold strategies with game-changing innovation. It is these types of organizations that McKinsey found consistently provided higher returns for companies than those who limit themselves to incremental innovation efforts.[32] In their article "The Faster They Fall," Caroline Thompson and Patrick Viguerie reported that the successful business innovators who unseat incumbents and create industry change are doing so nearly twice as fast as they did thirty years ago.[33] Rising challengers are creating new solutions faster with more rapid adoption and generating new market opportunities.

This book focuses on a cohort of such companies that have achieved success through a set of common transformative principles and actions. Their actions produced better results for their customers, growing markets and creating larger opportunities while enabling them to create lasting company advantages. They are transformative organizations because each has achieved success by not only innovating new solutions, but by radically changing the markets they enter. We will see similar patterns across these organizations in rethinking customer outcomes, building company strengths and capabilities, and other game-changing moves that produce lasting market leadership and put incumbents at a disadvantage. These patterns are important because they demonstrate repeatability with a high probability of success. Together, they can help form a model for others to create an effective innovation strategy.

In chapter 1, we discussed one such company, Intel Corporation, and how they shifted the landscape for semiconductors and created a market advantage that has endured for 35 years. We'll see many others that reached similar results, including newer technology-driven companies such as Airbnb, Lyft, Netflix, Zappos, Amazon, and Apple as well as organizations in more traditional industries such as Cirque du Soleil, McDonald's, and Walmart.

There is a common pattern among these organizations of creating dramatic and market-shifting success. Key attributes they share include the following:

1. **They are market innovators.** Transformative companies are not often first movers. They are market innovators, frequently competing in existing

and well-established markets by shifting them to create playing fields where they can win. The companies in this book compete in markets as diverse as hospitality, retail, entertainment, travel, dining, and transportation. Significantly, they do not limit themselves to existing market definitions and often change or even cross over multiple existing markets to create new customer solutions. They are proficient at achieving market leadership by leveraging important scale accelerators that fast-track market growth and change.

2. **They are category creators**. Because transformative organizations produce solutions that fulfill customer needs in new and unique ways, they are category creators. In most cases, these solutions are so valuable that the new category eventually dominates the market and the category creator becomes the new market leader.

3. **They are natural advantage builders**. Finally, transformative organizations naturally knock down existing barriers to entry and incumbent advantages while building new ones for themselves. They leverage the structural rigidity of the industry against itself in ways that incumbents find difficult to replicate without damaging their own position. They also concentrate efforts on how to maintain continual advantage and adapt to changing conditions in the future.

As category creators, we often note how these companies as product innovators. But they are more than that; they are business innovators. At first glance we look at them as having created the right product at the right time for the right market, but what they do is more than competing in a game of chance. When we dig deeper, we see that they altered the very nature of the solution, the industry, and what it takes to compete. This type of innovation is not a roll of the dice but a game of innovating in a way that increases their odds of success.

The Transformative Framework		
	Principles	**Key Transformative Actions**
Principle One	Game-changing innovation is founded on building different and better customer outcomes.	Change focus to the customer's objective and seek to deliver new and differentiated outcomes.
Principle Two	Structural innovation improves outcome innovation and delivers distinct strategic advantages.	Deliver critical strategic capabilities to support unique customer outcomes.
		Create market asymmetries by rethinking and reframing industry structure.
Principle Three	Markets that are expanding and transitioning are the easiest to enter and lead.	Take a market-expansion orientation and develop scale accelerators.
Principle Four	Organizational culture sustains ongoing innovation and adaptation.	Actively engage in developing intentionality, a strong organizational culture, and a challenge-setting clock speed.

Figure 2-1: The Transformative Framework

I believe you can increase those odds of success in achieving transformative outcomes by selecting the right approach. Fortunately, the transformative organizations researched in this book point the way with a common pattern that redefines value creation for their customers, opens and expands markets, and provides clear and lasting advantages for their organization. To that end, this book will focus on bringing to light four fundamental principles of transformative success and the deliberate, transformative actions companies can use to create an innovation strategy of their own. These principles, shown in figure 2-1, include the following:

Principle 1: Game-changing innovation is founded on building different and better customer outcomes. Fundamental to transformative success is a focus on developing solutions that deliver a new and unique customer outcome. These category-creating solutions change the very reason why the customer buys and starts a new competitive dynamic.

Principle 2: Structural innovation improves outcome innovation and delivers distinct strategic advantages. Companies create transformative advantage when they innovate the required company capabilities and industry structure needed to deliver the targeted customer outcome. Changing industry structure creates asymmetries, leveraging traditional incumbent strengths into disadvantages and changes the competitive dynamics of the market.

Principle 3: It is easiest to enter and lead markets that are shifting and expanding. Transformative organizations recognize that the best markets to enter are the ones they actively expand and change. They know how to take advantage of scale accelerators to promote a new-customer-first approach that aids market entry and the rapid ascent to market leadership.

Principle 4: Organizational culture sustains ongoing innovation and adaptation. Lasting transformative advantage comes from creating an organizational culture that feeds its innovation strategy and cultivating a challenge-setting organization.

In the next chapter, I will introduce questions to support exploration of these four principles that organizations can use to define and achieve a game-changing position and sustain ongoing innovation. Together, they can help leaders create a foundational path to creating their own winning innovation strategy.

There are infinite opportunities for producing better, more innovative customer outcomes when leaders are willing to break out of existing product, market, and industry structure to find new ways to deliver value. That interest in breaking out, to "walk back in the door" is the core of innovating to win. An effective innovation strategy requires creativity. It requires momentum. And it requires persistence. Yet, when it happens, the results are truly transformative.

Over the next chapters, I will begin to introduce the principles of the transformative framework, detailing how organizations create effective innovation strategies. We will start in chapter 3 by focusing on the first two principles of the framework to produce category-creating solutions through the example of one startup's dramatic transformation of a 100-year-old industry.

From Concept to Action

1. Are we overly reliant on technology as our primary competitive advantage?
2. Has technology innovation made our industry easier to enter?
3. If we were to reinvent a new way of doing business to put ourselves out of business, what would that be?
4. What digital catalysts will have an impact on our industry?
5. How could we use digital catalysts to improve customer outcomes?
6. How can new competitors counter our strengths using digital catalysts?
7. What changes can we make to improve our growth strategy?
8. Do we fall into any of the errors of the confidence bubble?

Chapter 3

Building Category-Creating Solutions

Victorious warriors win first and then go to war, while defeated warriors go to war first and then seek to win.
Sun-Tzu

Our tendency to think about markets progressing linearly limits our ability to create game-changing innovation. Successful companies break out of the linearity of traditional product trajectories to define category-creating solutions that change markets, attract new customers, and build strong competitive dynamics. The most effective way to do this is by focusing first on innovating customer outcomes, which reveals innovation options beyond the product itself and results in a change in customer priorities. Structural innovation, which includes innovating company capabilities and thinking outside the industry framework, supports and improves outcomes and reinforces advantages.

Rethinking Your Market

Consider a particular market you're familiar with, perhaps one where you currently compete, and review the various competitors, the customers they target, and how their solutions differ. Think about the way those products or services are designed, developed, and assembled. Consider where, how, and how long they are consumed and how they are disposed of, reused, or resold. Finally, think about the business models employed along with pricing, distribution, and any variations among competitors.

Now, after taking in the big picture, imagine you are in senior management of a new company looking to enter the market. It's your role to create a new product or service and an accompanying strategy that will put you in a market leadership position, giving you a tremendous advantage and competitive leverage. Where would you start? Could you envision a way to change the product or service to make it more attractive to current customers and open the market to new customers? What would you do differently from your competitors? Would you change any industry practices or structure to improve your competitive position? What would give you an advantage?

These may be tough questions to answer on the spot. However, they are answerable, and I will help you develop the skills to answer them for yourself.

Hopefully, you had some ideas about what you would do. But you probably also recognize that game-changing strategies are not necessarily easy to develop. One reason is the difficulty we have in looking beyond what we currently know and accept as the products, markets, and industries in which we are presently immersed. We spoke about this anchoring bias in chapter 2, which grounds us in accepting what we already know. The more expert we are, the more likely we will take what we already know as fixed and the less likely we are to think of alternatives. Even when we have a vision of where to go, we generally start from what we know, creating a linear perspective grounded with where we are now.

Linearity, the property of a straight line, dominates our thinking. We use it frequently in business, science, technology, the arts, even in our personal performance. It is foundational to our view of progress. Most companies track metrics for sequential improvement, often measuring efforts to improve one variable with the expectation that it will improve the performance of others. Product roadmaps start from the current product, adding features over time from today's version of the product. We can all see the future, and usually it is in a straight line.

We think of innovation in the same linear fashion. In our industry exercise above, you likely thought the right solution would be to improve the existing performance of the product or service in some way: faster, better, or more features. But those performance improvements keep the solution on an existing basis of performance, making it better but rendering only a temporary advantage.

In contrast, the most significant game-changing innovation strategies produce nonlinear innovation that puts solutions on a different track altogether. Possibly the most important takeaway from this book is this: there is greater opportunity in breaking out of traditional product and market definitions than there is in trying to follow them.

Take the fitness company Peloton as an example. Breaking traditional market boundaries, this startup created a new solution to personal fitness by combining the benefits of fitness center coaching and group classes with the convenience of superior quality at-home exercise equipment. Peloton didn't just offer a better stationary bike; they created a unique customer outcome of more engaging, impactful, and convenient workouts that became a new category of fitness. Their ability to create a new customer outcome combined with a new business model has led Peloton to over a billion dollars per year in revenue and a market capitalization of more than $13 billion.

Peloton took its inspiration from existing markets and solutions and developed something altogether different. We have a name for these types of companies that cross over market definitions to deliver unique solutions: *category creators*. Category creators defy current market definitions and often solve problems customers didn't even know existed. In this case, customers didn't usually think of the "problem" of going to the gym for their spin class until they were offered a better option of high-quality classes at home.

A solution like Peloton may seem like it was born of some epiphany, a sort of "eureka" moment of genius. Such innovation seems out of reach for most of us because we often limit our thinking in two ways. First, we tend to orient innovation around products, features, and functions, anchoring us to what already exists and limiting the scope of what we can improve. Second, we draw boundaries around innovation to keep it within the confines of markets (a group of customers), company capabilities (what organizations do well), and industries (the external structure of how the solution is delivered).

Transformative organizations are category creators that don't anchor themselves in existing solutions. Instead, they focus on redefining innovation by creating new outcomes for the customer. In the case of Peloton, they created a new outcome by upleveling—focusing on the customer's ultimate goal to be more fit. In this chapter, we'll examine how transformative companies succeed in creating outcome and structural innovation—the first two fundamental principles of the transformative framework. This will lay the groundwork for the next section when we discuss the components of creating a game-changing innovation strategy.

But first, let's start with a view of how we traditionally see markets evolve.

First Movers, Fast Followers, and Transformers

Humans naturally gravitate to structure. For good reasons, our brains are pattern recognition machines. As a result, we continuously seek to order and categorize things within the context of what we already know. Doing so gives us a sense of stability.

Pattern recognition is undoubtedly beneficial. When we see a repeated structure, we defocus on those things that fall into the natural order and put them aside to concentrate on what is different. Recognizing patterns and structure helps us to not overtax our brains. But this type of structure seeking can also hold us back when we accept things as given and assume linearity.

There is no better example of our acceptance of linearity than our view of markets and how they form and progress to maturity. We view markets as sort of fixed swim lanes, rising over time as successive waves of technology make products cheaper or more appealing with new features, developing into broader markets, and eventually peaking or declining as they become saturated.

Since the publication of *Diffusion of Innovations* in 1962 by communications professor and author Everett Rogers, we have viewed markets as progressing along a steady path that matures through the sequence of customer adoption stages as conceptualized in the adoption life cycle model shown in figure 3-1.

The orderly, smooth, predictable adoption life cycle shapes our views of how markets progress as each successive group finally finds a solution that is just better enough that they are willing to purchase it. As the first customers, innovators, and early adopters enter the market, the curve rises from the left side, growing in size as customer adoption progresses to early and late majority buyers, on through to the laggards at the right side, represented by a perfectly distributed bell curve. While the bell curve may not look quite so linear, each stage of customer adoption adds to the previous one, so that if we placed them all on top of each other sequentially, we would have a nice linear progression of adoption by the total market that goes up and to the right.

New competitors tend to build on previous solutions. This starts with first movers, those early entrants who fulfill the initial needs of early adopters and initiate markets. Research shows that first movers draw early advantages as their reward for the risk of being first to market, including getting a jump on the initial technology, early and exclusive access to the assets needed, and high switching costs for those early customers.[1]

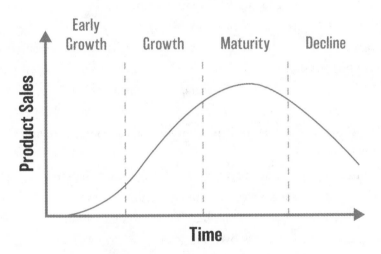

Figure 3-1: The Adoption Life Cycle

Next come fast followers who enter the market once it is established with competitive solutions. Fast followers are often some of the most successful organizations, coming to market quickly after the first movers and often overtaking them by offering improved or less costly solutions that spur greater demand. Fast followers tend to take less risky positions, largely copycatting first movers, and therefore fail less often.[2]

First movers and fast followers vie for leadership and market share, pursuing more significant innovation or greater efficiencies to maintain cost competitiveness, thus benefiting the customer with better, more cost-effective products. In this competitive dynamic, first movers and fast followers lock in on developing a structure that permits them to create their respective advantages. These competitors build in structural rigidity, solidify their capabilities, and define the industry around them to support building and delivering a standard solution over time. The resulting industry structure includes traditional operating models, business models, processes, know-how, and a supporting set of substructures, from supplier relationships to distribution, to help each company do what they do better.

As companies engage in a competitive battle, first movers and fast followers progress along a path of incremental and linear product improvements, governed by a limiting force that is anathema to innovation and competitive differentiation: regression to the mean.

Regression to mean is a statistical concept that tells us that no matter how good or bad our short-term performance, our overall performance will generally fall back in line with long-term average performance of the group. Suppose any variable rises to be higher than average at any point in time. In that case, it will likely be lower than average in the subsequent periods, regressing around an overall normal growth rate.

From a competitive standpoint, regression to the mean says that even when your organization has an occasional burst of innovative success, it will likely be followed by an innovation lull that allows the competition to catch up. It results in performance that is, over time, no better or worse than average. This continues until someone steps up to change the trajectory altogether.

The Power of Category Creators

Untethered from a specific product, performance trajectory, or market definition, transformative companies focus on solving customer problems in a way that creates a new set of valuable and distinguishing benefits. They are category creators because they step over product boundaries to deliver different and better customer outcomes.

Category creators are intriguing because they deliver something so new and unexpected. They redefine our traditional views of the product and its benefits. They alter product and market boundaries to the point that we classify them as something different.

Category creation is highly successful, but it is not a new concept. Some of the oldest companies that I describe in this book, including the Ford Motor Company, McDonald's, and Walmart, were pioneers of category creation. Each created a unique solution that redefined then-current solutions: automobiles *that every family could afford,* a *fast-food* restaurant, and a *discount* retailer. Each of these categories subsequently became a large and dominant segment of the market.

Category creators are at the heart of Joseph Schumpeter's concept of creative destruction, the process of industry destruction which produces new markets. Schumpeter notes that "it is not [perfect] competition which counts but the competition from the new commodity, the new technology, the new source of supply, *the new type of organization...*competition which commands a decisive cost or quality advantage and which strikes not at the margins of the profits and the outputs of the existing firms *but at their foundations and their very lives.*"[3]

Although they share the same pedigree with existing solutions, category creators defy contemporary classification. The new benefits they generate pull customers away from existing solutions and drive new demand from previously unserved and underserved customers.

In their groundbreaking article "Why It Pays to Be a Category Creator," Eddie Yoon and Linda Deeken highlight the fact that category creators generate a majority of market growth and profits.[4] They do this by creating new, more profitable business models to accompany the solution. In pursuit of their solution, they often cross over traditional market boundaries that had previously formed natural defenses and inhibited competition.

Category creators are not first to market, nor are they generally niche players. They are market expanders, providing significant new benefits that attract new customers and grow markets. Their course is to dominate the market or carve out a significant, new market segment. Starbucks created a massive new category for coffee consumption outside of home or traditional restaurant settings. This new consumption model enabled a new market segment and grew the coffee market with new ways to consume coffee and new customers.

Category creation often crosses over traditional market and industry swim lanes to create higher demand from new customers. European airline provider Ryanair created a new category of vacation-focused air travel, providing everything from travel to hotel and rental cars as well as destination activities. They are now the largest air carrier in Europe. Lyft and Uber created a new category for on-demand personal transportation, crossing over the markets for taxis, black car services, rental cars, and even automobile ownership, thus producing new levels of consumption. A few examples of category creators are shown in figure 3-2.

Market	First Movers and Fast Followers	Category Creator
Video Entertainment	Blockbuster, Hollywood Video, broadcast television providers	Netflix, Redbox, YouTube
Mobile Phone	Motorola, Nokia, Sony-Ericsson	Apple
Portable Media (MP3) Player	Audio Highway, Diamond Rio, Creative Labs	Apple
Personal Computers	IBM, Commodore, Compaq, HP	Dell
Personal Razors	Gillette, Schick	Dollar Shave Club
Meat Production	Tyson Foods, Pilgrim, Sanderson Farms	Beyond Meat, Impossible Burger
Fitness Center	LA Fitness, Lifetime, 24 Hour Fitness	Peloton
Hotels/Hospitality	Hilton, Marriott, Wyndham	Airbnb

Figure 3-2: Category Creators

Given that category creators have been so successful, it might be surprising that more companies don't pursue it. But category creation is not easy. It requires more than the power of customer observation. It requires creativity.

Category creation involves a common set of actions and approach to the market, resulting in a change in the way customers use the new category of product or service. Figure 3-3 shows what category creators do differently and what they don't do. Of these actions, I will focus on the two that form the foundation of the transformative framework: outcome innovation and structural innovation.

What category creators do:	What they don't do:
Create unique customer outcomes (outcome innovation)	Focus on adding more features or functionality
Cross over market swim lanes to create new markets	Act as first movers
Appeal to underserved and unserved customers	Focus exclusively on winning existing customers of competitive solutions
Derive a new set of customer benefits—often coupling previous benefits with new ones	Create incrementally more of the same benefits
Facilitate or change consumption	Maintain the same availability of consumption
Reinvent the way people think about how to use or consume	Stay within traditional product conventions
Produce a unique and defensible market position	Carve out niche markets or specialized solutions
Create clear positioning, including what they don't do	Rely on rebranding
Change how the outcome is achieved (structural innovation)	Use industry-standard approaches
Create new and accessible business models	Shift to lower prices or premium pricing models
Generate a new, broader market opportunity or a significant market segment	Fight for existing market share or create a niche product only
Cross over markets; borrow and recombine ideas	Stay in their swim lane of market or product type

Figure 3-3: Category Creation Attributes

The Basis of Category Creation

The great mathematician Archimedes asserted, "Give me a lever long enough and a fulcrum on which to place it, and I shall move the world." In a similar vein, the best way to move markets is to use as much leverage as possible. For transformative organizations, the fulcrum and lever to develop category-creating solutions are outcome innovation and structural innovation.

Together, these first two principles of the transformative framework provide the innovation leverage that shifts existing markets by changing both the solution and the structure required to create it. The alternative—the brute force method of spending the time and effort to copy and linearly improve on what exists in the market and extend it—is expensive and unattractive.

So let's look at how these two principles work together to create true business innovation.

Outcome Innovation

The first transformative principle is that game-changing innovation is grounded in changing customer outcomes. A customer outcome is defined as the extent to which a customer reaches their intended goal, or has better solved their problem, along with the resulting additional benefits.

Outcome innovation does not mean more of the same value. It is an upleveling of the outcome that provides new and different value they seek, helping the customer better accomplish their ultimate objective.

The leading indicator that you've changed the customer outcome is that they make their purchase decision based on a new and different set of purchase criteria. This changes the entire basis of competition—the reason why a customer buys one solution over another. The key is to center around innovating customer outcomes. Whitney Wolfe Herd, founder of the dating app Bumble, created a different outcome for women by challenging dating norms and empowering women to become the decision-maker. We will uncover how transformative companies find and deliver new outcomes in chapter 4.

Peloton's combination of high-quality fitness equipment and streaming or on-demand video classes delivers a new outcome because it gets the customer closer to their main objective along with all the accompanying benefits. It created new value that neither fitness centers nor fitness equipment vendors could adequately provide. Peloton upleveled the outcome of their solution to closely match the customer's actual goal. In this case, the goal is not to buy a better stationary bike; it's to become more fit, perhaps lose weight, and Peloton helps customers achieve their goals with the added value of being motivating and convenient.

Despite the iPod's beautiful design and features, Apple had only moderate success against incumbents Diamond Rio and Creative Labs when it was released in 2001. But two years later, Apple created a new category of personal music players by combining the iPod with the iTunes store, giving customers access to buy and download songs directly. This solved a significant problem of buying music and loading it on a portable device.

This produced a change of value by upleveling the outcome to achieve the customer goal to conveniently find and play the music they love. As a category creator, Apple quickly grew to dominate the market, and iPod sales rose fourfold the next year and fivefold in 2005. By 2006, five years after its release, the iPod accounted for 40 percent of Apple's revenues. The company also created a new business model that earned them billions of additional revenue in music sales.

Typically, and tellingly, one can't even compare category creators to incumbent solutions with the same purchasing criteria. Lyft, Uber, and other on-demand personal transportation services compete with other substitutable solutions such as taxis, black cars, and even rental car services, but do you compare the two under the same criteria? No. Although the use case may be the same, say to get you from the airport to your hotel, the benefits are so different that a customer doesn't evaluate the two the same way.

Outcome innovation provides an advantage in creating more options for innovation. As we will see, focusing on outcomes overcomes product myopia and presents opportunities for innovation, even when the product or service itself offers little prospect for innovation.

Some category creators use outcome innovation to solve problems or create new outcomes that the customer isn't even aware of. It results in distinct value that changes the customer's purchasing habits and decision criteria. There are enough distinct benefits in picking up a Starbucks Blonde Café Americano on the way to the office versus brewing a cup of coffee at home that Starbucks is a category creator on that basis alone.

However, by combining the morning beverage of choice with a welcoming store setting to work, socialize, or just get time away, Starbucks created that third place environment—a place outside of work or home—which produced a new customer outcome and a new model for consuming coffee.

The examples of Peloton, Apple's iPod, and Starbucks reveal an essential concept behind outcome innovation and category creation: the power of coupling. Coupling is the added value that helps the customer better reach their objective. The presence of coupling is indicated in an "and" statement of added value: quality fitness classes *and* the convenience of being at home, a beautifully designed portable audio player *and* easily purchase the music you love, great coffee *and* the third place where you can consume it while working, socializing, or escaping. Coupling is a sign of significant value add that redefines the category.

Outcome innovation is critical to transformative success, but to be truly effective and create long-term advantage, you must engage the second transformative principle: structural innovation.

Structural Innovation

While outcome innovation is easy understood, structural innovation may be less intuitive and the importance less obvious. But we'll see how transformative companies consistently leverage structural innovation to improve outcome innovation and create additional advantages.

Structural innovation focuses on creatively looking at the company's capabilities, resources, relationships, assets, knowledge, and the industry structure required to deliver a better customer outcome. It involves actively looking at changing how something is delivered to produce a better customer outcome.

There are two types of structural innovation. The first looks at innovating the internal structure of the firm, the capabilities it optimizes to achieve the intended outcome. Company capabilities are those things the company needs to do well, including the right skills, technology, processes, assets, and know-how.

The second type of structural innovation looks at how the organization aligns itself with the external structure of the industry and the norms of how things are done. External structural innovation involves challenging the standard assumptions that frame an industry, including who designs, develops, and produces the solution, the value creation activities, the way value is exchanged, suppliers, distribution, implicit and explicit market rules, and even the definition of the product or service. Both types of structural innovation require de-anchoring from industry norms and practices.

Structural innovation is essential to changing customer outcomes and altering the competitive dynamics of the market. It enables creating new advantages and overcoming incumbent strengths and barriers to entry. It often helps transformative companies leverage the rigid structure of existing markets to their advantage.

How well incumbents respond to new competitive solutions often depends on whether or not that innovation fits within the way they currently do things. If an innovative product or service still fits within the incumbents existing capabilities, business model, and source of suppliers and distribution, it is much easier for them to replicate. But when the solution goes against the industry structure and the way that incumbents deliver their current solutions, it is much harder to adjust and compete. Referring to the concept of structural innovation as "architectural innovation," strategy expert Tim Harford sums it up:

> Dominant organisations are prone to stumble when the new technology requires a new organisational structure. An innovation might be radical but, if it fits the structure that already existed, an incumbent firm has a good chance of carrying its lead from the old world to the new. An architectural innovation challenges an old organisation because it demands that the organisation remake itself. And who wants to do that?[5]

Not all category creators use structural innovation, but those that do can create a true transformative advantage. As it's easiest to see this transformative advantage through an example, I'll show you how outcome and structural innovation are used together effectively through the story of Dollar Shave Club, an upstart category creator that changed the market for men's personal grooming.

Dollar Shave Club: Transforming Men's Grooming

Dollar Shave Club transformed the billion-dollar personal grooming market, throwing big incumbents Gillette and Schick into a tailspin as they first ignored and then struggled to contend with this new competitor. What is so interesting about the Dollar Shave Club example is that it was able to create a category-changing solution even when the opportunity for product innovation was low and the traditional barriers to entry and incumbent advantages were high.

The consumer packaged goods industry has been one of the most resilient and resistant to change for many decades and with good reason. This diverse group of products—including food and beverages, clothing, and personal grooming—is dominated by big brands such as Nestlé, Procter & Gamble, Unilever, PepsiCo, and The Coca Cola Company. Incumbents are sustained by stable demand and protect themselves with massive investment in brand, marketing, product innovation, and distribution. Even markets that face a long-term shift in preferences, such as carbonated beverages, change over the course of many years, and companies are able to make adjustments and acquire smaller companies with interesting products to stay competitive.

Possibly, no one has benefited more from these protections of innovation, brand, and distribution than Gillette. Now owned by Procter & Gamble, Gillette is a 115-year-old business with near-universal distribution for men's razors—known as safety razors. Gillette has used its brand to maintain as much as 70 percent market share, dominating the list of top products in the men's razor category while maintaining premium pricing.[6]

Gillette had previously maintained a dominant share of the market based on four key advantages.

The first was product innovation. While it may not look like it at first glance, men's razors are the result of over 100 years of continuous product innovation based on large R&D investments. Gillette spent an estimated $750 million on the R&D behind its Mach3 razor alone.[7]

Excusing the pun, Gillette has been at the cutting edge of razor technology since launching its first safety razor blade in 1901. The last 50 years have been an intensive innovative fight between Gillette and Schick. For example, Gillette launched the Trac II twin-blade razor in 1971; Schick matched it shortly thereafter. Gillette added the Mach3 with a third blade in 1998; Schick countered with the four-blade Quattro in 2003, and Gillette fired back with the five-blade Fusion in 2005. The two companies introduced innovations, including flexible blades, pivoting razor heads, moisturizing strips, and vibrating handles. Supported by heavy investment in patent protection, these innovations are the cornerstone of product lock-in achieved through selling a low-cost razor handle, which generates future purchases of high-cost blades.

Manufacturing was the second advantage held by Gillette. The company manufactures its own razors, enabling direct control of new features, materials, and quality. The company manufactures from 64 locations in 27 different countries. Its high-capacity manufacturing supports very high-volume production and gross margins of as much as 60 to 70 percent.

Those product margins make it easier for Gillette to invest in its third significant advantage: marketing and brand. Gillette invests heavily in brand development and advertising. Gillette often buys some of the most expensive ad placements—especially during high-profile sporting events targeting male demographics. Gillette accounts for a significant amount of Procter & Gamble's massive ad budget, which reached $7.1 billion in 2017. In comparison, Schick's parent company, Edgewell, spent $336 million in advertising in the same year.

Gillette's fourth major advantage was its vast worldwide distribution. Ensuring repeat purchases of blades requires that they are available wherever consumers choose to purchase them, in grocery stores, pharmacy chains, and discount retailers.

These four cornerstones of advantage—product innovation, manufacturing, brand and marketing, and distribution—made Gillette one of the most profitable and best-defended consumer products for Procter & Gamble.

In 2011, a new challenger to Gillette arose from an unlikely background: a venture-backed company started by a team with no consumer goods pedigree whatsoever. That startup, Dollar Shave Club, was started by Mark Levine and Michael Dubin, who met at a party and expressed a mutual distaste for the high-prices and inconvenience of purchasing razors. Their focus was to conveniently deliver high-quality shaving products to consumers via mail for a fraction of the cost of razors sold at retail. Despite raising over $160 million in venture capital funding, Dollar Shave Club (DSC) was largely derided as an unlikely new competitor to the industry goliath, Gillette.[8]

That skepticism was valid given Gillette's overwhelming advantages. Neverthe-less, Dollar Shave Club entered the market in 2012 with an unusual marketing splash. With few resources and having raised only $1 million in funding to start, DSC launched with a YouTube video featuring founder Mike Dubin titled, "Our Blades Are F***ing Great." The video went viral and resulted in more than 12,000 orders on the first day. Offering subscription pricing and direct delivery via mail, the company skyrocketed from zero to nearly $200 million in annual-ized revenue and three million club subscribers in just over three years.

This was an earth-shattering shift in the glacially slow-moving market for men's personal grooming. In just four years, Dollar Shave Club became number two in US market share and reduced perennial competitor Schick to third place.[9] By 2015, Dollar Shave Club had grown to $152 million in revenue and was well on the way to over $200 million when Unilever acquired it in July 2016.

So how did a startup like Dollar Shave Club, starting with just $1 million in funding, disrupt the men's shaving market, and create a superior offering while rendering Gillette almost helpless from competitive response? DSC created a superior and highly leveraged position by using the fulcrum and lever of outcome and structural innovation.

Focusing on Customer Outcomes

Dollar Shave Club first focused on innovating a new customer outcome. It changed razors from a product to a service by creating a new category: the men's grooming club. First, Dollar Shave Club's service solved two immediate customer pain points: the cost of blades and their availability. A customer using a single Gillette blade per week spends over $300 per year on razor blades. Also, since blades are sold in multi-packs, the purchase price often would be $20 or more, making it a noticeable item on the grocery receipt. Dollar Shave Club's subscription was just $2 to $9 per month, a significant savings.

DSC also solved the pain point of availability. While from Gillette's perspec-tive availability begins and ends with the storefront, from the customer's point of view, availability comes down to having a sharp blade when you reach for it—provided you remembered to buy it.

Both pain points were never more evident than in the retail buying experience. As DSC CEO Mike Dubin describes it, purchasing blades requires a visit to the "razor fortress," a section of the retail store where the razors are behind lock and key, reinforcing the feeling that the blades are expensive.

Dollar Shave Club eliminated both problems with a simple low-cost monthly subscription service that invited customers to "Stop forgetting to buy those blades every month" with a membership that automatically ships the blades to the member's home. Conveniently, members can easily turn off or pause memberships at any time.

By reducing the cost and mailing blades directly to members with automatic reordering, DSC already created a new outcome for shaving customers based on four criteria: price, convenience (shipped to the customer), reduction of friction (automatic reordering), and personalization (you choose how many blades you want per month).

However, Dollar Shave Club did more than make razor blades cheaper and more convenient. Dollar Shave Club changed the customer outcome by developing a broad range of grooming products and connecting a community of like-minded men who cared about their grooming through their direct relationship with Dollar Shave Club. By sharing help, grooming tips and information to this community, they upleveled the customer outcome to make grooming easy and convenient by providing everything men needed to be well-groomed.

By offering a community, value, customized plans, the convenience of direct shipment, and reduced friction through automatic reordering, DSC created a new category in men's grooming: the men's shaving club. They altogether changed the buying criteria for customers in a way that Gillette found challenging to match.

Delivering Structural Innovation

Much of Dollar Shave Club's advantage came from the way it supported its unique customer outcome with significant structural innovation. Specifically, they completely changed the concept of what capabilities a razor company needed to compete and the external structure of how the industry typically operates.

DSC invested in a set of company capabilities that reinforced the delivery of its new customer outcome, providing the company with unique and differentiated advantages while turning Gillette's advantages into weaknesses. Those unique capabilities that gave them an advantage included:

- **Exceptional and cost-effective marketing.** DSC countered Gillette's massive marketing budgets using a nearly free social marketing presence without paying for multi-million-dollar athlete endorsement deals or expensive ad placements. Its swelling customer base became company ambassadors, influencing others to join the club.
- **Direct customer relationship management.** The company's ability to sign up and manage millions of customers directly gave it a cost-effective way to communicate, lower costs, manage demand, and shorten the product innovation cycle.
- **Data-driven customer intimacy.** Leveraging its direct customer relationship, DSC built a data analytics capability that created customer understanding and customer intimacy in a way that would make a Procter & Gamble product manager envious. Collecting data directly from the customer, DSC quickly tested and optimized offers and promotions, text messages, emails, and new products.

Similarly, Dollar Shave Club's innovative rethinking and reframing of external structure—the norms, assumptions, and written and unwritten rules—changed the field of play, generating advantages over traditional industry strengths. In particular, DSC made three critical decisions to innovate on standard industry structure and practices:

- **Outsource the razor.** DSC countered the long-held industry focus on design and manufacturing by outsourcing the design and production to a manufacturer in Korea. DSC recognized that product innovation (goodbye six blades and vibrating handles) was a losing battle and instead focused on delivering a good razor that was more than adequate for customer needs.

- **Bypass distribution.** DSC bypassed Gillette's distribution strengths by using its direct customer relationship management and analytics capabilities. Just as important, DSC decided to manage what was important (direct customer relationship and analytics) while outsourcing order fulfillment to a partner. This avoided a direct battle on Gillette's home turf of retail stores and enabled its most important structural innovation: creating a men's grooming platform.
- **Create a platform.** Finally, Dollar Shave Club used its capabilities to create an entire platform around convenient and cost-effective personal grooming products and grooming tips and information. Platforms, a hub for creating and retaining improved economic value, are a core strategy for transformative companies. Its platform moved quickly from a single razor to offering a full line of products, including shaving creams and gels, facial scrubs, shower gels, shampoo, conditioner, hair care, and even oral products. Just as important, DSC became a trusted grooming advisor through its online content.

Using its intimate customer knowledge and direct relationships, DSC innovated and developed products and quickly brought them to market. By reframing the market from a singular focus on razors to an expanded competitive playing field of men's personal grooming while developing the concept of membership in a club, Dollar Shave Club created a new category for men's grooming and reset the way companies compete. In a market where Gillette and Schick worked in monolithic product lines managed by different divisions, they couldn't easily counter the platform and club concept. Dollar Shave Club won by crossing over traditional product categories and reframing the industry's competitive requirements to its advantage.

Rather than investing to match Gillette's formidable capabilities and incrementally improve upon them, Dollar Shave Club built new company capabilities and external structural innovation that supported their outcome innovation and multiplied its advantage. Those, in turn, permitted DSC to counter or ignore many of Gillette's advantages with strengths of its own, as shown in figure 3-4.

Gillette Advantage	Dollar Shave Club Counter
Heavy spending on brand and marketing	**New advantage:** Cost-effective, social media-focused campaigns
High R&D and product innovation	**Reduced importance:** OEM design
Manufacturing in 64 locations world-wide	**Reduced importance:** Outsourcing to a Korean manufacturer
Near-universal retail distribution	**New advantage:** Direct distribution; out-sourced product fulfillment
Market research, segmentation, and broad customer understanding	**New advantage:** Analytics and the ability to experiment with new products enabled by direct customer relationships
Product technical superiority	**New advantage:** A community information platform and complete line of men's grooming products

Figure 3-4: Structural Innovation Counters Incumbent Advantages

Competing with a Category Creator

Dollar Shave Club's new category-creating solution resulted in rapid gains in the market taken mainly at the expense of Gillette, whose share of the market fell to 54 percent by 2017. That same year, five years after DSC launched their club, Gillette finally responded by reducing the price of razor cartridges by 20 percent and started providing direct subscriptions and text-by-phone ordering, but the damage was already severe.

Gillette and parent company Procter & Gamble had failed to take in the full extent of the threat early enough. In 2012, P&G's annual report to shareholders warned that "The emergence of new sales channels, such as sales made through the Internet directly to consumers, may affect customer and consumer preferences, as well as market dynamics. Failure to effectively compete in these new channels could negatively impact results." A potential change in sales distribution turned out to be a complete upending of the basis for competition.

While Dollar Shave Club could never have managed to match Gillette's strengths in branding, product innovation, manufacturing, and retail distribution, it could find game-changing results by changing the customer outcome and supporting it through structural innovation. Just four years after starting, in 2016, Dollar Shave Club was acquired by Unilever for $1 billion. At the time of the acquisition, *Fortune* magazine observed the following of DSC's improbable success:

> None of this was supposed to be possible. No company that five years ago consisted of two guys could disrupt a 115-year-old brand like Gillette that's backed by a global champion brand builder like P&G, right? Nope. The lesson for incumbents is to stop asking "Can it happen to us?" and to start asking "How will it happen to us?"[10]

Setting Game-Changing Innovation Priorities

The question "How will it happen to us?" is one that companies should ask, but even more pressing is to ask, "How can we do this ourselves?" Incumbent organizations that fail to ask themselves what new, better customer outcomes look like and set those as the goal of their innovation strategies will face formidable competition from those companies who have.

Whether you are an incumbent or challenger, the opportunity to transform markets and lead new opportunities lies before you. Starting by seeking to change customer outcomes opens far more options for innovation than improving what already exists. Combining that with structural innovation improves how customer outcomes are delivered and creates the lever and fulcrum that together achieve extraordinary results.

Sample Transformative Questions
1. How do we generate unique and more valuable customer outcomes?
Can we uplevel our focus to the customer's ultimate goal?
What existing problems we can better solve or new outcomes can we create?
What new benefits can we provide customers that will become the new basis of competition?
2. How do we best align our organization's capabilities to deliver an optimized outcome and create organizational advantage?
What capabilities are vital for us to achieve the target customer outcome?
What are the core capabilities our organization needs to differentiate ourselves?
What systems and processes do we need to manage and track to be successful?
3. How do we create market asymmetries by rethinking and reframing industry structure?
What is the accepted industry framework today? What is not necessary?
How would we change the structure of our industry to better optimize our business?
What are emerging the political, economic, social, technological, environmental, and legal trends we can take advantage of?
4. How do we innovate to win our market?
How can we break down barriers to market adoption?
What additional consumption models can we create to attract new customers and use cases?
What new business models would expand access and opportunities?
5. How can we create an organizational culture that helps us to create advantages now and adapt in the future?
How can we align our organization to improve our innovation capacity?
How can we use culture to adapt to future needs?
Can we increase the clock speed of our organization by taking a challenge-setting approach?

Figure 3-5: Transformative Questions

Together, outcome and structural innovation represent the initial innovation options companies can use to compete in a way that is game changing. Achieving them starts with a series of transformative questions shown in figure

3-5 which covers key questions organizational leaders should be asking. Each set of questions directly links to the four transformative principles that will be discussed in subsequent chapters. Following these principles will lead organizations to greater opportunities, including:

- Shifting and expanding markets;
- Generating solutions that are difficult to replicate;
- Creating new, distinct company capabilities;
- Overcoming existing entry barriers and competitive advantages;
- Turning incumbent strengths into weaknesses; and
- Creating new, natural defensive moats against competition.

Author Rashmi Bansal notes that, "An entrepreneur is one who chooses to solve old problems in new ways." Increasingly, digital transformation technologies are enabling entrepreneurial organizations to cross over market boundaries and solve problems in new ways by creating more intimate customer relationships through data.[11] These relationships will allow companies to break out of conventional market swim lanes to achieve new and better customer outcomes. In the quest for better outcomes, companies will increasingly cross over and blur formerly distinct market and industry borders, a topic discussed in chapter 6. Indeed, today nearly 60 percent of CEOs believe that their next significant competitor will come from *outside* their industry.[12]

Category creators ignore boundaries and set out with a clearly defined goal to produce something unique and valuable—the basis for any effective innovation strategy. Section II of this book focuses further on outcome and structural innovation.

From Concept to Action

1. What are the possible changes in customer outcomes we can envision?
2. If we were to start over, what would be the path we could take to create a better customer outcome?

3. Are there areas we are overinvesting in that are providing marginal returns for our solutions?

4. What capabilities would we need to provide the solution?

5. What structural innovations could we make that would change the *how* our solution is provided?

6. What do we take for granted as an industry norm—something we all accept that could change? How could it change? What impact would it have if it did change?

7. Do we have strengths that could be turned into a disadvantage by a competitor?

8. Who are potential cross-sector competitors outside our traditional industry boundaries?

9. Which potential competitors have the most incentive to step away from the traditional industry structure?

10. What possible business models could be offered to our customers that would be more attractive?

11. In what ways can we use data to understand our customers better?

12. What adjacent industries could we potentially target? How could we achieve a better outcome for those customers?

Section II

Building a
Game-Changing
Innovation Strategy

Chapter 4

Generating Unique Customer Outcomes

Every once in a while, a revolutionary product comes along that changes everything.
Steve Jobs at the 2007 iPhone launch

Transformative organizations are adept at producing category-creating solutions by delivering unique and valuable customer outcomes. Changing outcomes creates value by upleveling to help the customer reach their ultimate goal or solving new customer problems and delivering distinct benefits. Transformative companies frequently share five traits that help produce new outcomes: 1) taking full ownership of the outcome, 2) working backward, 3) flipping the script, 4) changing consumption models, and 5) mastering flow. One powerful result of changing outcomes is companies create natural defensive moats that protect them from competition.

Creating a Transformative Customer Outcome

We have already established that transformative organizations win by focusing on generating unique and valuable outcomes for their customers. This starts by envisioning and embracing the core objective of the customer—the ultimate "why?"—and involves getting them closer to their original objective or defining a new objective by solving new problems. Focusing on outcomes always leads to new and better opportunities for innovation and creates the foundation for a game-changing innovation strategy.

As we learned from chapter 3, this type of innovation leads to category-creating solutions. Category creators preserve the customer's original objective and provide compelling new value that redefines the category.

For example, when someone uses Airbnb to find accommodations, they go beyond seeking a place to stay to feel more part of the community, stay closer to a specific location, or have access to other amenities they couldn't get at a hotel. It reaches the customer's core objective with a better and different outcome.

In the first iteration of Netflix as a mail-order DVD service, what we'll call Netflix 1.0, the company still achieved the customer's foundational objective to be entertained. However Netflix delivered a different outcome by providing access to an extensive library of DVDs that customers could consume at their own pace. This had the bonus of being attractive to customers who were underserved or unserved by the traditional blockbuster-oriented video stores.

Even retailer Zappos took a new-customer-first approach to online shoe shopping. By creating a model with fast delivery, exceptional customer support, and the ability to buy and try on multiple pairs at home, they appealed to those underserved or unserved by existing online shoe retailers. They did it by replicating the in-store experience at home and accelerated the market for online shoe sales, winning over both customers who would shop online and those who previously wouldn't.

In each case, the new outcomes these companies produced were unique with benefits that set them apart. And in each case, those benefits became the new priority to win over the existing, underserved, and unserved markets.

The best opportunities are available for category creators who can shift an existing market by creating new customer outcomes. This triggers a change in customer preferences that produces a transformative shift in market momentum. Apple's entry into the smartphone market with the iPhone is a classic example of a company that shifted an existing market and expanded it further, and it's one that we will highlight later in this chapter.

The question is, how can organizations consistently produce these types of category-creating solutions? In this chapter I reveal five traits that lead organizations to develop new, category-creating solutions that produce new and better customer outcomes.

These five traits appear consistently across transformative organizations and shed light on how you can lead your organization to the same game-changing outcomes. They are consistent practices that are instilled in the very DNA of the organization. A few organizations, like Amazon, Apple, and Netflix, have mastered them to the level that they can consistently use them to create and launch new category-creating products and services.

The Five Traits of Outcome Innovators

While these five traits can be used independently with some success, trait three is central because it focuses on creating a customer outcome that switches out old priorities for new ones, known as flipping the script. The other four traits contribute to that primary goal of providing a solution that is unique with *new* benefits that are higher priority than the old. Companies that practice any of these traits will create better customer outcomes. Learning to master them all will produce solutions that are that much more impactful. So, let's run through them.

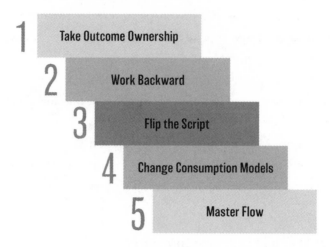

Figure 4-1: Five Traits for Changing Customer Outcomes

Trait One: They Take Full Ownership of the Customer Outcome

The first distinguishing trait among transformative companies is that they accept ownership of the customer outcome, reflected in their obsession with helping customers reach their objective and receiving the full benefits that accompany it. The first trait is so fundamental, yet most organizations don't even realize its importance.

That ownership of the customer objective causes them to widen their scope of innovation and look beyond traditional product definitions.

Apple's success as a category creator is enshrined in its practice of rethinking solutions in terms of the customer's goal or desired outcome. Former CEO Steve Jobs continually advocated a benefits-focused approach, stating, "As we have tried to come up with a strategy and a vision for Apple, it started with, 'What incredible benefits can we give the customer?' 'Where can we take the customer?'"[1]

Jobs disdained the alternative, technology-focused approach of product development, which he once derided as "Let's sit down with the engineers and figure out what awesome technology we have and then how are we going to market that."[2] A technology- or feature-focused view anchors organizations into building on what they have or what already exists and centers them on a transactional customer relationship, always seeking to add something more to get the customer to buy.

That may come naturally for Apple, but all other transformative organizations share this same trait of outcome ownership, even when they are distant from the customer. Although Uber uses contract drivers and cars, they obsess over the passenger ride experience, down to using telematics to track how smoothly drivers accelerate and brake. Even Intel, though a component manufacturer, owns the PC ecosystem from the motherboard to how peripherals interconnect, and how software is tuned for performance. Like other companies, they seek to control as much of the customer outcome as possible.

Trait Two: They Work Backward

The second trait is that category creators work backward. That is, they start from the outcome they want to achieve and work backward to understand how to deliver it.

Sam Walton sought to bring the same retail shopping experience that urban shoppers had to rural communities. That intent and defined customer outcome led Walton through a natural process of thinking about what Walmart needed to do to create that retail experience provided by stores such as Kmart and Target to a smaller community.

Walton knew that rural residents would be interested in discount retailers because they already shopped in those stores when visiting larger cities. So he started from the experience he wanted and learned to adapt it to rural needs and a business and operations model that would allow him to set prices that no one could beat. Doing so required creating improving store layouts and better merchandising, logistics, inventory management, and supplier relations. In other words, Sam Walton guided his company to work backward from their vision of the customer outcome.

Working backward is a common approach across transformative companies to achieving an intended outcome. Starting with the end in mind, they challenge themselves to a defined outcome and benefits and find a way to achieve it.

When online shoe retailer Zappos created an e-commerce site for buying shoes online, there were already many sites selling shoes over the Internet, but they represented only a small fraction of total shoe buying. Zappos CEO Tony Hsieh knew that the way to succeed at online shoe sales was to create a customer outcome that would "take the risk out of buying online."

Working backward from the intent to create a risk-free online shoe shopping experience, Zappos transformed the customer outcome to be *superior* to in-store shopping. They made it easy for customers to call them by putting their phone number on every webpage, building an incredibly helpful customer support staff, and encouraging customers to order multiple pairs of shoes with free shipping. This way, customers could order multiple pairs of shoes and try them on in their homes with different outfits. They could also take their time to decide and easily return the shoes they don't want to Zappos any time within 365 days, no questions asked, with free return shipping. Zappos, which was acquired in 2009 by Amazon for $1.2 billion, remains a pioneer in online commerce because of the principle of working backward from their desired outcome.

Working backward is at the core of Amazon's approach to new products and services, a methodology that forces product teams to focus on building something that matters to the customer. Based on the Amazon leadership principle of customer obsession, "Leaders start with the customer and work backward."[3] This forces the product champion at Amazon to focus all their attention on the customer outcome in painstaking detail.

Counter to the traditional method of starting with a product specification and detailing the product features and functions before the product is approved, Amazon's approach to developing a new product proposal is to have the product champion write an overview in the form of a press release as if they were announcing it to the public, extolling the new product's customer benefits in a one-and-a-half-page document. This is not a trivial exercise, as product leaders obsess over how to describe the benefits of their product or service in great detail. Andy Jassy, the CEO of Amazon Web Services, and his team purportedly went through 23 revisions of the press release for their new cloud service before taking it to the management team for review.

At Amazon, the press release is often accompanied by a Frequently Asked Questions (FAQ) document that highlights potential questions and answers in more detail, again from the perspective of the finished outcome. The Amazon management reads these documents together in a meeting, reviewing them, marking them up, and discussing them from the customer's perspective.

Working backward and focusing on benefits centers the team discussion on outcomes rather than features and forces the product champion to prioritize and simplify the solution, concentrating on only those most important outcomes rather than a laundry list of features that could be put into the product.

This approach also prevents the team from spending time on the topic that most often dominates new product discussions, the "How do we build it?" that focuses on whether the company has the capabilities to develop the product. Instead, the approach narrows the focus to one thing: "What is the ideal customer outcome?" Doing so lifts the limitations of what is possible and concentrates on what is needed, forcing the team to think about how to overcome the challenges to achieving it.

Focusing on the outcome also ensures that the organization finds and gains a market foothold with something that is valuable and unique. In the words of Amazon's former CEO Jeff Bezos:

> There are many advantages to a customer-centric approach, but here's the big one: customers are always beautifully, wonderfully dissatisfied, even when they report being happy and business is great. Even when they don't yet know it, customers want something better, and your desire to delight customers will drive you to invent on their behalf. No customer ever asked Amazon to create the Prime membership program [Amazon's subscription service], but it sure turns out they wanted it, and I could give you many such examples.[4]

Contrast this to linear-focused innovation that advocates adding new features or giving customers more of the same by increasing performance while delivering the same customer outcome. This approach alone leads organizations down a dead-end path of overshooting customer needs or confusing them with too many features. The result is failing to define new benefits, creating niche market applications, or complexifying the solution. Products often turn into Swiss Army knives, filled with more and more functions without producing anything of significant benefit.

In comparison, working backward allows organizations to start with a clean slate to answer the question of what is most valuable. That opens leaders up to the next trait identifying how to swap out new customer benefits for old ones in the minds of customers.

Trait Three: They Flip the Script

The third trait, flipping the script, is foundational to new category-creating solutions. Category creators deliver new benefits that are so important that customers swap out old purchasing priorities for new ones.

These new benefits form a set of purchasing criteria that are so valuable to customers that they become the basis of competition. The basis of competition is the set of differentiating features that benefit the customer to such an extent that they become the reason why customers buy a solution over the competition. The more differentiated and valuable the customer outcome, and the more a company is distinguished in its ability to provide that outcome, the higher its appeal.

Consider how hospitality provider Airbnb was able to flip the script over traditional hotels by offering rooms, homes, and other unique accommodations. Much of what customers previously prioritized when seeking accommodations through a hotel was standardization and predictability—a no-surprises proposition. For hotels, that meant uniform, sterile, and often dull rooms with standard furnishings, located in geographic regions where masses of individuals would likely be working or vacationing. But Airbnb flipped the script to make uniqueness a differentiator while highlighting the little differences and surprises that make staying in an Airbnb a different customer outcome, to give customers more of a feel of really being part of their destination. In doing so, they successfully relegated what was previously important to customers to a lower priority in place of the Airbnb local experience.

The purchase consideration matrix in figure 4-2 is a useful way to visualize customer priorities and purchase decision factors. It is also handy for planning how to change those priorities.

	Low differentiation	High differentiation
High value	Hygiene factors 1	Basis of competition 2
Low value	Standard Factors 3	Avoid 4

Figure 4-2: Purchase Consideration Matrix

The purchase consideration matrix highlights how customers prioritize their decision about which product to purchase based on two dimensions of benefits: the value it provides and the level of differentiation from other options. The combination of these two factors produces four possible categories represented by the quadrants shown in figure 4-2.

Quadrant 1 represents hygiene factors—those features that deliver important benefits to the customer but have little differentiation from one competitor's solution to another. Features in this quadrant are relatively fixed and receive little attention in competition.

Quadrant 2 represents essential features that offer both high value to the customer and the best opportunity for differentiation among competitors. This quadrant forms the basis of competition for the product or service—the bundle of factors that form the most consequential purchasing decision criteria for the buyer. It is in quadrant 2 where companies can differentiate their product or service.

Quadrant 3 includes base factors for a decision. These features are necessary to the product or service, but they offer little value to the customer and little opportunity for differentiation.

Quadrant 4 covers those features that offer a high prospect for differentiation, but they are of little value to the customer. As a result, the "nice to have" features in this quadrant are often viewed as an investment trap—you can spend a lot with little payback.

Product strategists might use the purchase consideration matrix to determine where they should invest their time and effort, improving on those existing customer priorities in quadrant 2 that carry high value and high ability to differentiate. The logical conclusion for most product managers is to continue to invest in those quadrant 2 features that deliver the most valued customer benefits. Taken to extremes, this strategy results in overinvestment in features or capabilities that eventually provide little marginal benefit for the customer. Alternatively, they may try to add so many quadrant 2 features that they create a complicated solution with no clear distinction.

By contrast, category creators flip the script by focusing on changing customer outcomes to swap out the benefits that typically come from quadrant 2 features for new ones. The resulting advantage creates a new basis of competition while shifting out the features that at one time were differentiating for competing solutions. It has the dual benefit of creating unique customer benefits while turning competitors' strengths into weaknesses.

Apple has long been a master at flipping the script, increasing the value of the benefits derived from their products to generate a new basis of competition. The iPhone created a new category of smartphones that changed the value of the mobile phone for consumers, effectively transforming the market for mobile phones into something completely new. Watching Apple's rise to dominate the market, Nokia CEO Stephen Elop correctly observed, "We didn't do anything wrong, but somehow, we lost."[5]

Given how much the mobile phone changed with the iPhone's launch in 2007, it may be challenging to recall how differently we once viewed mobile phones and how different the competitive landscape was at that time. In 2006, Nokia was the mobile phone industry's 800-pound gorilla and had just completed another year of strong growth. With over €41 billion in revenue, the Finnish phone maker held 36 percent of the mobile phone market and shipped almost twice as many phones as its next competitor, Motorola. Just as impressive was Nokia's more than 50 percent market of the smartphone market, a small market growing 30 percent per year.

Nokia and Motorola were prolifically innovative at designing and building new phones. In 2006, Nokia launched 39 new phones, including 23 in the mid-range "feature phone" and smartphone categories. Motorola launched 64 new phones that same year even as it continued to win new customers to its hit phone, the Motorola Razr, a flip phone that had sold a staggering 75 million units.

One particularly impressive new phone Nokia launched in 2007 was the N73, a full-featured smartphone. Running on the Symbian operating system, the N73 featured the ability to run multiple applications in the background simultaneously, an FM radio, and a 3.2 MB camera with a flash. It was available in both music and Internet editions, but not both in the same phone. The N73 even featured software for reading Microsoft Office and PDF documents and the ability to play a few games. Despite this compelling product, Nokia was about to face its most challenging competition from a company that had never produced a single mobile phone: Apple.

On June 29, 2007, Steve Jobs opened the iPhone launch event in San Francisco by announcing that Apple was launching three revolutionary products that day: a widescreen iPod with touch controls, a revolutionary mobile phone, and a breakthrough Internet communications device. A few minutes into the presentation, it became evident that those three products were actually just one device: the iPhone.

The iPhone launched to mixed, if not somewhat hostile, reviews. Bloomberg covered Apple's announcement, predicting the iPhone's impact would be minimal and that it would only appeal to "a few gadget freaks" and that Nokia and Motorola "haven't a care in the world."[6] Microsoft CEO Steve Balmer exclaimed, "There's no chance that the iPhone is going to get any significant market share. No chance."[7]

Perhaps the iPhone was so quickly dismissed because, despite the hype, there were really no new features in the iPhone that hadn't been available on some other phone. In fact, as shown in figure 4-3, every one of the features released with the iPhone had been previously released by Nokia at least three years before the iPhone launch.

Main iPhone Features at Launch (2007)	Phone and Time Nokia Released the Feature
Touch Screen	Nokia 7710 (2004)
Camera	Nokia 7650 (2002)
MP3 Player	Nokia 5510 (2001)
Wireless Internet	Nokia 3510 (2002)
Video	Nokia 3650 (2002)
Virtual Keyboard	Nokia 7710 (2004)

Figure 4-3: Nothing New Here: iPhone Features and Nokia Releases

Nokia aired its disdain for the iPhone publicly. Chief Strategy Officer Anssi Vanjoki openly declared that in the PC market, "Apple attracted a lot of attention at first, but they have remained a niche manufacturer. That will be their role in mobile phones as well."

Privately, Nokia scrambled to launch its first significant response later that year, the N95 smartphone. The new smartphone featured a much larger screen than the iPhone, full Internet access, a music player, and GPS navigation. In 2008, they countered again with Nokia's first touchscreen phone, the 5800, at a lower price point than the iPhone; the N97, the product designed to take the iPhone on head-to-head; and Nokia's own music store. In the end, neither product could compete with the growing momentum of the new iPhone. Nokia never recovered, and by 2012, its revenue had fallen by 40 percent to €30 billion. That same year, the company's market value had dropped to just 4 percent of its high in 2007, and it sold its handset business to Microsoft for €5.44 billion.

When writing the case history for Nokia, many would attribute its downfall to a failure to keep up with Apple's superior technological innovation. However, the iPhone was more than a technically superior product. By focusing on the right customer outcome, Apple flipped the script to reset customer priorities.

Apple accomplished this by focusing on two areas where Nokia would never adequately respond. The first was to make the basic phone features of the iPhone differentiated and valuable. Jobs stated this clearly on stage the day of the iPhone launch, saying, "We want to reinvent the phone. What's the killer app?" He answered his own question in the next breath, saying, "The killer app is making calls! It's amazing how hard it is to make calls on most phones."[8]

Apple shifted customer priorities by treating phone calls as a software application with a cleaner icon-based interface, keeping call logs, favorites, contacts, and voice mail packaged together in a single application. At the launch event, Jobs went into exquisite detail about how Apple had changed standard phone features, demonstrating how to make calls, retrieve voice mails, send texts, and sync contacts. He reviewed Apple's visual system to elevate the utility of voice mail that could be sorted like email. By the end, it was clear that what had been taken for granted as basic features on current phones had now become a significant point of differentiation. Apple elevated basic phone features to become valuable and differentiated purchase decision factors.

The second way Apple changed customer priorities was by combining three functions into one simple design. As Jobs described it, the iPhone became three devices: a widescreen iPod with touch controls, a revolutionary mobile phone, and a breakthrough Internet communications device. This brought two highly differentiated features, the iPod-based entertainment system and Internet communications, together in a way that made them highly valuable, turning the iPhone into the customer's center of entertainment, communications, and information.

Was Apple's iPhone a real transformation of the customer outcome or just a smart bundling of features that worked well together? Looking at it through the lens of the purchase decision matrix helps us understand how Apple flipped the script to create new customer priorities by using features that already existed.

	Low differentiation	High differentiation
High value	Hygiene factors 1	Basis of competition 2
Low value	Standard Factors 3	Avoid 4

Figure 4-4: Apple Changed Customer Outcomes

Viewed through the customer priority matrix figure 4-4, we can see how Apple shifted features from lesser to greater importance to create a new outcome. They did this first by elevating basic phone features, which were previously quadrant 1 hygiene factors, shifting them into quadrant 2 by developing a new level of usability and customer experience that created unique benefits for the customer. They turned basic phone features into the new "killer app."

Second, they improved several quadrant 4 features to turn them into valuable features with quadrant 2 benefits that were highly differentiated and valuable. In this case, Apple made Internet access and a built-in media player more valuable by creating a new user experience for each, shifting them to become quadrant 2 priorities.

The result was a new category of smartphones: software-driven, application-based, with integrated functions of separate special purpose phones in a single device. In turn, that shifted customer priorities away from the old purchase criteria and toward the new basis of competition—flipping the script from old buyer priorities to new.

Significantly, this shift displaced previous customer priorities that Nokia was good at—cost, phone size, hardware design, and camera resolution—to become less important and less differentiated characteristics.

Other organizations have used this concept of flipping the script by making latent features more valuable and, therefore, a priority. Fast-food giant McDonald's flipped the script to change buyer priorities by dropping quadrant 1 features found in traditional restaurant offerings such as plates and utensils, table service, and broader menus. By emphasizing new quadrant 2 purchasing criteria such as value, speed, quality, consistency, and convenience to a much higher level, they transformed the restaurant industry and created a new dining category.

Google dominated the search engine market by flipping the script with a new customer outcome of a cleaner, more accurate search engine that was simpler to use than Yahoo, which had previously dominated the market. At the time of Google's launch in 1998, Yahoo was still putting resources into being a directory of the Internet, with categories of topics and links that permitted users to browse websites. Yahoo focused on getting people to its website, where it made money as an advertiser. Google created an outcome around a cleaner, more accurate search engine and created a new business model along the way of paid search page ads. The result for Google (which evolved into the tech conglomerate Alphabet) has been two decades of search dominance with a 92 percent market share in search.[9]

As you have likely noted, flipping the script is essential to producing category-creating solutions and is a prerequisite for getting customers to prioritize new customer benefits. And one way that companies achieve that is through the next trait of mastering the ability to change the customer's model of consumption.

Trait Four: They Change Consumption Models

The fourth trait for achieving transformative outcomes is to focus on changing the consumption model, which includes where, how, and how often a solution is consumed. Few companies have been as transformative as Netflix has been in the last 20 years. There are many reasons for Netflix's success. However, one stands out: no company in any industry has changed the way customers consume their product or service more than the way Netflix has changed how we consume video entertainment. To understand this and the fourth trait of changing consumption models, let's go back to the beginning, back to 1997, to look at Netflix 1.0, the DVD rental company.

Netflix started as a true David and Goliath story: a small startup that took on billion-dollar behemoth Blockbuster Video and its rental late fees in a head-to-head competition and won. But the reality is much better and revealing when you understand that Netflix did this, not by taking on Blockbuster directly at their own game, but by offering video renters an entirely new way to consume movies. The result was an upleveling of the customer outcome, getting the customer closer to their goal of being entertained with a near-continual stream of movies. It also resulted in a change in customer benefits, which drove new purchasing priorities.

The Blockbuster movie renting experience was much worse than putting up with their late fees alone. The entire physical video rental experience, the journey customers took from rental to return, was fraught with problems as it was mainly focused on one objective: efficiently delivering the most recent blockbuster movie releases to customers.

That renter's journey started with the inconvenience of driving to the Blockbuster store to look for a specific new movie release, but it didn't end there. The search for a particular video in the store, the uncertainly of finding it, and the cost and inconvenience of returning it to the store within 24 hours to avoid a late fee were all a drag on the experience.

Many of those problems were easy to fix, and a rational approach by a competitor might be to try to solve Blockbuster's "product" issues with a better rental service—more convenience, stocking more copies of the same recent video releases, or developing a faster process to check out customers during peak times, along with notifying customers to avoid late fees. All of these would seem logical because they would fix customer problems by improving on the existing, highly valued purchase criteria that formed the basis of competition.

This type of transactional, problem-focused approach, however rational, would only provide marginal improvements to current customer outcomes.

More importantly, it would likely elicit a competitive response by Blockbuster to match or improve on those same features, with little ability to differentiate themselves in the long run.

Netflix, founded by CEO Reed Hastings in 1997, took an entirely different approach by concentrating on creating a new customer outcome that was distinctively valuable and something that Netflix could uniquely provide. As Hastings explains it himself, "It's possible to totally misunderstand Netflix. Some people think of us as just a DVD-rental service. But the real problem we are trying to solve is, 'How do you transform movie selection so that consumers can find a steady stream of movies they love?'"[10]

Rather than replicating or improving on the Blockbuster Video experience, Netflix created an entirely new customer outcome that included curated, convenient access to a deep "long-tail" DVD library that became the customer's new on-demand library of DVDs. This deeper content was far beyond what Blockbuster, who focused on the latest releases, could stock in their stores. This resulted in a shift to a new "slow consumption" model, allowing customers to rent and watch TV series and movies at their own pace.

Building on that model, Netflix realized that an extensive DVD library alone was insufficient to optimize a new customer outcome. A deep inventory of content offered little value for most customers if it was difficult to find what they wanted. The shallow stock of older release videos on the shelves at Blockbuster generally was a poor second alternative to the new releases for just that reason. Searching that inventory of older videos involved wandering the aisles, browsing through movies until the customer stumbled upon something worth watching.

The genius of the Netflix model was to use its vast DVD inventory and monthly subscription to enable a latent consumption model, unlocking access to a deep and appealing inventory of videos that customers only had superficial access to at Blockbuster. This new-customer-first approach appealed to customers who were unserved or underserved by Blockbuster's hit-oriented video stores.

To enable this new slow-consumption model, Netflix added four key features that brought that deep inventory to the forefront and became the new quadrant 2 features.

First, by fulfilling DVDs by mail from regional distribution centers and allowing customers to keep the video for as long as they wanted, Netflix gave subscribers the convenience of always having one or more DVDs at hand, depending on their subscription. This created convenience as a priority feature.

Second, by providing an online ordering queue of preferred videos, Netflix gave customers the ability to prioritize their queue of DVDs and then forget it, automating the process of receiving their entertainment on demand. The result was a friction-free delivery of the customer's next DVD as soon as they sent their previous movie back.

Third, Netflix's created a recommendation engine to help customers add new video selections to their queue based on personal preferences and previously viewed DVDs. The engine enabled customers to navigate the deep inventory and build their own personal, curated video list.

Finally, Netflix enabled its new model of consumption through a subscription business model that enabled the new slower consumption pace. Netflix's model also allowed the company to be much more efficient in using its DVD stock as 70 percent of its total inventory was deep, long-tail movies vs. new releases, compared to just 25 percent for Blockbuster.[11]

This new, virtual DVD library enabled Netflix to change the customer consumption model from chasing blockbuster movies to more in-depth video consumption and flipped the script of customer purchase decision criteria in Netflix's favor. For Blockbuster customers, the compelling quadrant 2 benefits of the purchase consideration matrix included cost, convenience of location, and the availability of new releases. The inventory on Blockbuster store shelves was not a priority because it just wasn't as accessible. Netflix enabled the foundational customer objective of having something interesting to watch at home but changed the outcome with a new consumption model. Convenience, friction reduction, and personalization along with a subscription model became the enablers to make a deep DVD library more important, effectively moving it from a quadrant 4 to a quadrant 2 feature, as shown in figure 4-5.

	Low differentiation	High differentiation
High value	Hygiene factors 1	Basis of competition 2
Low value	Standard Factors 3	Avoid 4

Figure 4-5: Netflix Changes Customer Outcomes

This focus on a new customer outcome propelled Netflix to become a dominant force in DVD rentals before it eventually moved to online video streaming and then created its own content. With each transition for the company, Netflix accomplished a game-changing outcome by creating a new consumption model as shown in figure 4-6.

Phase	Consumption type	Explanation
Netflix 1.0 DVD rental	Slow consumption	Friction-free DVD queues, recommendations, and subscription model permitted deeper exploration of content.
Netflix 2.0 Video streaming	Curated consumption	Curated consumption model based on its highly refined video recommendation engine.
Netflix 3.0 Own content creation	Binge consumption	Releasing the entire content of a new season all at once, enabling binge-watching.

Figure 4-6: Netflix Consumption Models

In the 20 years since its launch, Netflix has extended its video service into over 190 countries, and the company is valued at over $200 billion. Notably, only a few years after launching Netflix in 2000, CEO Reed Hastings approached Blockbuster CEO John Antioco with an offer to sell Netflix's DVD business for $50 million. Antioco dismissed the offer, calling it a niche business.

Just seven years later, John Antioco was fired by activist investor Carl Icahn after he announced his intent to eliminate all late fees to copy Netflix's business with a new service called Blockbuster Total Access. Blockbuster continued its steep decline for another three years before announcing bankruptcy in 2010.

Changing the consumption model is multi-dimensional and can include altering where, when, how frequently, and how easily a product or service is consumed. Category creators such as Peloton, Keurig, Zappos, Starbucks, Apple, and even McDonald's have all mastered changing the way customers consume to create new customer outcomes.

Trait Five: They Master Flow

The fifth trait of companies changing customer outcomes is the ability to create product flow, an essential element for altering consumption. Product flow is an elusive element that makes a product or service easier to find, purchase, and consume. Primary ways organizations create flow include reducing friction, increasing convenience, personalizing, and altering the business model.

Reducing Friction. Friction is the antithesis of flow. It's a business killer. Friction reduction focuses on removing the effort required for a customer to go through the journey from identifying, searching, and finding your product to purchase, fulfillment, and consumption. Like its physical counterpart, business friction occurs when that journey is slowed down through tension or reduction in motion.

Transformative organizations are expert at reducing and removing friction. Dollar Shave Club removed friction with automatic shipments. Netflix 1.0 removed friction with its rental queue. Lyft/Uber eliminates friction by making hiring a car, identifying the vehicle, and even paying as fluid as possible, with minimal customer interaction, taking an entire customer experience down to a few simple steps.

Increasing Convenience. In a time-strapped world, convenience has historically been a compelling benefit. There is a reason that convenience stores, which sell high-priced basics and crave-worthy snacks, have had a 15-year history of record profits in the US.[12] Making the product or service more available and proximate to the customer has the added benefit of breaking out of traditional industry structure in a way that brings lasting advantage.

IKEA created a new consumption model by creating convenience with inexpensive flat-pack furniture that could go from the store to the home the same day. IKEA's furniture appeals to all ranges on the economic scale as an easy way to inexpensively and quickly buy furniture. The outcome of same-day furniture the customer could take home in their car completely changed the basis of competition for buying furniture to focus on convenience.

Personalization. Personalization, the ability to create a solution tailored to individual customers' needs and usage patterns creates flow when it is provided in a manageable and scalable way. As the options for purchase increase exponentially, as with Netflix's long-tail inventory of streaming movies, for example, the prediction and automation of personalization becomes more important.

Starbucks transformed the coffee consumption model by creating a highly organized coffee personalization system that allows for easy selection of the "right" coffee from more than 80,000 possible combinations of types, sizes, and options. They enabled this level of personalization by simplifying the selection process for what could otherwise have lost customers in a sea of possible combinations.

Business Model. Nearly every change in the consumption model is facilitated by a change in the business model, both how the company creates value and how they charge for it. Changing the business model enables different modes of consumption, lowers barriers for consumers, and deters incumbent competitive response.

Could you imagine Netflix without a subscription business model? When the company initially implemented a DVD rental by mail business, it looked just like Blockbuster, including single video rental fees and late fees. After a year of operations, the company debated whether to shift to a subscription business.

After careful deliberation, the company changed to a subscription-based service that allowed customers to rent and receive by mail between one and six DVDs at a time. This enabled consumers to watch the videos at their leisure and return them at their own pace. This change demanded the rental queues and automatic fulfillment that became distinguishing features of the service, finally delivering the company's vision of a consumption model in which customers could "find a steady stream of movies they love."

Creating a Protected Position: Natural Defensive Moats

A significant benefit of changing customer outcomes is to create natural defensive moats, structural barriers that make it difficult or impossible for incumbents to copy a company's solutions without significantly changing or hurting their own business or abandoning their own advantages.

One benefit of category-creating solutions is that incumbent competitors often suffer from belief perseverance, the tendency to continue to believe something even when new evidence contradicts it. Even as transformative companies launch new category-creating solutions and start to show success, incumbents continue to cling to their outdated notions of products and markets. Incumbents dismiss their new competitors as niche solutions, as Nokia and Blockbuster did.

But belief perseverance is temporary. In the long term, transformative companies are effective because incumbent competitors find it difficult to copy them since doing so is counter to their existing way of doing things. This type of defensibility comes from three barriers:

Structural Barriers. Structural barriers are processes and products that competitors can't match because doing so would go counter to the incumbent competitor's assets, resources, and know-how or would operate outside the industry structure they work in and from which they find it difficult to escape.

Business Model Barriers. Business model barriers exist when the transformative organization creates models that an incumbent can't copy as doing so would directly hurt the existing business or operational model that they use to create and capture value. A strong incumbent business model is often one of the most significant barriers to entry, and a company will go to great lengths to protect it. Thus, the most significant transformative outcomes include a change in the business model that operates outside the standard industry current model for capturing value.

Cumulative Knowledge Barriers. Finally, one distinct barrier for the transformative company involves accumulating the knowledge others would find necessary to copy the new solution. This is especially true with the type of knowledge gained with experience, trial, and error.

Netflix was able to avail itself of all three defensive moats by changing the structure of how to fulfill their service (through mail versus Blockbuster's nine thousand brick-and-mortar stores), business model (subscription versus rental charges and late fees), and cumulative knowledge such as how to optimize regional DVD distribution and customer analytics.

How to Find New Outcomes

Adopting the five traits of outcome innovators is an effective way to ensure that you define and achieve category-creating solutions that produce new customer outcomes. However, sometimes you just need a kick start to find that opportunity. Consider these three options for where to hunt for further inspiration:

Thinking in Terms of Consumption. We often think in terms of altering products to address underserved or unserved segments of the market. An alternative approach is to think in terms of consumption, which opens up opportunities to reach both new and existing customers. I will explain this concept further in chapter 8.

An example is Zipcar, which provides short-duration rental cars in urban locations as an alternative to car purchases or rentals from traditional rental agencies. Founded in 2000 by Robin Chase, an MIT graduate and then a stay-at-home mother, and Ante Danielson, a Harvard professor of geochemistry, Zipcar was built on their interest in reducing consumer reliance on single-owner vehicles and a growing trend towards environmentalism. Meeting through a chance encounter through their children's kindergarten class, the two formed the company with the idea that an environmentally-focused organization could also be a profitable one.

Zipcar's solution is tailored to the underserved urban market by changing the consumption model: making it convenient and frictionless to go directly to a car in their neighborhood to rent for as little as an hour, opening up rentals to those whose needs were not being addressed elsewhere.

Creating Extremes and Constraints. Interestingly, you can also pursue outcomes by looking to lift or add constraints relative to current solutions. Think in extremes and create "what if?" scenarios. The exercise of adding constraints, such as "How could you build a video rental service without the use of stores?"

or lifting them, as in "What if we gave consumers unlimited access to DVDs?" is beneficial in breaking old models to achieve better outcomes. Organizations can run these "what if?" scenarios regularly to identify opportunities and work backward from the result or forward from the constraint.

Borrowing and Recombining. Outcome innovators know how to borrow and build on ideas of others to create new innovation. Companies such as Starbucks, Apple, Salesforce, Amazon, and Dell have learned the power of recombination, borrowing from other industries to improve their solutions.

In Section III, we discuss using recombining, democratization, simplification, and other scale accelerators as catalysts to address the needs of underserved and unserved customers and facilitate market entry.

Creating new customer outcomes takes customer understanding, observation, creativity, and the willingness to experiment to develop better solutions. Such outcomes are often the result of an iterative process.

As a single rental model with DVD fulfillment by mail, Netflix was good, but it represented a linear progression in the movie rental model—a more straightforward way to receive and send back DVDs. It was only after an iteration of experimenting and observing that Netflix resolved to move to a subscription model and achieved a new, category-creating solution with a new customer outcome.

Moving forward, we will shift our discussion from customer outcome innovation to look at how organizations approach structural innovation to support and enhance their newly designed outcomes. In the next chapter, we'll review how organizations think in terms of capability sets—a unique bundle of skills and assets they develop and invest in to support their outcomes.

From Concept to Action

1. Is the objective of our current product or service roadmap to change the customer outcome or simply to improve it at the margins?

2. Do we take a technology approach or problem-oriented approach to product or service development?

3. What trends might affect our industry and facilitate the change in customer outcomes?

4. What digital catalysts could assist us in creating new customer outcomes?

5. Using the Customer Decision Matrix, what is the existing basis of competition for our product or service? What are the hygiene factors?

6. Are there hygiene features (quadrant 1) today that could be enhanced to become part of the basis of competition? What could we do to change the customer outcome by enhancing those hygiene features? What would be required to make them the center of focus in the customer's decision?

7. Are there undervalued but differentiated (quadrant 4) features that could be enhanced and turned into purchase decision criteria?

8. In what ways could we change the consumption model of our product or service?

9. How could we use convenience, reduction of friction, or personalization to enhance product flow to change the customer outcome?

10. What new problems can we resolve to improve the customer outcome? How can we enhance the customer outcome with practical value tradeoffs?

Chapter 5

Aligning and Investing in Capabilities

We are honing the businesses that we're in and making them as efficient, as profitable as possible, while also investing very pointedly and very wisely, we believe, in things that will enhance customer experience and create lasting businesses for us down the line.

Amazon CFO Brian Olsavsky

Capabilities are the things that organizations do well and that deliver meaningful business results. They include skills, processes, know-how, and unique ways of using assets and resources. Transformative organizations master the ability to build capability sets that support customer outcomes and give their organization an advantage. Transformative organizations develop capabilities called scale accelerators that help them enter and transform existing markets.

Defined by Capabilities

Think for a moment about a successful company and what it is you admire about it. If you're like many people, you might start by pointing to the company's unique and awe-inspiring products or services. Or perhaps you identified an incredibly charismatic leader who has driven the company forward to success.

These are reasonable answers, and they both can be critical to success. But the question was, what do you admire about the company? When you dig a little deeper, you will likely point out what the organization does well. Take Apple, for example. We might say that we like the way they design products, their attention to detail, how well they integrate hardware and software to simplify how to use it, their incredible brand image, or how everything just comes together for a fluid customer experience. A similar assessment of Walmart might bring to light their ability to consistently lower prices and expand selection while maintaining higher than average operating margins. These things come from their exceptional logistics and data-driven customer insights and efficient inventory and supplier management—all things they do well.

These things that Walmart, Apple, and other companies excel at are what enables them to be great companies. They are called capabilities. McKinsey defines capabilities as "anything an organization does well that drives meaningful business results."[1] This includes their skills, processes, know-how, and unique ways of using assets and resources they have developed.

This chapter will start the first of two discussions on how transformative companies use structural innovation to their advantage. I'll show how companies answer the question of what core company capabilities they need to support an optimized customer outcome and create a set of organizational advantages.

Capabilities are critical to supporting customer outcomes and executing on strategy. Intel Corporation created a unique customer outcome by taking ownership of the PC architecture from beginning to end and supported that strategy by intentionally developing a unique set of capabilities. They defined the customer outcome as a personal computer with a fully integrated architecture from the processor and motherboard to the operating system and peripheral systems. The customer could identify and trust this ubiquitous system as identified by the Intel ingredient brand "Intel Inside." The company supported its strategy by developing the best-in-class capabilities that you would expect for a large semiconductor manufacturer: processor design, material science expertise, and manufacturing.

But Intel also developed capabilities that you might not expect to see in a semiconductor manufacturer, capabilities that gave them a distinct and layered advantage. Creating capabilities in strategic partner relationship management, systems design, and ingredient brand marketing differentiated them and enabled them to achieve their unique customer outcome and strategy. They created a unique set of capabilities that, together, have been extremely difficult to replicate, enabling them to lead their industry for decades.

Because capabilities should be enduring and provide advantages that are difficult to replicate, organizations need to focus on identifying and investing in a set of capabilities that, when layered together, create their unique advantage.

Aligning and Investing in Capabilities

Leaders in most organizations recognize the need to build strong capabilities, but they often fail to create them. In a recent corporate survey by McKinsey, 58 percent of respondents ranked building capabilities among their company's top three priorities, and 90 percent place it among their top ten.[2] Yet only one-third of companies focus effort on building the capabilities they see as necessary, and only 25 percent rated themselves good at building capabilities at all.

Why such a disconnect between aspirations for creating company capabilities and reality? I have seen from my own experience that organizational leaders don't prioritize establishing core capabilities because they haven't expended the effort to identify which capabilities their business requires to set them apart. This failure results in being unexceptional at nearly everything. It results in a missed opportunity to create real advantage.

The lack of leadership emphasis here may have more to do with a general unawareness of what capabilities are and how to identify and prioritize those most critical to their business. Often capabilities are generally important to organizations but don't receive the proper investment to rise to a level of industry leadership. In the Harvard Business Review article "Capitalizing on Capabilities," Norm Smallwood and Dave Ulrich identified 11 such capabilities that well-managed organizations tend to have. They include talent, speed, shared mind-set, coherent brand identity, accountability, collaboration, learning, leadership, customer connectivity, strategic unity, innovation, and efficiency.

Becoming good at this set of capabilities may get you to the realm of being well-managed, but they alone won't lift you to achieve industry-transforming status. To do that, each organization needs to define what it needs to support its unique customer outcome and differentiate itself from competitors. This set of capabilities that are unique to your organization is what lies at the center of achieving the results you seek.

Becoming a Capabilities-Driven Organization

Transformative organizations are exceptional at creating and developing their capabilities. They have identified what they need to be good at and are willing to invest in it. They are capabilities driven.

Being a capabilities-driven organization is different from being capabilities led. A capabilities-driven organization identifies and invests in the few distinctive and critical capabilities they need to support their targeted customer outcome and organizational strategy. It focuses on capabilities that drive the most important results, regardless of what they are, and changes them as needed.

By contrast, a capabilities-led organization emphasizes the capability itself, focusing on taking advantage of what the organization does well, without thought about a capability's current or changing importance. Such a stance locks the company into doing what it does well to support its existing model and strategy, subjecting it to potential capability traps, as I will discuss later in this chapter.

Being capabilities-driven helps an organization identify the most critical areas for investment. Because they see capabilities as supporting their goals, such organizations are free to divest, discontinue, or adapt capabilities when outcomes or strategy changes.

Amazon stands out for its ability to develop and layer the right capabilities that distinguish the company and drive superior customer outcomes. Amazon's former CEO Jeff Bezos's obsession with logistics started from the earliest days of the company as it made steps toward creating an e-commerce giant. Bezos chose books as Amazon's debut product because they were durable and could withstand the postal system abuse, were relatively small, and could easily ship. Amazon focused on logistics, which has helped it grow to an organization that sent more than 3.5 billion packages in 2019 and topped $280 billion in revenue.

Amazon has become a logistics powerhouse but hasn't stopped there. It has achieved impressive results by creating and investing in a set of world-class capabilities that support its unique customer outcome, including:

1. **Reducing Friction.** Amazon obsesses over friction and has developed a deep focus on eliminating it. It has capitalized on reducing friction through high search engine placement, one-click purchases, Amazon Dash buttons (battery operated one-button ordering devices), and Amazon Echo's ordering system to create friction-free ordering.

2. **Analytics.** Amazon's website is backed by analytics and recommendation engines that tailor offerings and sell additional products to its customers.

3. **Amazon Prime.** Amazon's Prime service functions as a unique capability that includes free shipping and many other services, including access to Amazon's video and music catalog, Kindle books, shopping deals, and discounts at Whole Foods. With more than 150 million members paying up to $119 per year, if Amazon Prime were its own company, it would have revenue of nearly $18 billion and sit at #181 on the Fortune 500. Prime is a crucial capability designed to keep customers from shopping elsewhere.

4. **Logistics.** Amazon's logistics platform provides the tools for planning, guidance, and customer service around its delivery services with partners.

5. **Warehousing.** In a recent annual report, Amazon revealed that it owns more than 253 million square feet of space, including 70 regional warehouse facilities in the US. Beyond the sheer square footage, Amazon has established advantages, including robotics, algorithms for grouping and locating products to optimize order processing, and worker tracking.

6. **Amazon Marketplace.** One of Amazon's fundamental innovations is its e-commerce platform, Amazon Marketplace, which allows third-party vendors to sell on Amazon's website alongside Amazon's products. Many of the products are stored and fulfilled directly from Amazon's warehouses.

7. **Delivery.** Through partnerships with the United States Postal Service, other delivery partners, and increasingly, delivery entrepreneurs that it has encouraged through its own program, Amazon has developed multiple methods to fulfill the delivery of its products.

Amazon continues to maintain its advantage by investing in the people, processes, and technology behind these capabilities, and that provides a distinct advantage over its competition to deliver on its unique customer outcome. Not only has no organization been able to replicate this combination of capabilities and compete with Amazon directly, but many have also actually adopted Amazon's platform for selling and delivering their products.

Like Amazon, other transformative companies have built capability models that support their unique customer outcomes and generate competitive advantage. Walmart's ability to bring the large-format discount stores to small towns across the US and eventually to more population-dense regions depended on many critical capabilities, including:

1. **Logistics and warehousing.** Walmart combined its 160 regional distribution centers with its unique cross-docking capabilities to lower inventory costs.

2. **Cost controls.** The company is famous for cost management, including employee travel, which is ingrained into its culture.

3. **Merchandising.** With a tradition born from Sam Walton's early days of running Ben Franklin stores, Walmart built a strong merchandising capability to present and promote goods in stores and boost sales.

4. **Supply chain management.** Walmart is known for its diligent management of supplier pricing and for sharing point of sale analytics and logistics information with suppliers, while requiring suppliers to help manage store inventory.

5. **Price cutting orientation and process.** Walmart's philosophy of lowering supplier costs and using those costs to continually maintain low prices enables the company to avoid sale prices, generate consistent customer loyalty, and maintain a price advantage.

6. **Store management learning and independence.** Walmart's fosters innovation across the organization by giving store managers the freedom to implement their own improvements in their stores and bringing managers together regularly to their Bentonville, Arkansas, headquarters to share these ideas and successes.

Walmart's unique combination of capabilities enables them to maintain a long-term advantage in the retail market and consistently generates margins that are double the rest of the industry, a large advantage in the competitive retail market.

In short, Amazon, Walmart, and so many other transformative companies are capabilities-driven organizations because they use their focused customer outcomes to dictate what capabilities they need to become successful.

Looking from the outside with hindsight, it's clear which capabilities are strategic to Amazon or Walmart. But it may not be so clear for your organization what is essential and what isn't. So, let's look at what makes a capability strategic.

Strategic Capabilities

To answer that question, you must determine what the company needs to be great at delivering the right outcome to their customer. In the ocean of possible capabilities that a company can choose to develop, one capability is strategically more important than another based on how it addresses three key questions:

1. **Does it drive value?** Capabilities are strategic when they directly contribute to the basis of competition, improve the buying criteria for the customer, or provide distinct value. Such a capability should be something that the company does well that supports something highly valued by the customer. For example, all of Amazon's capabilities support key customer benefits to form the basis of competition: low prices, breadth of selection, personalization, and fast delivery.

2. **Can you be industry-leading?** Because capabilities are tied to the basis of competition and are driving value, the company must be able to uniquely and sustainably lead the industry in that capability. Otherwise, the company risks losing to others as a high-value differentiator. Amazon is world-class in each capability and continually improves upon them.

3. **Is it difficult to copy?** On its own, the capability should be difficult to copy, replicate, or substitute in the long run.

In the end, the most objective way to determine if a particular capability is strategic is to answer the question, "Would we be able to differentiate ourselves effectively if we didn't have this capability?"

While individual capabilities are essential, the best organizations look at capabilities collectively as a set. The goal should be to form a capability model, a complete set of capabilities that together support the targeted customer outcome and create a distinct advantage.

Building the right capability set was critical to Salesforce's early success. It delivered its first large scale successful Software as a Service (SaaS) application, Customer Relationship Management (CRM) software, in 1999. As a pioneer in cloud-based SaaS software delivery, Salesforce developed a capability to create and deploy its cloud platform to deliver a multi-tenant application (one platform for many users) in central data centers, permitting it to serve customers worldwide.

The company based its original design on Amazon's e-commerce website with an unmistakably similar appearance to the online bookseller. In an era when software was developed mainly to run on personal computers or servers, Salesforce developed the capability to deliver a simplified solution that was configurable for each customer, not an easy feat at that time. Salesforce also created a more agile way to deploy their application, albeit slow by today's standards. By rolling out new features in one of three annual feature releases, the company became faster than competing software companies.

These capabilities enabled Salesforce to deliver a cloud-based solution that transformed the software industry and lured customers away from incumbents such as Seibel Software. It provided a unique customer outcome of the application without the hardware, software license, and complexity of on-premises software.

The company's core capabilities may seem typical for a cloud-based software company today, but they were unusual in the late 1990s. Since then, application developers have honed capabilities in cloud-based SaaS application design.

However, Salesforce has continually developed new capabilities to maintain its market leadership. Among them is its ability to create an application ecosystem of third-party developers that develop solutions that sit on top of the Salesforce platform, enabling better and more diverse applications than the company could offer on its own. This has created even more value for customers by delivering faster solutions in vertical markets or specialized applications that Salesforce could not achieve independently. These third-party solutions also create platform "stickiness," making it more difficult for customers to leave without losing significant value.

This combination of capabilities that supported Salesforce's unique customer outcome of applications through cloud delivery has enabled the company to maintain consistent growth as one of the fastest-growing application companies of all time. In its most recent year, Salesforce reached over $21 billion in sales.

Salesforce's progression is an encouragement for any company not to be complacent about their capabilities. It also demonstrates the importance of creating capability sets that layer company strengths built on various capability types.

Let's look at another transformative company that reshaped the European air travel industry. Starting as Europe's original discount airline, Ryanair provided a unique customer outcome of low-cost leisure travel. It has dramatically expanded the market for travel across Europe and is now Europe's largest airline. Despite the major airlines' attempts to replicate its model, Ryanair has grown its business by cultivating a unique capability set to support its low-cost strategy. That set includes:

1. **Access to secondary airports.** Ryanair's well-developed expertise in working with smaller, less expensive secondary airports has given it cost-leading access to more than 26 countries, much to the delight of its vacation travelers.

2. **Operational efficiencies.** Ryanair's ability to control costs is a significant capability. Using a single aircraft type, the Boeing 737, permits easier planning, fast turnaround of aircraft at the airport, and staff interchangeability to improve efficiencies. The secondary airports also contribute to operational efficiencies since such airports charge lower fees, may even pay Ryanair to fly there, and support outsourcing and fixed-price contracts to maintain the most cost-competitive flights in the industry.

3. **Subsidized low-price model.** Ryanair subsidizes its flight revenue by selling merchandise, charging for additional frills such as snacks, offering additional travel bookings for hotel and rental cars, and even advertising on planes' seatbacks.

4. **Online booking.** Ryanair was an early adopter of online booking, avoiding the high costs of phone-based reservations. Today, over 90 percent of bookings are done online through the company's website, reducing customer contact costs.

Like many other companies, Ryanair developed capabilities that aided its strategy execution and delivered its defined customer outcome. In this case, the airline's capability of using secondary airports was critical to their low-cost strategy.

Perhaps one of the most significant benefits of Ryanair's use of secondary airports was that it neutralized the incumbent competitors' strengths. Primary airports have limited capacity and are difficult and expensive to use. Ryanair's capabilities that support using smaller regional airports counter and neutralize those incumbent strengths.

New capabilities can often replace or nullify incumbent strengths, whether they are asset or capabilities-based. This helps counter strong incumbent positions and the advantages they accumulate. As in the case of Ryanair, this can often be done through direct substitution, replacing one capability or asset with another capability that improves the customer outcome. Netflix 1.0 would never have been able to match Blockbuster Video's 9,000 video stores. Still, they didn't need to. Instead, Netflix developed capabilities around regional warehouses and logistics to fulfill DVD rentals by mail. Redbox took a different approach, developing capabilities around microsites—small, high-traffic areas such as fast-food restaurants and convenience stores. By creating and developing low-cost video rental kiosks and placing them in more than 43,000 convenient locations, they eliminated the need to compete directly with Blockbuster Video.

It may not always be practical or necessary to substitute a competitor's capability with a superior one. But capabilities that are bundled together may achieve the same result of new and better customer outcomes and diminishing an incumbent competitor's strengths. We saw this in the case of Dollar

Shave Club as it competed with Gillette by building critical new capabilities around online marketing, direct customer relationship management, and data analytics. This strategy enabled Dollar Shave Club to compete effectively even though it outsourced everything that Gillette saw as a competitive advantage: product development, manufacturing, and distribution.

Dollar Shave Club, Ryanair, and others highlight a critical aspect of creating a capabilities-driven model: capabilities always work better when created in sets. Reliance on a single-threaded capability will always be more vulnerable because while any individual capability may be replicated or substituted, it is difficult to recreate a full set of comparable capabilities.

Creating New Capabilities

McKinsey's capabilities study found that while 50 percent of organizational leaders stated that they prioritize building capabilities, most faced substantial hurdles in building them. Over one third reported that one of the largest impediments to creating capabilities was internal resistance to change. Another 34 percent cited the lack of company vision as the cause of not adequately investing in the capabilities the company requires.[3]

Organizations can overcome these hurdles by identifying which competencies they require, challenging their organization to invest in them, and then resolving to address them continually for improvement or adaptation. This is particularly beneficial when setting out a new strategy or as part of a company's periodic strategic planning process. I have personally implemented this process as part of an annual strategy planning process using what I call the CMOGS method, which stands for Capability Model, Objective, Goal, and Systems. When instituted as part of a strategy review, this method links capabilities in supporting the company's overall strategy and requires leadership teams to prioritize where to invest their time and resources to help the company reach its overall strategic objectives.

- **Capabilities Model.** There is no magical capability, or even set of capabilities, that an organization can use to gain an advantage in its market. In most cases, capabilities are what an organization makes of them. A seemingly standard capability can be powerful if executed well. Likewise, if a potential core capability is not fully exploited, it may bring no advantage at all.

What is more important is to think about what set of capabilities your organization can commit to that will maximize the ability to deliver the best customer outcome and offer the highest value and differentiation for the company. Using a capability model similar to the examples we've reviewed in this chapter would orient an organization to focus on three to five capabilities that you should excel at doing better than your competition.

- **Objective.** Ensure that each capability maps to a specific objective. Most will tie to the seven major capability types outlined in figure 5-1. These are the most frequent categories of capabilities that companies draw from to build value and differentiate themselves. Some will tie very specifically to the customer outcome or to a particular change to the basis of competition, as we discussed in chapter 4.

  For companies entering an existing market where incumbents have substantial advantages, an objective may be to build a capability that is a direct substitute for an incumbent competitor's assets and capabilities. Identify competitor capabilities and look for ways to serve customers differently or for trends and technology advances that may support improving or substituting new capabilities for old ones.

- **Goal.** Identify how you will track this capability in its optimized state in an objective and measurable way. Too often, organizations settle for uninspiring and ill-defined aphorisms such as "world-class" and "industry-leading." Take the time to identify what leadership means for your organization with a defined outcome and metric, measuring the capability or its impact.

- **Systems for Improvement.** Recognize that capabilities are not static and require constant investment and development. Organizations need to put in place the accountability, systems, and processes for measuring, tracking, and improving their core capabilities and create a roadmap of committed improvements with defined timelines and objectives.

Major Capability Categories		
Category	**Description**	**Examples**
Leadership, execution, and talent	The company's ability to manage vision, talent, resources, performance, and culture of the organization to create advantages.	Hiring, training, and retaining talent, leadership development, creating context, communication of vision, employee communication and collaboration, intentionality and sense of mission, ability to see macro trends, speed, accountability, agility, responsiveness to change, sense of urgency.
Customer insight and customer outcome creation	The ability to create unique insight and vision of what will benefit the customer and look beyond existing products and features to develop new categories of solutions.	Customer insight and empathy, analytics-based insight, acuity, creativity and innovativeness, ability to borrow and recombine ideas from others.
Operational	Capabilities that improve the organization's operating model, directly improve efficiencies of processes, and leverage its assets to create advantage.	Speed, cost focus, process development, supplier relationships, logistics and shipping, warehousing, inventory management, automation, third-party management.
Market approach	The capabilities that improve the organization's ability to understand the customer from a broad perspective and deliver the solution before sales.	Customer insight, buyer definition, branding, strategic marketing and positioning, data analytics-focused customer insight, distribution management.
Go to market	The sales and marketing capabilities required to reach and sell to the customer.	Sales lead generation, sales model management, customer relationship management, sales value proposition development.
Ecosystem development and management	The ability to manage outside partnerships and relationships to create an optimized solution.	Partnership development and management, supplier management, information sharing, joint venture development, partner program, technical API development, data analytics, business development.

Major Capability Categories (cont.)		
Category	Description	Examples
Business model	Those capabilities that improve the value created or the way or frequency in which value is captured by the organization, including improving how the company can make money.	Creativity, business model development, innovation outside the product, partnerships and cooperation, consistency, data insight, sales execution.

Figure 5-1: Capabilities Categories

The goal of developing a set of strategic, overlapping capabilities across the organization requires direction and oversight from the senior leaders of the organization to coordinate across functional groups and set the tone.

Capability Traps

Understanding the difference between being a capabilities-driven versus a capabilities-led organization helps leaders avoid developing the wrong capabilities or even overinvesting in good ones. Nevertheless, even the best organizations can make mistakes when developing or continuing to invest in capabilities that align with their needs.

There have been few competitive rivalries as intense as between Walmart and Kmart for the US retail shopping market. Being in the same industry, you would expect that both would have focused on roughly the same capabilities. Logistics, vendor, and inventory management are among the core capabilities needed to compete in the price-competitive retail market. But the capabilities one company builds to get there can be much different, and where one company sees no advantage, another may create one. In this case, Kmart failed to see opportunities while Walmart chose to invest for long-term advantage and create their own.

While Kmart decided to outsource its trucking requirements to lower costs, at about the same time, Walmart had invested in building its own trucking line as part of its logistics competencies. Investing allowed Walmart to have more control over the timing of delivery and the costs, which they could steadily lower over time. And while Kmart approached vendor management by constantly switching suppliers and pitting them against each other to squeeze out lower costs, Walmart took a different tactic, retaining vendors and making Walmart a larger portion of each supplier's business. They were able to gain efficiencies by sharing logistics information, integrating vendors into their inventory planning software, and sharing store analytics with suppliers. This made suppliers more efficient and increased their dependency on Walmart as a partner.

Walmart's different approach reminds us that although the goals can be the same, companies may achieve them through different capabilities. It also demonstrates that it is much easier to dismiss a potential capability for short-term gains and more challenging to explore how to turn it into a longer-term advantage.

One way to overcome the tendency to discount seemingly low-priority capabilities is to think about what this capability would do for you if it delivered extreme benefits. Maybe owning its own trucking line didn't seem like the best option, but if Kmart saw that it could cut shipping costs by 50 percent, it might approach this decision differently. Suppose you could define an extreme point at which that capability could provide very attractive advantages, and you could work out a path to get there. In that case, it's worth pursuing that capability further.

Yet another common trap is confusing new technology with a capability. Given the rapid pace of technology development, and the ability to use it to gain operational efficiencies, the temptation of associating technological advancement with a strategic capability is high. This is especially true for new digital technologies such as data analytics, machine learning, and artificial intelligence. Adopting these digital transformation catalysts often leads to the technology paradox we spoke about in chapter 2. When a company pursues digital transformation technologies but needs to rely on cadres of consultants, contractors, and off-the-shelf software to create it, those advantages won't last.

Technology can be a significant capability and an advantage, as we've seen from the examples of Dollar Shave Club, Netflix, and Amazon. All have been able to build strategic capabilities from data analytics. But the advantages from these capabilities come from their early adoption and the cumulative gains over years of investment and refinement. Stand still, and those advantages dissipate over time.

Finally, the most common trap that companies fall into is becoming tied to a specific capability rather than focusing on the capabilities required to deliver the best customer outcome. This trap is called capability lock-in. It occurs when an organization becomes blinded by what it does well and focuses on improving it continually, even when it provides decreasingly marginal benefit.

Many incumbents fall into this trap and create an overreliance on what they do well now. Gillette's highly valued distribution channel was vital until it became a disadvantage relative to Dollar Shave Club's direct model. Blockbuster video found an advantage in its 9,000 stores until Netflix found a better way to distribute DVDs by mail and then video over the Internet. Nokia relied on its prolific hardware design capabilities to developing dozens of phones each year, but Apple showed it could focus on delivering better outcomes with one iconic and elegant design. For each of these companies, the bias of overvaluing the capabilities at which they excelled resulted in a disadvantage when competitors introduced a more effective capability.

Creating a Continuing Capabilities Perspective

Henry Ford developed one of the best capability models with a combination of manufacturing, distribution, and cost controls to deliver the revolutionary Model T. He offered the best remedy for capability lock-in and the other capability traps when he said, "Be ready to revise any system, scrap any method, abandon any theory, if the success of the job requires it." In like manner, transformative organizations know how to adapt capabilities to provide better customer outcomes or even discard them when something better comes along.

Amazon, for example, has invested heavily in capabilities that support fast delivery but avoided the type of capability lock-in that creates a potential Achilles' heel. By continually reinventing how to improve on two-day shipping, Amazon has improved the customer outcome, adding one-day and same-day delivery by continually investing in multiple options for delivery logistics. In just the last few years, Amazon has enhanced its logistics capabilities with innovations such as:

- **Amazon Deliver.** Amazon's partnership with the United States Postal Service has given it advantages, including dedicated vehicles and off-hours and Sunday deliveries.
- **Amazon Hub Lockers.** Permits faster customer pickup of goods at nearby locations.
- **Amazon Flex.** A pool of individual contractors who work shifts delivering on behalf of Amazon.
- **Amazon Delivery Service Partners.** A system to work with entrepreneurs to develop their own delivery businesses under the Amazon Prime brand.
- **Amazon Prime Air.** Amazon's active drone development program has developed at least 64 patents filed on drone design and delivery, which will likely improve Amazon's delivery capabilities in the future.

By focusing on the customer outcomes, Amazon has improved performance (such as same-day and two-hour delivery for Prime Now), building its logistics capabilities in aggregate rather than facing the risk of someone else disrupting it with a better, more efficient way to deliver goods to customers.

Sometimes companies need to invest far afield to continually create a better customer outcome, even scrapping and replacing their current set of capabilities with a new set. No company has done this more than Netflix, which has reinvented the way to deliver movies to customers three times in less than 25 years.

In the previous chapter, we described Netflix from the standpoint of the traits companies need to succeed in transformative innovation, but its reinvention of its capabilities is just as impressive. From the beginning, Netflix CEO Reed Hastings knew there were two things that he needed to be good at: helping customers find the movies they would want to watch and delivering them efficiently. He has focused the company on building strong capabilities to support both needs and evolved them over time. Early on, Hastings recognized that companies face significant hurdles in moving away from what had previously made them successful. He once reflected that "most companies that are great at something—like AOL dialup or Borders bookstores—do not become great at new things people want [streaming for us] because they are afraid to hurt their initial business."[4]

Nevertheless, the Netflix CEO understood that there was "a finite market for DVD-by-mail, and the growth over the next 10 years will be in stream-ing." In fact, according to Hastings, he always knew he would be in the streaming business but realized the company needed to wait until Internet bandwidth was sufficient to do it. So, in 2007, the company launched video streaming, building a new set of capabilities to support streaming while continuing its DVD mail-order business. While doing this, the company still built on its core capabilities around customer analytics and its video recommendation engine.

The move to streaming improved the customer outcome by changing the consumption model for the second time. Netflix became a category creator in its market with online and on-demand streaming movies because it didn't tie itself to what it initially did well: DVD delivery. Netflix maintained its market-leading position by transforming its industry with a new customer outcome and the new capabilities to support it.

Netflix made a third transformative change just a few years later by creating its own content and developing additional capabilities to support it. Beginning with purchasing the rights to produce the show *House of Cards*, a television series originally produced in the UK, and launching it in 2013, the company has had tremendous success in creating and offering its original content. Netflix quickly built off its core capability—customer data analytics—to identify the types of shows it should create and developed a new capability—original content development.

Netflix now reportedly spends upward of $8 billion on content production annually. Has it been successful? Original shows now constitute 20 percent of Netflix's viewed content and reinforce a strong Netflix viewer behavior in a new consumption model: binge-watching. According to a survey released by Morgan Stanley, 39 percent of US consumers said that Netflix offers the best original programming, compared to HBO at 14 percent and Amazon at 5 percent.[5]

Throughout its transformation from the DVD-by-mail business to online streaming and then to content developer, Netflix has consistently focused on the requirements for its business's two core elements: helping customers find movies and delivering them. The company built capabilities around these two requirements and adapted them as needed, creating new outcomes as a result. In this way, capabilities can have a reciprocal impact on outcomes. Focusing on improving or changing a capability can directly result in improvements to the customer outcome.

Mastering Market Leadership

In addition to producing unique, category-creating outcomes and mastering core capabilities, the transformative companies in this book demonstrate significant skills in their ability to enter and change existing markets. This includes mastering a distinct set of capabilities to produce widely adopted solutions, overcome barriers to market entry, create profitable business models, and creatively draw from and adapt ideas from other markets and solutions. This set of scale accelerators is shown in figure 5-2.

These scale accelerators facilitate making solutions accessible to broader potential markets, finding initial points of market entry, and generating creative ways to overcome barriers to entry. It encapsulates the new-customer-first orientation that we previously discussed, looking at developing customer outcomes that open up and expand markets by focusing on winning new customers first.

Organizations like Amazon, Apple, and Google show that companies can learn these market capabilities and repeatedly apply them to different markets with success. Using both their core capabilities and market approach capabilities, these companies have entered and transformed markets as diverse as discount retailing, cloud storage, books, groceries, consumer goods, video, music, portable music players, smartphones, and enterprise applications.

Scale Accelerators	
Scale Accelerator	Description
Democratizing	Creating near-universal availability of a product or service and lifting constraints for customers to find, access, and buy it where and when they want.
Simplifying	Taking a product or service down to the most basic and essential elements, resulting in a significantly expanded market opportunity.

Scale Accelerators	
Scale Accelerator	**Description**
New-Customer Focusing	Targeting initial beachhead markets that give organizations the traction to create a broad market opportunity.
Model Building	Creating new profitable business models that accompany innovation and add to company advantage.
Recombining	Creatively borrowing and recombining existing ideas from other markets to introduce innovations into their own market.
Rule Breaking	Breaking rules, dispelling beliefs, and eschewing accepted practices to change customer outcomes and create a sustainable advantage.

Figure 5-2: Changing Market Approach through Scale Accelerators

These companies and others are increasingly moving into new markets, leveraging their core capabilities, and taking advantage of these scale accelerators to facilitate how they approach and take on new markets. For example, Uber applies the capabilities it developed in the personal mobility and transportation market to food delivery, trucking, and even emergency transportation. Amazon, Apple, and Google have likewise looked to enter such diverse markets as transportation and health care services and benefit from the capabilities they have learned entering other markets.

The classic Harvard Business Review article "Competing on Capabilities: The New Rules of Corporate Strategy" proposed that organizations that become experts at a highly developed set of core capabilities in their own market could, in turn, use those capabilities to enter other markets with equal success. Once a company refined its capabilities, it would be easy to use those same advantages to enter other markets, essentially becoming a "capabilities predator." In the authors' words,

> Competing on capabilities provides a way for companies to gain the benefits of both focus and diversification. Put another way, a company that focuses on its strategic capabilities can compete in a remarkable diversity of regions, products, and businesses and do it far more coher-

ently than the typical conglomerate can. Such a company is a 'capabilities predator'—able to come out of nowhere and move rapidly from nonparticipant to major player and even to industry leader.[6]

This concept of a "capabilities predator" is based on the idea that companies can transfer core business capabilities from one market to another with success. At a practical level, understanding and using these six scale accelerators can help organizations overcome barriers to entry existing markets and innovate to win by shifting markets into motion. We will explore each of these capabilities in further detail in Section III, unpacking how leaders can use them to improve market entry and create a path to market leadership.

In the next chapter, we will move to the second way companies can use structural innovation to their advantage by turning outward to rethink and reframe their industry, leveraging industry structure to their advantage.

From Concept to Action

1. What current capabilities does our organization have? Are we leading? Are we investing in those capabilities? Do they pass the test as a strategic capability?

2. Which capabilities are vital for us to support our customer outcome?

3. What are the best capabilities required to fulfill the aspirational customer outcome? Do they truly change the customer outcome?

4. What trends and technology advances may support improving or changing capabilities? Look for trends and technology advances that facilitate a change to or improvement in capabilities.

5. What organizational changes do we need to make to support these newly defined capabilities, who owns those changes, the processes to manage them, and setting metrics for managing them?

6. What systems do we need to track and improve on those capabilities over time?

7. How can our organization avoid capability lock-in with our existing capabilities by continually looking for ways to evaluate their importance and adjust as needed?

Chapter 6

Rethinking and Reframing Your Industry

There exist limitless opportunities in every industry. Where there is an open mind, there will always be a frontier.
Charles Kettering

Transformative organizations create asymmetric competition by actively reframing their industry, seeking to change the rules and structure to gain leverage against incumbents and create a playing field where they can better compete. Reframing looks for alternative ways to create value and advantage and turn incumbents' strengths into weaknesses, forcing them to maintain existing assets that are less competitive in the new industry model. The three most effective reframing methods are developing platforms, crossing industry swim lanes, and democratization.

Winning in a World of Constraints

If you could rewrite the rules of your industry, what would you change? That is a difficult question for most leaders to answer. It's difficult because they have spent so much time working in their industry that they are comfortable with how it works and how they have built their organization specifically to compete in that environment. Changing the rules is hard when you've played by them for so long.

If I were to ask you a slightly different question, say, how you would compete with a specific new constraint on your organization, you'd likely find it easier to respond. For example, if you could no longer use a current channel to market, a specific supplier, or your preferred business model, could you come up with an alternative? What if you were not able to produce your product in its current form? Would you be able to come up with a solution? Likely you would because constraints force you to think, to resolve specific problems, and to create successful adaptations that you need to survive.

You compete every day under constraints, rules, and norms. Your ability to think around them helps create an environment where you have an advantage. This chapter is the second of two discussions on structural innovation. In it I'll show that transformative organizations are especially adept at creating competitive asymmetries by actively rethinking and reframing the basic assumptions of their industry.

Perhaps one of the most notable stories of successfully overcoming constraints and reframing a situation to create an advantage is the biblical account of David and Goliath. Those familiar with the story may think of it as the classic tale of the triumph of the little guy. But the details of this underdog-inspiring story unveil a more profound lesson on creating a playing field on which you can win.[1] The book of Samuel in the Old Testament recounts how ancient Israel was forced to face the war-favoring Philistines, their continual foe, in the Valley of Elah at the time of King Saul. Although the Philistines had numerical superiority, they offered the Israelites a commonly used way to resolve conflict while avoiding much bloodshed: Israel could send out their best warrior to face combat mano-a-mano against the Philistines' top warrior. The stakes for the contest were high: whoever won by killing their opponent would enslave the entire opposing army.

The Philistines' combatant of choice was Goliath of Gath. He was a giant of a man who stood much taller than any of the Israelite adversaries at six-feet-nine (2.06 meters). Goliath was large enough that his copper coat weighed some 126 pounds (57.3 kg), and the head of his spear alone weighed 15 pounds (6.8 kg).

For 40 days, no one was willing to fight the seemingly invincible Goliath. No one until David, shepherd, future king of Israel, and possibly the earliest inspiration for Grubhub, came to the battlefield to deliver food to his brothers. Hearing of the standoff, David, with more courage than strength, offered to be the one to fight on Israel's behalf.

More worrying than David's size and lack of experience was his refusal to use the usual but likely ineffective defenses of helmet, shield, and armor that accompanied warriors of his day. Instead, he opted for his sling and few smooth rocks from the river.

As the battle commenced, David bypassed the expected hand-to-hand combat that favored Goliath and changed the rules of engagement. Taking to the open field, David used his size and speed—and his lack of a bulky sword and shield—to avoid direct contact with his larger opponent. From afar, David used the sling to strike the giant in the forehead. The young man, smaller, weaker, inexperienced in traditional battle, felled his more massive, more experienced foe with just one stone. The battle ended in victory for the Israelites, and the Philistines, seeing their best fighter killed before them, fled to avoid enslavement.

The story of David and Goliath resonates as an inspiring story for anyone, company, or individual looking to overcome enormous odds. But looking a bit deeper, there is a lesson for aspiring transformative companies: it pays to not play by the rules.

While the battle's objective was set, the rules of engagement were entirely up to his choosing as far as David was concerned. Instead of accepting them, David set convention aside to fight on his own terms. To start, David selected his own weapon of choice, the sling, rather than the expected sword and shield for close combat.

While David was forced to accept fighting on the battlefield, he used that field in a way that played to his strengths, keeping his distance and using the sling from afar.

David also altered the engagement itself. He made speed, agility, and accuracy a benefit over size and strength, taking down Goliath before his large, lumbering opponent could attack.

David had no choice but to change the rules. To have gone with convention would have been certain death. And by breaking those rules, David turned

Goliath's advantages of size, strength, armor, and weapons into disadvantages.

In any normal situation, Goliath's advantages would have led him to victory. His size, strength, and his skills were well-honed for combat. He undoubtedly was well-trained and well-practiced in battle to have such high confidence. So as long as the rules remained the same, Goliath was guaranteed a victory.

This type of asymmetric competition, in which one side holds a great advantage, happens all the time. And when organizations accept the industry structure rules and norms, it puts them at a disadvantage against their larger competitors' assets and resources. As in the story of David and Goliath, there is no competition until someone reframes the engagement so that incumbent strengths no longer matter. When David changed the rules, it created a weakness in Goliath's conventional approach where there was none previously.

Research indicates that later market entrants tend to have a broader product/market scope and enter the market with more innovative and differentiated solutions.[2] Transformative companies are more likely to rewrite their industry's rules and norms, creating a new form of competitive asymmetry in which they have the advantage. That asymmetry begins with resetting what customers value and includes developing new company capabilities that support the customer outcome and give the challenger an advantage. Creative rethinking of the industry structure can enhance it further because as long as the rules remain the same, the incumbent is more likely to win.

This type of innovation of the industry structure is known as reframing, and we've already explored examples of it from transformative companies like Dollar Shave Club, Dell, and Netflix. Each chose to operate contrary to standard industry practices, changing the rules that other industry participants accepted as given. In doing so, they leveraged competitor strengths into weaknesses while creating their own advantages.

Reframing an industry is a powerful concept because it creates a new competitive dynamic by actively looking for opportunities to change the rules. Yet I believe it's difficult because we have a fixed mindset about the industries in which we compete. As we saw from our previous exercise, even a question as simple as "What would you change about your industry?" is difficult to answer because it is hard to objectively view established structures in a new light. A fixed mindset focuses on competing in an existing market and takes existing assumptions, rules, methods, and structure as given.

Reframing is founded on a growth mindset. It is often fundamental to expanding and scaling existing markets. Reframing focuses on the opportunity without presupposing existing market definitions as limitations. It embodies the new-customer-first approach we've spoken about in earlier chapters, empowering companies to rethink their industry's structure to attract and win new customers. A growth mindset opens up the opportunity for changing the industry to improve both the customer outcome and its potential market reach. What often results is a breakdown of traditional market boundaries to create something entirely new. Figure 6-1 contrasts the differences between fixed and growth industry mindsets regarding market and industry structure.

This chapter will explore the tools you have available to explore how to reexamine, rethink, and reframe industry structure. But first, let's look at what is meant by industry structure.

Perspective	Fixed Mindset	Growth Mindset
Product focus	Improve current product performance and/or cost	Creating new solutions that deliver new and unique value
Market orientation	Better competing in an existing market	Creating new market opportunities
Target customer	Winning currently defined customers	Winning new and existing customers
Industry structure	Fixed industry; focus on cost and efficiencies	Structure adapts to best the customer solution
Approach to barriers to entry	Emphasis on how to break through them	Building solutions that makes traditional barriers irrelevant
Industry rules and constraints	Assumed to be constant	Existing rules become incumbent weakness

Figure 6-1: Fixed and Growth Mindset Approach to Industry and Market Structure

What Makes Up an Industry?

How do we look at an industry? For 40 years, Michael Porter's Five Forces model has been the standard tool to model industry structure, evaluate industry competitiveness, and assess relative power. It looks at five forces or factors that influence whether an industry is attractive to new competitors: customers, suppliers, the threat of new entrants, the threat of substitutes, and the level of rivalry between competitors.

Porter's Five Forces is an excellent tool for evaluating an industry, but it is also problematic because it influences us to view the industry through the lens of a fixed mindset. Used as a tool for determining the attractiveness of an industry to new entrants, it encourages us to accept the industry structure and only think of how easy it is to enter and compete in a particular market, rather than how to change that market to our advantage.

It's essential to think about reviewing an industry in a way that enables us to evaluate it and decide what is worth adopting and what can and should be changed. A simple industry structure model like that in figure 6-2 gives us a different perspective, examining industry structure with a view toward how to change it.

An industry is defined as a set of economic activities that can be grouped together around the objective of delivering a product or service to a customer. It is a classification of the actors, including companies, customers, and suppliers, along with the activities, practices, and norms used to produce and deliver that product or service. I characterize that structure by dividing an industry into its front end, core, and back-end components, as shown in figure 6-2.

The back end of the industry includes those activities that fuel the development and sourcing of solution elements, including the suppliers, factors of input, how a solution is produced, the methods to create scale, and the limitations on scale. This last factor is essential for understanding how to move beyond the barriers to profitable growth. The front end of the industry includes those elements that characterize the marketplace for end customers, go-to-market activities, the business model of value exchange, and the customer attributes and activities.

Between these two, in the industry core, are the activities and factors used to create a valuable solution, including the product or service itself, how value is created, substitutes, alternatives, and the parts of the market ecosystem that need to be in place to create a complete solution. While some areas such as co-consumables and ecosystem partners may seem a stretch, they are essential to identify and explore ways to improve the outcome or change the structure to your advantage.

Finally, stretching across the entire industry is a list of the assumptions, rules, and regulations that govern the industry. For a complete analysis, this list should be as comprehensive as possible and extend to the unwritten rules that govern industry actions and limitations.

Model of Industry Structure		
Back End	**Industry Core**	**Front End**
Suppliers	Value creation	Value exchange
Factors for input	Product offerings	Customers
Methods of production	Competitive offerings	Marketplace
Methods and limits of scale	Ecosystem partners	Distribution
	Substitute solutions	Basis of competition
	Co-consumables	Consumption model
The rules, assumptions, practices, axioms, and industry regulations		

Figure 6-2: Industry Structure Model

It is a helpful exercise to spend time writing out each of the components for your industry. As you do so, you will start to recognize areas where the industry could be improved, viable alternatives, and practices that you have accepted as a given. As industries progress, each of these attributes tends to become more established and industry attributes fixed. Competition stabilizes as companies figure out their own strategy and their core operations model.

Identifying and understanding each of these elements individually and specifically, we better understand how an industry works and how to change it. That is where reframing comes in.

Reframing an Industry

Incumbents hold every advantage in maintaining an industry structure that they have optimized as it is. Supplier relationships, distribution agreements, economies of scale, partnerships, and proprietary technology and methods can all be advantages and barriers to entry. When a company changes a factor in an industry, it is usually a challenger who takes that bold step. More Davids taking on Goliaths with a different view of the battlefield will increasingly transform the structure of many industries in the process.

We could have precisely defined the broadcast television industry in the United States just 30 years ago. There were essentially three significant competitors at that time: CBS, NBC, and ABC. In addition, there was the Public Broadcasting Service (PBS) and an upstart broadcaster, Fox. That industry was framed by a set of rules, regulations, content producers, distribution arrangements, rules for station ownership, a defined value exchange model, and other factors. It was also governed by symmetric competition with competing parties on close to equal footing.

However, since that time, technology, demographic changes, viewing trends, and regulatory modifications have enabled a reframing of the industry. These changes have included an increase in cable television options, the Internet and availability of online streaming, wireless broadband, and the introduction of mobile devices. The shifts have altered the entire structure of the market, including competitors, content suppliers, consumers, devices, and business models. While the main broadcast networks still exist and retain remnants of their historical model, they face a new set of competitors, including Netflix, Hulu, Amazon, and YouTube. They also compete with video content from Facebook, Instagram, and TikTok. Today, we find broadcast, cable, and streaming markets to be very different and difficult to define compared to 30 years ago.

Reframing, consciously rethinking, and reshaping the structure of an industry requires examining the dynamics, rules, and parameters that make up the industry with an eye toward how to change them to create better customer outcomes and improve a company's ability to compete.

Constraints are often the genesis of innovation. As most companies enter or create change in a market after it starts to mature, they face countervailing forces. Frequently there are barriers to competition that limit the ability to meet competitors head-to-head with any chance of success. Reframing is an exercise in rethinking and navigating around those constraints.

Netflix overcame industry structure to deliver a better video rental business without stores by focusing on DVDs and mail delivery. Uber and Lyft created a ride-sharing service without the benefit of a fleet of vehicles. Despite constraints on owning hotel properties, Airbnb has become a leading accommodations provider. Walmart developed new methods to overcome the logistics of offering a wide selection of goods at low prices to sparsely populated areas.

To better understand options for reframing, I will discuss three standard ways that transformative organizations reframe their industries: creating platforms, crossing swim lanes, and democratization. These forms of reframing are not mutually exclusive and can work together. Then we will finish with several ways to create alternatives to the existing structure.

The Rise of Platforms: Recentering on New Value Creation

There is probably no reset of industry structure more impactful today than the rise of the platforms. While platforms are nothing new, the platform economy has grown exponentially over the last 20 years under the momentum many of the transformative companies examined in this book.

A platform is a foundation that serves to organize economic, social, or innovation activity with financial or other benefits to those that participate, with the greatest benefit going to the platform owner. Platforms can be transaction-oriented (such as Uber/Lyft, Airbnb, Netflix, Craigslist, and Amazon) or innovation-orientated (such as Apple, Salesforce, and Intel). While they are primarily digital, they can include non-digital components and may be asset-heavy (Walmart and Ryanair) or asset-light (Airbnb).

The important, defining characteristic of a platform is the presence of network effects in which the platform becomes more valuable with an increase in the number of participants. This is evident in transaction platforms like Craigslist or Uber/Lyft, where more users, including suppliers and customers, create more value and in technology platforms, such as the iPhone, in which more developers and content providers generate more content and applications for consumers. More users on the platform, such as iPhone users, create more value for developers, who produce more valuable content and applications. This reciprocal relationship that occurs through the platform creates an upward value spiral for all parties, making the platform itself more valuable.

The benefits that aggregate to platform providers are tremendous. Accenture estimates that platform companies represent some $2.6 trillion in market capitalization worldwide.[3] Underlying this market value are the benefits that platforms create for themselves, including not just network effects, but speed, higher innovation, access to assets, better business models, and, increasingly, analytics-based insight from the data generated on the platform.

Platforms are a valuable reframing method because they can create profound changes to industries and disrupt traditional industry structures. Attracting industry participants into a common platform creates a hub of innovation, creating pooled assets and resources, ecosystem partners, interactions, transactions, and, increasingly, activities that can be tracked and analyzed to produce better results. This gives them the power to dramatically disrupt and reframe industry structures and permit new forms of asymmetric competition. For example, Airbnb uses a platform approach to completely change the competitive requirements of the hospitality industry. It creates a platform of accommodations for renters without Airbnb owning any of the assets.

The customer relationship management application company Salesforce uses a platform-centric model to create advantages and deliver better and broader customer solutions. AppExchange enables third parties to develop business applications built on the Salesforce platform. AppExchange now includes more than 3.5 million applications delivering business solutions to customers and creating broader and more significant innovations than Salesforce could have created on its own.

Apple has successfully created platforms around its computing and mobile platforms, including integrated applications and media. The development of the iPhone as an innovation platform for the use of applications, books, video, and music changed the structure of the mobile phone industry forever. It also opened up a business model that included multiple new revenue streams for Apple and content developers.

Amazon's platform has turned into the world's largest online marketplace. The vast number of vendors selling on Amazon Marketplace has created tremendous value while lowering the barriers for sellers to enter the retail market. In 2020, Amazon reported $80.46 billion of revenue that was fulfilled by these independent vendors, many of whom store their products in Amazon warehouses. Amazon Marketplace takes advantage of network effects by collecting vast amounts of data, including what customers buy, how they shop, what food they eat, the videos customers watch, and the music they listen to.

Even Walmart has established itself as a retail platform that now incorporates both its own services and an ecosystem of partners to supply other services, including pharmacy, financial services, eyeglasses, healthcare services, and money transfer. Walmart integrates both digital and physical elements to round out its platform.

Increasingly, with the use of data analytics, platform-based organizations gain advantage in their ability to track and analyze the interactions and transactions on their platform, accumulating data that helps them better target customer offerings.

Uber created a platform that has used data to optimize the rider experience, placing drivers in the right locations for shorter ride times and fine-tuning their ride with driver feedback. Now, as a company it has extended its data capabilities to launch other services as platforms, including Uber Eats food delivery.

Crossing Swim Lanes

Another way organizations reframe industry structure is by crossing over the traditional swim lanes that define product and market boundaries. As they focus on helping the customer achieve their objective, organizations often find it advantageous to cross over, ignore, and blur traditional industry lines.

As organizations become more customer-focused, traditional demarcations fade away. This creates hardships for incumbents, who have optimized for competition in a discrete industry with a fixed set of rules.

Nowhere has blurring industry lines to create a new solution set been more obvious than at Apple. Apple has had one of the most successful track records of transforming industries by blurring industry lines. Particularly successful has been Apple's convergence of media and devices that started with the iPod. Using the iTunes Store, Apple created a seamless solution that allowed users to easily buy and download new music, creating the ideal user experience and disrupting the MP3 player market with something that the incumbents were not prepared to provide.

With the introduction of the iPhone, Apple blurred industry lines by turning the iPhone into a mobile computing and media consumption device that included an almost unlimited number of ways to use the device for entertainment, communications, news, fitness and health, e-commerce, and more. This convergence of functionality has allowed Apple to use the iPhone to offer movies, streaming services, news subscriptions, and applications, crossing traditional market boundaries.

Uber crossed traditional swim lanes to create a new personal transportation industry that pools customers from multiple discrete markets, a common sign of asymmetrical competition. Is Uber competing with taxi companies? Rental car agencies? The auto industry? Trucking? The answer to all is yes. Conceived initially as an application for calling "black car" services, it transformed transportation services as a taxi competitor. It has also replaced rental cars for some customers, and, for others, it is a viable alternative to car ownership. Crossing swim lanes allows companies to aggregate customers from multiple markets, creating more massive market opportunities while better serving customer needs.

Starting as an e-commerce platform, Amazon's solutions have crossed over traditional industry lines as well. While it currently represents 43 percent of all e-commerce transactions, Amazon has blurred the lines between e-commerce and physical retail by creating its own Amazon stores as well as by purchasing Whole Foods in 2017.

For Amazon, it doesn't stop there. It has become an electronics and media provider, offering devices such as the Kindle e-reader, Amazon Fire TV, and Echo smart speaker. The latter features the Alexa virtual assistant, which connects with Amazon's e-commerce platform, provides information, and integrates with other devices, including Amazon's newly acquired home security company Ring. Wrapped around much of this is Amazon's lucrative and category-defying membership club, Amazon Prime, which provides free shipping, music, movies, original content, and discounts as part of the subscription, further blurring traditional swim lanes.

Democratizing

As it implies, democratizing entails a focus on creating a solution that is universally available and accessible. By nature, democratization efforts break down industry structures and the barriers that inhibit broad adoption. It replaces them with more efficient and universal ways to bring solutions to market.

Well known for his early focus on democratizing the automobile, Henry Ford restructured an entire industry that had already existed around mass-market development. By developing new manufacturing structures and supplier integration, Ford developed an industry structure that supported reducing the price on a Model-T by more than 70 percent from its initial price and created the first mass-market for automobiles. Ford also created an industry structure of vertical integration, a new concept at that time, that was adopted by other auto manufacturers and eventually other industries.

In yet another market, Amazon Web Services has democratized cloud hosting and computing to create on-demand services that allow users to spin up new computing resources as needed. This has resulted in a new, compressed industry infrastructure that would otherwise demand separate decisions about data centers, server configurations, bandwidth, and the like. By putting all of that into its service, Amazon created a dynamic platform that could be used with little upfront investment and paid for only as consumed, creating a new business model that has competed effectively against hosting on-premises or with more traditional infrastructure providers.

Democratizing is a powerful strategy because the actions that support it result in reviewing and reframing industry structure. A more in-depth examination of how companies democratize is a central topic of the next chapter.

Change Challenges Incumbents

Transformative companies benefit from orienting themselves to a customer outcome and creating a position for themselves by blurring an industry's boundaries, whether they seek to be a new market leader or a niche player.

The blurring of industry lines that accompanies creating new customer-oriented solutions makes the competitive landscape more challenging for incumbents. They must also face competing against a transformative competitor who has developed an advantage with its own unique capabilities model.

As the long-held framework of the old industry falls away and a shift happens, the likelihood of radical industry change increases. Incumbents in markets that are transforming struggle to compete against a new customer outcome that is outside of their ability to replicate and one that often goes counter to their assets, capabilities, and the industry structure they know.

How to Kickstart Reframing

Industry reframing begins with leaders that take a proactive approach to look for change. It is a process of discovery that requires open-mindedness. It should not be a surprise that most of the transformative companies researched in this book were founded and run by an industry outsider who had no previous experience at all in the industry. Those who had previous experience in their industry, including Henry Ford (Ford Motor Company), Marc Benioff (Salesforce), and Sam Walton (Walmart), all showed a high level of openness and interest in experimentation and shedding existing convention.

Common across these transformative leaders is the ability to take an outsider's view of their industry. They share an ability to see the potential for change, opportunities, and alternative solutions in an industry where others don't.

Not everyone has the visionary capacity of Henry Ford or Steve Jobs, but creativity and openness are skills that can be learned and developed. Organizations can also foster them with the right culture, including hiring people from diverse backgrounds and industry experience. Steve Jobs advocated hiring people from diverse backgrounds, observing, "A lot of people in our industry haven't had very diverse experiences. So they don't have enough dots to connect, and they end up with very linear solutions without a broad perspective on the problem. The broader one's understanding of the human experience, the better design we will have."[4]

To aid in looking for ways to broaden perspective we'll use the remainder of this chapter to discuss two tools that help provide that perspective: lateral thinking and creating contextual awareness.

Use Lateral Thinking

Lateral thinking is an approach to "out of the box" thinking developed by physician, psychologist, and author Edward de Bono. It creates a thinking process to develop alternative solutions, bypassing the existing way of solving problems, common assumptions, and traditional linear thinking. Lateral thinking is a crucial method of achieving transformative outcomes.

One exercise to apply lateral thinking to an industry is by using the industry framework outlined earlier in this chapter to lay out all the assumptions that frame the industry as you now see it: Who are the customers? What are the characteristics of the product? Who pays for the solution, and how do they pay for it? Who owns it? Who produces it? What are the activities that create value? How is value exchanged? Where is the market? Where is value exchanged? Who are the suppliers? What is the current channel to the customer? Thinking about those questions helps identify and document the rules, both written and unwritten, and the regulations we think govern our industry.

Identifying the underlying dynamics and assumed structure of the market gives you a list that you can then challenge by creating an alternate universe of industry structure. After making the industry structure explicit, address each element individually, exploring alternatives and enhancers. Challenge each component separately with questions such as "How else could our product be distributed to the customer?" and "If the customer didn't pay, who could, and why?" The process of challenging each assumption develops a keen recognition of those elements, how important they are, and, most significantly, what can be improved upon or changed and how.

Alternatively, you can use lateral thinking to work backward from the desired outcome to create alternatives to achieve it. Working back from an idealized outcome overcomes traditional assumption-based methods and can suggest multiple paths to that same outcome and ways to break from conventional industry structure.

Working backward avoids following the well-known path of the current industry structure and facilitates addressing how an outcome can be accomplished and highlights the value of creating intentionality, a topic we will discuss in chapter 10.

Ridesharing services were a radical departure from traditional taxi, black car, and rental car services. They feel like a radically brilliant solution because they have completely shifted our experience and the traditional industry structure. Particularly interesting to me is the unique customer outcome they provide. There is a flow in the user experience from the time a customer pulls out their phone to call a driver in a ride-sharing app to the time they step out of the vehicle at their destination without having to act to pay the driver. Their vision of making transportation as easy turning on water, or as pulling out your phone, helps dictate how to dictate industry structure to achieve that outcome.

While lateral thinking is used for sweeping changes, it can also be used to focus on overcoming specific barriers and problems. It is helpful for focusing on developing alternatives to specific problems that may also have a broad impact on breaking traditional industry structure. One powerful tactic is to take extreme positions by removing a building block of the current industry structure and examining alternatives to competing without that specific element. By running alternative scenarios, you can envision and create alternatives that may become the building blocks of your industry reframing strategy.

Create Contextual Awareness

Foundational to rethinking and reframing an industry is the development of contextual awareness—that is, an understanding of what changes may impact the industry and create opportunities. Leaders often fail to cultivate this baseline understanding of the market and industry environment that paints the background of the bigger picture.

Often industry change is enabled by outside forces, so leaders must maintain a keen awareness of the environmental factors that can influence the industry. This is done by creating context.

Developing a common set of assumptions and trends that may impact the industry and the organization allows leaders to create a map of current conditions, revealing threats and opportunities and informing how to use those changes to create advantage. The extension of this thinking unveils the opportunities to reframe the industry.

Recognizing contextual changes drives the creation of great companies. The initial impetus for the creation of Netflix 1.0, the company's DVD mail-order business, may have come from Reed Hastings's displeasure over a $40 video late fee. However, the real foundation for the solution came when a friend told Hastings of the coming trend of movies moving to the digital video disk, or DVD. Understanding this trend, Hastings created and tested the hypothesis that this more durable media could be mailed without damage. He purchased several CDs and, shipping them to himself, proved his hypothesis. DVDs available at retail for $20 when Blockbuster was buying VHS cassettes for $45 helped Hastings recognize that fundamental change to the industry was possible: a company could purchase inexpensive and durable DVDs and mail them cheaply. This allowed Hastings to develop a competitive offering by using regional distribution centers to distribute the DVDs by mail.

As with Amazon selling books over the Internet, Netflix was able to take advantage of a fundamental trend or change in conditions that enabled a concept not previously possible. Similarly, Lyft and Uber were able to take advantage of the advancement of analytics, greater societal openness for consumer-to-consumer transactions, and the common practice of using rating systems to create a ride service that would not have been imagined previously.

This ability to recognize trends and capitalize on them is not limited to recent transformative companies either. Sam Walton of Walmart recognized and benefited from key trends that permitted him to build his retail empire, including the development of the interstate highway system that linked major rural areas together, enabling his logistics strategy. Walmart also took early advantage of technology changes by adopting new computing systems that facilitated their logistics, merchandising, and supplier strategies. Perhaps most importantly, Sam Walton made the keen observation that an increasingly mobile rural population that more frequently visited cities and had seen their large, well-stocked stores would return to their rural homes wanting a similar product selection.

After Walmart had established itself in rural areas, the company could expand rapidly by taking advantage of the broad shift in population out of cities and into suburban areas. This allowed Walmart to build ahead of the migration to the suburbs, finding inexpensive locations and meeting customers as they moved in rather than locating in already contested locations.

Charles Darwin observed, "It is not the strongest of the species that survives, nor the most intelligent that survives. It is the one that is the most adaptable to change." That ability to change is predicated on the skill of observing and understanding what is changing. An essential tool for identifying and analyzing trends that have the potential to impact an industry and enable transformative approaches is the PESTEL analysis. PESTEL is a mnemonic for the category of trends can have an impact on your industry and includes:

Political—This covers the extent to which government policies are impactful on the industry. This can include government policies on tax, trade, labor, environment, competitiveness, and other regulations.

Economic—Factors can include overall economic growth, inflation, interest rates, exchange rates, degrees of income inequality, regional changes, changes in spending and savings habits, business spending, and investing.

Social—Social analysis may include changes in the population, such as growth, age distribution, changes in attitudes, sentiments, beliefs, and accepted cultural practices.

Technological—Technology has a massive impact on our society, as manifested in new products and how they are made, sold, distributed, and consumed.

Environmental—Environmental factors can include societal attitudes about the environment as well as changes to the physical environment including weather, landscape, pollution, and availability of raw materials.

Legal—This can include changes in societal laws, product regulations, consumer rights, commerce laws, and regulations governing specific industries.

Each of these categories has the potential for significant impact on your industry. Using this PESTEL framework helps identify those changes that most impact your industry today and where you can focus and facilitate change. Organizations should spend time reviewing trends affecting their organization at least twice per year. One of the most helpful ways to do this is to pose the question of what is currently affecting your organization to multiple smaller teams, having them present and debate their views.

One CEO I worked with exemplifies the effective use of contextual awareness to identify what trends were impacting her organization, how they were affecting customers, the opportunities created, and what capabilities the company needed to build to take advantage of the opportunities. In every board meeting and company meeting, she would display three slides describing the management teams collective view of what was happening in the market, reminding everyone why there was an opportunity for the company, and explaining what the company was currently focused on to meet that opportunity head on. She would always give her audience the chance to challenge the context, adding insight and noting observed changes to that reality. Those simple actions created an environment for everyone to think about what was happening and challenge how the company was addressing it. We'll discuss that topic more in chapter 12.

In the next section, we turn our attention to understanding how to master market entry by exploring scale accelerators and explore how organizations can use these capabilities to innovate customer outcomes and industry structure.

From Concept to Action

1. What is our accepted industry framework today?
2. What are the key assumptions of the framework today? What alternatives exist?

3. What constraints and barriers to entry would exist if we were a new competitor trying to enter this market? How could we overcome them?

4. What is the desired outcome for our customers? How can we work backward and create other ways to reach an ideal outcome?

5. What is emerging in political, economic, social, technological, environmental, and legal trends?

6. In what ways can we use these trends to change our industry?

Section III

Innovating to Win:
Scaling to Market Leadership

Innovators spend significant time focusing on building new products, but when they fail it is often due to problems with market entry. McKinsey's review of market winners and losers found that four out of five new market entrants fail, and the most common reasons were not product factors.[1]

Too often leaders, in the words of General Motors CEO Mary Barra, "confuse progress with winning." Innovating to win represents the way that an organization approaches and re-defines the market it enters. It reflects the type of business innovation that has made so many transformative companies successful. Market leadership involves creating markets where they play, making it easier to win customers and dominate a market in transition.

Because of this, most companies included in my research have been successful despite lacking the most obvious predictors of market entry success: early timing and order of entry, a less mature industry to enter, significant complementary assets, or even experience in the market. Almost all were founded by leaders who had little or no industry experience, entered late into mature markets, and lacked most or any of the traditional requirements or assets to be competitive.

Economists have long argued about the effectiveness of barriers to entry for incumbents, which can include early access to resources, economies of scale, customer switching costs, and intellectual property protection. Barriers are important in defending an existing industry structure and business model. But research on industry competitive structure from Helen Salavou and others shows that high barriers to entry lead to higher levels of innovation by new firms seeking to creatively go around those barriers.[2]

Underscoring the concept of innovating to win is principle three of the transformative framework: it is easiest to enter and lead markets that are shifting and expanding. Transformative organizations side-step traditional barriers and even head-to-head competition by targeting new customers with new outcomes (outcome innovation) in new ways (structural innovation), which shifts the market and eliminates traditional barriers. Shifting markets makes old barriers to entry ineffective. Transformative companies then protect themselves simply by doing things that incumbents don't find logical to do because it goes against their established practices and assets. This is at the heart of business innovation.

Successful market entry for these companies arises, in part, from a distinctive and unique approach to addressing the market, starting with a new-customer-first approach that focuses on drawing in new customers to expand the market. Their innovate to win strategy is based in part on their ability to shape and expand markets with the set of recognizable scale accelerators shown in figure III. These capabilities reinforce a new-customer-first approach that looks to expand the market by attracting unserved and underserved customers, creating new consumption models, developing attractive business models, and efficiently identifying innovative substitutes to current practices.

Scale Accelerators: Enabling Market Expansion and Industry Reframing	
Scale Accelerator	Description
Democratizing	Creating near-universal availability of a product or service and lifting constraints for customers to find, access, and buy it where and when they want.
Simplifying	Taking a product or service down to the most basic and essential elements, resulting in a significantly expanded market opportunity.
New-Customer Focusing	Targeting initial beachhead markets that give organizations the traction to create a broad market opportunity.
Model Building	Creating new profitable business models that accompany innovation and add to company advantage.
Recombining	Creatively borrowing and recombining existing ideas from other markets to introduce innovations into their own market.
Rule Breaking	Breaking rules, dispelling beliefs, and eschewing accepted practices to change customer outcomes and create a sustainable advantage.

Figure III: Scale Accelerators to Facilitate Market Leadership

Together these accelerators form a set of options that will boost your odds of success when entering a new market with a differentiated offering, winning new customers, and creating a favorable competitive position. The three chapters in this section will describe these accelerators in more detail and highlight how organizations can use them to their advantage.

Chapter 7

Democratizing and Simplifying

Democratizing and simplifying are foundational scale accelerators that lead to increased adoption and market expansion. Democratization focuses on creating universal availability of a product or service and lifting constraints for customers to find, access, and buy it where and when they want. Simplification creates high customer value by streamlining a product or service down to its most basic and essential elements.

Democratizing

I'm going to democratize the automobile.
Henry Ford

Democratization is defined as "the action of making something accessible to everyone."[1] Whether it is the desire to bring to the world a good cup of dark roast coffee, affordable furniture, or a ride on demand, organizations such as Starbucks, IKEA, Uber, and many other transformative companies share a common aspiration to make their solutions as widely available as possible.

Democratization is both a capability and a mindset. It is more than just making something more widely available. It is a reset of the "why?"—the customer outcome—which instantly makes a product or service more widely appealing, creating an inflection point in the market and accelerating growth. It focuses on lifting constraints for customers to find, access, and use it where and when they want.

When Henry Ford launched the Ford Model T in 1908, he wasn't the first to manufacture a production-level car. Karl Benz had already accomplished that with the Benz Patent Motorwagen in 1888, the first commercially available automobile. Benz licensed the three-wheeled, open vehicle design to Emile Roger, who produced it in France.

Ransom Olds ushered in the manufacturing production line when he started the Olds Motor Vehicle Company (later known as Oldsmobile) to produce the very Tesla-sounding Model R, also known as the Olds Curved Dash, in 1901. He sold 425 Model Rs that year for around $650 each, approximately $18,000 today.

After apprenticing for Thomas Edison, Henry Ford started the Ford Motor Company in 1903 and produced several models before creating and launching the Model T in 1908. Sporting a 20 HP engine and two forward gears, the Model T sold 11,000 vehicles that first year for $825 each, almost twice the average worker's salary in the United States.

Ford had bigger aspirations for the automobile, stating in 1909, "When I'm through, everybody will be able to afford one, and about everybody will have one." The next year, he sold just over 19,000 units of the Model T at about $900 each. While paved roads were rare and automobiles were mainly purchased by wealthier customers, Ford's vision was to "build a car for the great multitude." His dream: "It will be large enough for the family, but small enough for the individual to run and care for. It will be constructed of the best materials, by the best men to be hired, after the simplest designs that modern engineering can devise. But it will be so low in price that no man making a good salary will be unable to own one."[2]

It took 12.5 hours on the product line to build a Model T in 1909. Ford set out to improve on that by breaking down production components, documenting and refining skill sets, reducing complexity, and introducing machinery to replace manual processes. When the company opened its new Highland Park

Complex in 1914, it took only 93 minutes to build a Model T. Selling cars for $440 each, Ford produced 200,000 vehicles that year.

Ford used production efficiencies to eventually drop the price of the Model T to $260, selling around two million cars per year by the 1920s. By the time Ford replaced the Model T with the Model A in 1927, Ford had produced 16.5 million vehicles, making the Model T one of the most popular automobiles of all time.

Ford demonstrates a common drive of transformative organizations to push and expand markets through democratization. Walmart brought discount retailing first to rural markets and now has 12,000 locations throughout the world. Google made advertising on the Internet available to anyone with Google Adwords. In a market dominated by cheap, basic phones, Apple democratized the smartphone, creating the core functions for mass appeal.

Ireland-based airline Ryanair democratized vacation travel in Europe by building on the low-cost airline model pioneered by US-based Southwest Airlines, targeting vacation and low-cost business travelers. In 2019, Ryanair carried 148 million passengers across Europe, making it the continent's largest airline.[3] With flights priced as low as five euros per segment, Ryanair has genuinely democratized vacation air travel in Europe.

The Multiple Dimensions of Availability

Democratization means more than just availability or price. There is a depth to democratization that involves producing the right customer outcome at the right place and the right time for mass appeal. It lifts constraints to finding, accessing, buying, and using solutions with adaptations and trade-offs to optimize customer outcomes. Consider some of the multiple dimensions of democratization:

- **Location.** Location availability is a key distinguishing objective of many successful transformative companies. McDonald's, Starbucks, and Walmart have created available solutions through tens of thousands of physical locations.

- **Immediacy.** Amazon's e-book delivery through its Kindle reader and apps has created a precedent for immediacy. Amazon is increasingly focusing on providing near-immediate experiences with non-digital goods and services like Prime Now for two-hour delivery. Netflix likewise created a new consumption model with streaming access, breaking the traditional linear programming model of broadcast television.

- **The intersection of time and place.** Redbox takes a unique spin on democratization, providing access to DVDs for rent at the intersection of time and location with over 42,000 locations. Mitch Lowe, Redbox's president, observed, "Two-thirds of all films for rental are selected between four and nine in the evening."[4] So Redbox reached the customer by putting their bright red DVD machines at locations where customers stop by for dinner or the drive home: grocery stores, fast food restaurants, gas stations, and convenience stores. This two-dimensional form of democratization has also been successful for Lyft and Uber, who use algorithms and a fluid pool of drivers to support rides when and where they are needed.

- **Depth of availability.** Democratization can include access to depth and diversity as well. Amazon brought availability of millions of book titles to our fingertips, far beyond what any bookstore could provide. Netflix 1.0, the mail-order DVD provider, gave customers access to more than 60,000 DVDs, making an enormous DVD library available to anyone.

- **Access.** Access by curation is a unique form of democratization. Netflix's algorithms provide filtered access to the most relevant titles out of its vast supply of movies and TV shows, preventing customers from drowning in options. On the other end of the spectrum, Redbox trades off the location of kiosks and the reduction of selection, focusing on selling between 70–200 titles in each kiosk and presenting the most relevant new release titles first to make them more accessible.

- **Effort.** Reducing friction and increasing convenience are additional forms of democratization. Lyft, Uber, and Amazon all focus on eliminating friction in ordering. Subscription models such as Dollar Shave Club eliminate reordering effort with automatic renewals. Mobile apps from Redbox, Walmart, and Starbucks create fluidity from order to pick up.

Democratization as a Mindset

Democratizing goes beyond any single product, event, outcome, or achievement. Among transformative companies, democratization is a common mindset, leading to an ongoing process to continually improve upon it.

That relentless focus is visible in Intel's efforts to design and build the most powerful and cost-effective microprocessors in the world. Moore's Law, first observed 50 years ago, is less of a forecast and more a company objective. The result of Intel's focus on creating smaller, more powerful microprocessors is a transistor now 1/50,000 the cost, and runs 5,000 times faster, using 1/4,000 the energy compared to the transistors in Intel's first microprocessor introduced in 1971.[5]

In an increasingly digitized world, democratization means changing what is delivered to better fulfill customer needs. Amazon has transformed the concept of a book multiple times to improve access. From Amazon's beginning as a web-based bookstore, the company has concentrated efforts on making books more accessible. Its milestone efforts include:

- **Kindle eBook Reader.** Amazon launched the Kindle reader in 2007 and pioneered instant wireless delivery of books, making them available any time. Amazon now has five million books available for Kindle.
- **Kindle Lending Library.** Amazon permitted Prime members to borrow and read a book per month for free.
- **Kindle Unlimited.** The company created an eBook subscription-based library with unlimited reading rights that offers hundreds of thousands of books on demand.
- **Audiobooks.** With the acquisition of the company Audible, Amazon created the Audiobook Creation Exchange (ACX), a marketplace for turning books into audiobooks. From 2011 to 2012, ACX expanded the number of audiobooks available by tenfold in its first year.[6]
- **Audio narration.** Whispersync narration for Kindle eBooks has given customers audio narration to transition from reading to audiobook seamlessly.
- **Self-publishing.** Amazon acquired CustomFlix, a DVD on-demand provider, and BookSurge, a self-publishing platform, merging them

to form the CreateSpace self-publishing platform, opening publishing to any writer.

Amazon's democratization mindset comes from a developed intentionality—that persistent focus on the aspirational customer outcome which we will discuss in chapter 10. Its mindset, skillset, and persistence are visible in other areas of Amazon's business, like its continual effort to improve its ability to deliver physical goods. Amazon's experimentation with new delivery methods has included drone-based air delivery, package-carrying blimps, and a patented beehive-like Amazon tower that would allow for self-service customer areas, truck deliveries, and drones that fly into the beehive to pick up packages for delivery.

Deconstructing Barriers

Once they set democratization as a priority, transformative companies create a model of ongoing action that fosters democratization. IKEA incorporates democratization into their culture. The furnishings company's vision of "Democratic Design," as described on its website by head of design Marcus Engman, is "our way of doing the impossible: making good design available to many people."

IKEA centers democratic design focuses on five principles: form, function, sustainability, quality, and low price. The company sees achieving its vision as a process. Engman states, "Over the years we've learnt that by constantly asking ourselves, 'Is there a better way?', bright ideas can come from just about anywhere, from anyone."[7]

The process of routinely asking whether there is a better way encourages team members to continually search for new opportunities along one or more of the dimensions of democratization.

Success hinges on looking at every aspect of the product or service to objectively understand barriers and then creating the initiative to eliminate them. Removing common obstacles such as cost, supply, and availability is just the beginning. Other methods of democratization can go even deeper, such as:

- **Standardizing for general appeal.** Like Henry Ford's "Any color, as long as it's black" mantra, other companies democratize through standardization and mass customization. The iPhone started as a single model, compared to dozens of options from Motorola and Nokia. Apple recognized that the software-based customization was what would scale. And while McDonald's localizes some menus for regional tastes, it mostly standardizes its menus.

- **Unbundling.** Reducing barriers can include untethering or unbundling the product or service. Craigslist became the online platform for classified advertisement by unbundling that service from the newspaper platform and digitizing it. In another form of unbundling, Zipcar unbundled car rentals for urban residents by eliminating time constraints and friction and while increasing convenience by turning rentals into a digital membership with hourly rental fees.

- **Reducing risk.** Risk is a big barrier for purchases, especially online. There are probably few online purchases more challenging to make than shoes. Zappos lowered risk by offering free shipping and returns, thus encouraging buyers to purchase multiple pairs to try on at home, essentially replicating the in-store shoe buying experience. The result is a much more pleasant and risk-free buying experience. Likewise, the use of peer-to-peer reviews by Uber and Lyft lowers the risk of a potentially uncomfortable experience of stepping into a stranger's car.

- **Reducing upfront investment.** AWS, Amazon's online, scalable cloud platform has overcome the need for upfront investment in cloud hosting hardware and software. Making it fluid and available on demand allows users to grow incrementally without big upfront or step-function costs to install new servers, acquire rack storage, and the like. Similarly, cloud application provider Salesforce makes it easy to add customer relationship management (CRM) capabilities without significant hardware and software expense.

- **Saving time.** As on-demand transportation changes the options we have for hauling ourselves from one place to another, companies such as Uber and Lyft have the challenge of ensuring that the service is available with nearly the same speed as someone getting into their own car. The sharing economy and scale of driver availability, along with predictive algorithms, allows them to solve this better than a dedicated taxi service.

Simplifying

Simplicity is the ultimate sophistication.
Leonardo da Vinci

German mathematician and astronomer Johannes Kepler declared that "nature loves simplicity and unity." There is ample evidence to believe that customers love simplicity as well. While we are barraged continually by complex products and services, and we tend to gravitate to the simplest solutions, often with excitement or relief.

We live in a world where technical innovation is a constant, often bringing with it added complexity. Incremental innovation often causes companies to pile on new features. Simplified solutions, particularly those that offer a simple and clear value proposition, are the most attractive.

The best companies fully adopt the principle of simplification to their advantage. They create high customer value by simplifying their product or service down to the most basic and essential elements. They are also clear about what they offer and what makes them valuable and different.

This simplification is different from our concept of merely reducing the number of features in a product or service. It is a mission-driven approach that retains in mind the company's mission and the emphasis on value in the customer experience, focusing on that to the exclusion of all else.

No company embodies the art and the science of simplification as much as Apple. The organization has always found an advantage in focusing on the art of reduction. "Simplicity is the ultimate sophistication" was the headline of Apple's first marketing brochure back in 1977. "It takes a lot of hard work," CEO Steve Jobs once said, "to make something simple, to truly understand the underlying challenges and come up with elegant solutions."[8]

When Apple launched the iPod, that philosophy of focusing on simplicity came through again. He assessed that competitors' products were too complicated. "What made the Rio and other devices so brain dead was that they were complicated," Jobs observed. "They had to do things like make playlists because they weren't integrated with the jukebox software on your computer. So, by owning the iTunes software and the iPod device, that allowed us to make the computer and the device work together, and it allowed us to put the complexity in the right place."[9]

The company followed a similar path when launching the iPhone in 2007, delivering three main functions: a touch screen iPod, mobile phone, and an Internet communications device. Simplified designs like visual voice mail and quickly setting up email accounts made the product intuitive and drove demand. Detailed focus on physical design and interface led to more than 42 design patents filed under Steve Jobs' name in the first four years of the product launch.

Simple by Design

It's noteworthy that many features considered essential by competitors, including a physical keyboard, infrared data sharing, media card slot, stylus, radio, higher resolution camera, media buttons, podcast downloading, VoIP, games, and voice dialing, were not included on the iPhone.

Significantly, Apple simplified choice as well. While most mobile phone manufacturers were launching dozens of models per year, Apple only had one model. Tech columnist John Dvorak declared that Apple's "one phone fits all" concept was ridiculous. To generate broader appeal, Apple would need "half a dozen variants in the pipeline, otherwise it would be passé within three months." Apple succeeded in featuring just one model through 2013, and since the launch of the iPhone 5c, it has since carried only a few products distinguished by size.

Like democratization, simplification is not a one-time house cleaning or reduction program. It is an ongoing process derived from the organization's mission and is driven by its vision.

Mission Driven: A License to Kill from the Top

When driven from a sense of mission, simplifying is not just desirable; it is a means to accomplish the organization's vision of making the solution usable and available to a larger market, going hand in hand with democratization efforts. That vision often comes from the top of the organization, as in the case of Steve Jobs' vision for the computer to be like an appliance or Marc Benioff envisioning that Salesforce needed to be as simple to use as Amazon's website.

When mission-driven, transformative companies become ruthless about eliminating what is unnecessary, including many historically accepted practices, features, and benefits in competitors' products. Often, simplification removes the bottlenecks that have tied the industry to middling performance that fails to meet customer needs adequately.

This mission mentality provides companies with the freedom to trade current performance for superior performance based on what provides the most value and the broadest market opportunity. Both Redbox and Netflix became successful by chipping away at Blockbuster's business with distinctly dissimilar offerings. They did so by replacing the video giant's mediocre store inventory of 6,500 titles with better and simplified offerings optimized on two different dimensions.

Redbox simplified the solution by dramatically increasing the number of locations, which eventually has grown to 44,000 sites while reducing the number of videos to focus on convenience. Netflix's effort followed a different vector, creating a simplified service that provided curated access to unlimited rentals to a very long-tail library of 60,000 DVDs.

Great companies often employ a license-to-kill mentality, focusing on delivering a customer outcome that customers value more highly than existing offerings by lifting barriers and bottlenecks. This type of "greater good" approach involves optimizing the performance dimensions that matter to the experience. As shown in figure 7-1, this often involves eliminating what competitors see as vital.

Company	Simplification Focus
McDonald's	Table waiters and table service, reusable plates, and tableware
Apple	The floppy disk, DVD optical drive, phone keyboard, 30-pin connector, and headphone jack, among many other features
Amazon	Browsing bookstore shelves
Redbox	Brick-and-mortar stores. The gazillion movies you weren't going to rent
Netflix	The latest blockbuster movie releases
Ryanair	Free snacks on planes, more convenient primary airports
Zappos	Stores, sales, immediate availability
Google	Extra buttons, links, photos, and banner ads
Cirque du Soleil	Animal performances
Ford	Limit of color (black) and standardization of features
IKEA	Assembled furniture
Salesforce	On-premises software
Dollar Shave Club	The option of buying blades at a local store (initially)

Figure 7-1: A License to Kill

Getting to these more significant elements of simplification and democratization often requires managing customer expectations. To keep flight costs low, Ryanair limits the number of flights available, usually using less busy traffic times of the early morning or later in the evening and limiting staff-intensive duties such as onsite check-in. By making it expensive to use in-person check-in, for example, Ryanair sets passenger expectations and modifies customer behavior to fit its model.

Simplification Goes Beyond Product

Simplification can go beyond product features in improving the overall value delivered to the customer in four key areas: utility, choice, understanding, and availability.

Utility

Utility simplification involves making the product or service as easy to use as possible to maximize its benefit. Companies look at it first because the impact is high.

Amazon Web Services (AWS), Amazon's on-demand cloud hosting and data storage service, has created a unique and scalable cloud infrastructure designed to be fluid and scale on demand. AWS maximizes the utility of its cloud hosting platform, removing the need to manage the hardware, software, and network infrastructure directly. With virtualized systems available through a web interface, Amazon created a way to host applications and store data analogous to turning on a tap: it flows on demand. The AWS focus on simplifying the service to maximize software developers' ability to focus on their solutions instead of the hardware and software hosting it sets it apart for ease of use in a field of competitors that includes Microsoft, Google, Rackspace, IBM, and many others. When launching Amazon S3 cloud data storage, Amazon set simplicity as a requirement, stating, "Building highly scalable, reliable, fast, and inexpensive storage is difficult. Doing so in a way that makes it easy to use for any application anywhere is more difficult. Amazon S3 must do both."[10]

Early time to market and a focus on masking the complexity of its cloud infrastructure while maximizing its usefulness has enabled Amazon Web Services to take a dominant 47 percent share of the cloud hosting market.

Choice

Simplifying choice centers on creating factors that help the customer select the most appropriate product or service. Online retailer Zappos shows how choice can be simplified in a unique way to create an advantage.

Zappos has simplified choice by taking the risk out of buying shoes online, making it easy to return them with their no questions asked policy. Simplicity takes the anxiety out of making a challenging online purchase. In a contrarian approach, Zappos encourages customers to purchase multiple shoes, simplifying the purchasing process by facilitating returns. And Zappos encourages customers to use live 24/7 customer to help them choose, even publishing the phone number on every page of their website.

Understanding

Simplification of understanding means helping the customer to maximize the benefit of using the product or service.

Starbucks gives customers a unique and personalized coffee experience, which results in a massive number of options for their customers to choose from—more than 80,000 drink combinations.[11]

Starbucks overcame this potential problem by leveraging social learning and behavior norming to teach customers an ordering structure that has become a language all its own.[12] Customers initially only need to learn that there are two main choices they need to make: the type of drink with four options (espresso, drip coffee, Frappuccino, and tea) and size with four options (short, tall, grande, venti), followed by options. No matter how the customer places the order, they will hear the Starbucks barista repeat it back to them in a very precise order to establish that language in the customer's mind. As they hear this from the barista and other customers who have adopted the ordering language, they begin to learn it themselves. Both the barista and fellow customers teach new customers the ordering language, allowing them to start experimenting with options without confusion and creating a sense that they are now in the Starbucks community.

Availability

Simplifying availability can involve limiting choices on when and where the customer wants the product or service. Companies such as Dollar Shave Club, Netflix, Redbox, and Walmart have used subscription services, automatic renewals, and location availability to simplify customer decisions and drive market growth.

Sophisticated Simplicity

In our increasingly digitized world, providing customers with too much access and choice is a challenge. Democratization and simplification often reinforce each other, but it can take focus and effort to manage the trade-offs. That only happens when these values are ingrained the organizational culture and activated by clear intent. The result is a solution with an understandable message and differentiated product positioning versus the competition. When the intention is clear, there are no mixed messages.

Perhaps no company has continually balanced democratization and simplification more than Netflix. While creating a streaming service that is more widely available, by one estimate, it has reduced the number of movies in its inventory to just over 5,000 in any given country in 2020.[13] That is down dramatically from its early days as a DVD-by-mail company. Still, it is easy to overwhelm customers with the vast number of options they have. Netflix knows they have between 60 to 90 seconds to help a customer find something to watch. In the words of one of their algorithm designers, "The user either finds something of interest or the risk of the user abandoning our service increases substantially."[14]

About 80 percent of customer choices come from Netflix recommendations. Therefore, Netflix focuses on those "moments of truth" when it can help customers find the right content. While much has been made about its content matching algorithm and 2009 contest with a $1 million prize to find a better algorithm to improve on it, the original algorithm is now part of at least six different methods Netflix uses to connect subscribers with content.

By focusing on using data to lead the customer to the right content, Netflix creates hyper customization, creating more opportunities for helping customers find that moment of truth. This type of customization isn't cheap. Netflix spends approximately $150 million per year on developing better recommendation algorithms.[15] According to its top developers, those algorithms bring more than $1 billion per year in benefits to the company.[16] That estimate is conservative, considering Netflix has grown in value from $3.3 billion when it launched its streaming service to over $580 billion in 2021.

As Netflix demonstrates, much of the value from democratization and simplification comes from creating a broader market appeal that shifts existing customers and brings a mass of new customers to market. Apple did the same by winning over smartphone customers with the iPhone, even as it appealed to simpler feature-phone customers and attracted those who had not yet adopted a mobile phone. Likewise, Ryanair's simpler, democratized travel made it the leading airline in Europe by stealing from the large airlines as well as attracting new customers to market.

Simplification, in particular, is key to creating new and more profitable business models. Apple took on the smartphone market with one product compared to dozens of product options by its competitors and has been able to sustain that practice. Although Samsung has introduced ten times more phone models than Apple did, Apple's gross profits are ten points higher than Samsung's due to higher economies of scale. As a result, Apple takes in two-thirds of the mobile phone industry's profits. Likewise, IKEA, the world's largest furniture provider, has gross profit margins of at least 43–45 percent, much higher than the norm for the furniture industry.

Democratizing and simplifying improve upon profitable business models in other ways. Zappos has an incredibly high 12-month customer repeat purchase rate of 75 percent. Redbox's customers rent another DVD when they return the previous one 25 percent of the time. Netflix's subscriber churn is so low that their biggest retention issue is when customer's credit card expires.

This notable attribute of transformative companies, their ability to generate new and more profitable business models, is critical to their unique market approach and, along with their ability to attract new customers, is the topic of our next chapter.

From Concept to Action

1. How could we better intersect our customers along the dimensions of time, location, or availability?
2. What supply constraints exist for our customers today? Are there alternatives to supply that lessen the need for dedicated resources, time, availability?
3. What demand roadblocks exist? What would we need to change in our product to make it more available?
4. If we were to prioritize how to remove roadblocks, which would have the most impact on opening up demand? What would be next?
5. In what ways can we untether our offerings to make them have more mass appeal?

6. In what ways could our organization shift the location or time of what we are offering?
7. Could we provide deeper availability?
8. How could we improve access? Would it benefit us with some customer use cases to narrow choices to provide better or more universal availability?

Chapter 8

New-Customer Focusing and Model Building

New-customer focusing is the ability to find an initial market beachhead by targeting a specific customer, need, or consumption model that creates the protected space from which to move to broader market opportunities. Model building seeks a more profitable business model that expands the market opportunity and adds to your advantage with a difficult-to-replicate business model.

New market entry requires organizations to commit to answering critical questions of who to target and how to make money. Targeting an attractive initial market segment is the first important step.

According to CB Insights research, the most prominent reason for failure among venture-backed companies, resulting in 42 percent of flops, is no market.[1] While transformative organizations are dealing in existing markets, it's critical that they find a group of initial customers motivated to use them over existing solutions. Failure to find the correct target market puts them directly head-to-head with existing competitors. This chapter will explain the best ways to find a sustainable beachhead market.

One sure indicator of creating game-changing outcomes is the development of new, more profitable business models. In the second half of this chapter, we will discuss how organizations achieve more profitable models that reinforce their success.

New Customer Focusing

It is much easier to expand from something that a small number of people love to something that a lot of people love than from something that a lot of people like to a lot of people love.
Sam Altman, Y Combinator CEO

When Walmart went public and traded on the New York Stock Exchange in 1972, it had stores in only five states: Arkansas, Kansas, Louisiana, Mississippi, and Oklahoma. These states constituted only 6 percent of the United States population and were some of the most rural and sparsely populated areas. Coincidently, fellow retail giants Kmart and Target started in the same year as Walmart in 1962. These two discount competitors started in much larger Detroit and Minneapolis-Saint Paul markets, going head-to-head against larger retailers.

Walton, a famous contrarian, once explained, "If everybody is doing it one way, there's a good chance you can find your niche by going exactly in the opposite direction."[2] Following his own philosophy, his strategy was to launch stores in small towns and sparsely populated areas in the rural south of the United States where he knew there would be demand and little competition.

Critically, Walton knew he needed to develop essential capabilities to be viable in smaller markets. So he focused on improving logistics, distribution, customer analytics, supplier management, and merchandising that enabled Walmart to be consistently more profitable than other discount retailers. The advantages the company created by learning to survive in smaller initial markets helped it dominate, becoming the largest retailer in the US market by 1990.

Starting from a small niche market, Walmart is now the largest retailer globally with 12,000 stores worldwide. Its success came because it could hone its capabilities in an unserved segment of customers in smaller rural markets.

The Transformative Beachhead Orientation: Consumption

It is a widely accepted marketing principle for companies to initially target smaller markets to create a foothold for broader market opportunities. These smaller segments in newly emerging or existing markets serve as a beachhead, a protected space that gives the company time to focus resources and effort to dominate a niche and stake out a position. Companies then use that beachhead to move into adjacent market segments.

Companies traditionally find these beachheads by looking at geographic, demographic, or psychographic similarities to source a segment with a common need. Ideal beachheads create an initial protected space and enable the company to land and expand, quickly moving to a more considerable market opportunity. They must include a set of buyers with a similar buyer profile and a clear, compelling reason to purchase.

The prevailing perspective for identifying a beachhead position is to segment the market by customer. This involves dividing the potential market into three buckets of customers based on whether they are served, underserved, or unserved by existing solutions. When entering a market, organizations determine whether to outperform incumbents to win existing customer segments or create a product to focus on underserved and unserved customer segments, creating a solution that appeals specifically to their needs.

This logic of going after unserved and underserved customers is sound. The theory of disruptive innovation, in particular, hinges on targeting underserved and unserved customers. It advocates offering solutions that address their needs and then building on that solution to reach the broader market of already served customers, eventually taking on existing competition directly. This strategy requires companies following this path to initially ignore the primary market and then build on their initial solution until it finally meets the broader market's needs.

Because transformative companies develop category-creating solutions that produce new outcomes, their solutions are often both broadly appealing and uniquely differentiated. Still, they eschew the "go big or go home" approach and start with a smaller beachhead to hone their solution before going more broadly.

So what is the best way to find those beachhead markets? One successful approach to finding the right beachhead is to take a consumption perspective, looking at customers' varying consumption levels. This approach starts by asking who is currently consuming the product or service and why. That "why?"—the outcome they are seeking—is critical. Further insight comes from asking how, when, and where they consume it. At a foundational level, you can build a profile of who is or isn't consuming based on the following categories:

- **Current consumption.** Those customers that currently using existing solutions, and the benefits they seek.
- **Limited consumption.** Customers who may be using only part of the functionality or in minimal conditions or circumstances, with lesser benefits.
- **Nonconsumption.** Those who are not consuming the solution at all in its current form.

So far, the consumption approach may look similar to a customer-focused approach. However, adding two more categories provides us with more insight into opportunities. Those categories are new consumption and constrained consumption.

New consumption seeks to understand where there are opportunities for existing customers or new customers to use your solution in a unique setting or environment. These insights open up new views into how else it might be used or changing how, where, or when it creates new opportunities.

The first, new consumption, seeks to make the product or service available in new situations. Often, customers may already use the product or service but usage could be expanded. You can also obtain new customers by creating a different reason to consume it.

Starbucks is a prime example of a company that benefited from creating a new consumption model. While they have become the standard for picking up a morning coffee, changing and replacing the traditional consumption model, they extended coffee consumption well beyond that by creating a new model for anytime consumption. By pairing coffee with a unique setting of sleek cafes and comfortable seating, coffee consumption has become the means to indulge, recharge, work a virtual office, or create an ideal meeting environment.

The second new category, constrained consumption, looks for opportunities to target customers who, whether or not they use the solution currently, would be better served and often even consume more if they were not constrained in some way. Constraints may be due to limits on their ability to consume more or a lack of depth to the solution that prevents them from capturing the full benefit.

Constrained consumption is frequently found in solutions that are part of a bigger platform or product offering whose breadth is unneeded by the customer. Such customers are overserved by the existing solution and benefit when features are unbundled to create a stand-alone solution targeting their needs.

Applying a consumption-focused lens to customers is intriguing because it identifies customers based on needs and opens up possibilities for fulfilling them. This creates options for uncovering latent consumption that expands the market.

Figure 8-1 compares the consumption perspective to traditional customer segments, showing how this approach can expand opportunities even when targeting existing customers. Often the new consumption model approach fulfills needs at a new time, place, or for a different customer outcome that appeals even to existing customers.

Attribute	Segmentation Perspective	Consumption Perspective
Orientation	Distinct customer segments based on customer profile	Based on how and why the customer uses the solution
Approach	Win market segment by segment	Create mass appeal based on the customer outcome
Customer profile	Buyer orientation	Usage orientation
Entry point	Niche segment	Build for broad appeal
Expansion opportunities	Winning additional customer segments	Add new consumption models and removing barriers to constrained consumption
Tools for expansion	New features and fulfilling additional customer requirements	Curation, reducing friction, customization, pace or variability of consumption

Figure 8-1: Consumption Perspective

The unique vantage point of the consumption-focused approach enables organizations to define solutions that target multiple customer beachheads and eventually move to the broader market. For example, Ryanair's affordable travel solution found an ideal customer beachhead in non-consumers, those who would not normally fly for vacation, and created new consumption around low-cost weekend travel. With more affordable air travel and package offerings, Ryanair became a viable solution for short weekend holidays, expanding demand further.

Looking at constrained consumption can also yield new opportunities. The prime example of overcoming constrained consumption to create a large market is McDonald's and the rapid growth of fast-food restaurants. Traditional restaurants, with formal settings, service, and time requirements, overserve customers who simply want a quick meal. This type of constrained consumption limits demand. Cutting back on the elements of overservice opens up higher levels of consumption.

Today you are more likely to find opportunities in constrained consumption by looking at markets served by larger platforms and suites of solutions. These solutions seek to fulfill a broad base of customer needs but often fail to solve individual needs deeply enough. Craigslist, for example, has become a marketplace of marketplaces that is finding it increasingly difficult to compete with dozens of competitors that are unbundling those marketplaces into separate services to meet the needs of those customers better.

The importance of the consumption-oriented model is that it reveals the why behind customers, their motivations. In this way, it supports the jobs-to-be-done framework created by Harvard Business School professor Clayton Christenson. Jobs to be done takes the perspective of looking at what the customer is hiring your product to do.

In a similar vein, the consumption approach looks at who the customer is and why they are consuming the product. That is, what is the outcome they seek or what is the job they are hiring the solution to do? Each consumption category generates options for multiple market segments of customers and the outcomes they are seeking. Adding the dimension of how, when, and where creates more possibilities. With options to target underconsumption, nonconsumption, new consumption, and constrained consumption, the new entrant increases its chances of launching a category-creating solution into a beachhead it can win, thereby creating a platform to access the broader market.

Benefits of Market Focusing: Finding Protected Space

While transformative companies use these beachheads to unlock latent consumption first, the goal is to create a solution that can target the larger market segments. This new-customer-first approach allows them to gain traction in a market segment that is easier to win and defend. Defensibility, in the long run, comes from a unique and inimitable value proposition. Still, in the short-term, a defensible position may come by creating a beachhead in a market that appears limited or unattractive to competitors. Such a position can also be enhanced by structural innovation: creating something extraordinary to win these customers that the competition can't, won't, or doesn't know how to do.

Incumbents often view such solutions as extreme, a niche, or lacking in competitive features compared to the incumbent. Netflix was initially seen as a niche player. The iPhone was not viewed as a mainstream business product because of the lack of a keyboard, the cost, and difficulty integrating with corporate email systems. As more customers shift their preferences to the new solution, it eventually becomes apparent that the niche is an actually new and large market segment.

Finding a beachhead also gives companies a protected space to get their solution right. At times, companies starting up demand extraordinary measures that simply do not scale. When Airbnb launched in New York City, founders Joe Gebbia and Brian Chesky found that early listings often included low quality, blurry photos of the accommodation. So the two entrepreneurs rented a digital camera and walked from location to location in New York, taking photos of the listings for owners to improve their attractiveness. This would be impractical with a larger launch.

In the book *Crossing the Chasm*, author Geoffrey Moore described a beachhead strategy as a path to go from a narrow to a mainstream market and identified that the value in the first beachhead came by gaining knowledge from innovators and early adopters who could tolerate failings in the product. Only after the product was whole, with all the features in place and the bugs ironed out, could companies take their products to the mainstream.

A critical benefit of protected markets is how they help organizations learn and generate cumulative knowledge—the type of learning that happens over time and is additive, building on previous insights. This is increasingly important for organizations to find the time to develop and refine new capabilities, processes, and advancements that will give them a cumulative knowledge advantage.

Like Airbnb, Lyft, Uber, Netflix, and Amazon include among their advantages complex algorithms that learn and understand customer preferences, identify and predict behavior, and make recommendations. Each algorithm required base knowledge and abilities developed from early customers, which created a considerable barrier for other companies following them to market.

Finally, protected beachheads allow organizations to make mistakes in a less costly manner and recover from them more quickly than they could in a broader market.

With only basic functionality and a need to iterate, AWS was able to run through many life cycles of their cloud services service quickly and learn from its customers, many of whom were startups that could not afford the upfront cost of on-premises data centers. AWS leader Andy Jassy identified that the company needed to play in smaller market segments first to take advantage of "the ability to try a lot of experiments, and...not having to live with the collateral damage of failed experiments."[3]

Finding New Consumption Orientations

Finding ideal beachhead markets is not easy. But with options for targeting nonconsumption, underconsumption, new consumption, and constrained consumption, your possibilities increase significantly. Here are some suggestions on how to find and define your beachhead for market entry:

Targeted New Consumption. Psychographic segmentation looks at attitudes, aspirations, and other psychological attributes as the basis of segmenting the market. Uber launched its ride-sharing service as an alternative to expensive black car services. At the time of the launch, the service was as much as 150 percent more expensive than a cab, but it launched in the San Francisco Bay Area of California to great reception. Using geographic and psychographic segmentation, Uber determined that the convenience of a mobile app and one button ordering was highly appealing for the young Technorati of San Francisco. The company later focused on broader transportation needs, becoming the darling of the sharing economy.

Long-tail Product Interest. A concentrated and deep product interest can indicate an effective beachhead, much as books did for Amazon in its earliest days. In this strategy, organizations can provide increased access to variety or fulfill a specialized and specific customer need. In the early days, customers flocked to Amazon because it could offer a deep long-tail inventory, and the company was especially good at locating hard-to-find books for customers. Netflix was able to take similar advantage of long-tail interest.

Intersections. Some beachheads are created by intersecting the solution with a different situation. Redbox took advantage of the intersection of location and time to make a highly convenient service. The DVD rental company was started by McDonald's Corporation based on a time and location intersection that created a new beachhead. Redbox succeeded because it found a new consumption point different from the typical rental—finding a new movie on the way home from typical commute or at fast dinnertime locations.

Trend Interception. Netflix 1.0, the DVD subscription rental, was a born Blockbuster killer, but it only happened because they took advantage of the trend of DVDs replacing VHS cassettes. Netflix was born just two years after the first DVD shipped in 1995, benefiting from the small size and durability of the discs, which were ideal for shipping. The low cost of DVDs, with an average retail price of $20, created a better economic model, and the ability to enable a new slow consumption model (a beachhead) kept them off Blockbuster Video's radar until they snowballed with the adoption of DVD players.

Releasing or Imposing Constraints. Removing or imposing constraints and taking more extreme positions often creates opportunities with new market segments. Netflix has used constrained or curated choice as the hallmark of its offerings. When it first launched, it avoided offering the latest release movies that renters were looking for, giving them the long-tail inventory of TV shows and movies instead. Today, as a streaming service, it is on demand but with only about 10 percent of the number of movies and TV shows it had as a DVD rental company.

At the other end of the spectrum is Zipcar, which lifts constraints on renting a car in urban environments by placing cars on the street or in parking lots for convenient pickups and drop-offs.

Variable Consumption. Nonconsumption can often create a target when variable consumption models create access to assets that the customer would not own, as in the case of Zipcar. Zipcar uses an on-demand model to fulfill varying consumption needs, allowing customers to pay for access to a vehicle to use in one-hour increments. Although Zipcar would be more expensive for consistent use, it is reasonable for infrequent or low usage, and customers are willing to pay a premium for it. Similarly, Amazon Web Services provides variable consumption for customers who want the flexibility to use more or less cloud services on demand.

For much of this book, we have discussed how to look more broadly at innovation to deliver different and better value to customers, particularly at focusing on changing the outcome in a way that provides a different outcome. With a change in value, it's only natural to expect an opportunity to change the business model profitably. Evidence in the public markets shows that while category creators make up 22 percent of the market, they account for 52 percent of the revenue grown and 72 percent of market capitalization.[4]

As you would expect, transformative companies can give us insight into how to take advantage of these more profitable models.

Model Building

Products and services can be copied. The business model is the differentiator.

IBM CEO Survey Respondent

When Apple introduced the iPod in 2001, it was just one more entrant in a sea of existing Portable Media Players (PMP). Vendors such as RCA, Sony, Intel, and Diamond Multimedia with its popular Rio line had begun launching MP3 players four years before Apple and were established in the growing market.

The first-generation iPod's features, particularly its signature click wheel interface, improved on existing designs, and the device maintained a good balance between cost and song capacity. But it was not revolutionary. Because it was compatible only with Apple's Mac OS computers, it held limited market appeal. At $399 to $499, the iPod was not an overnight success, selling an estimated 25,000 units in its first year.

Sales of the iPod languished through 2003, when the company launched its third-generation device. The new release included improvements to the interface, support for Windows computers, and capacity up to 40 GB. Apple also lowered the price of its 10 GB model to $299. More importantly, Apple launched the iTunes Store, providing an easy way to purchase and download music onto the iPod. By the end of 2004, Apple had sold an estimated 10 million iPods since its launch and would sell another 20 million units in the following year. The product was on its way to becoming a success.

The launch of the iTunes Store was a turning point for iPod customers and Apple as a company. With iTunes, Apple provided a complete outcome to customers that combined both devices and access to digital music. For the first time, users had a seamless way to search for, purchase, and download music directly onto their device. It also gave customers the freedom to buy individual songs instead of being forced to buy an entire album, giving customers the option to pick the music they wanted.

The iTunes Store also provided Apple with an additional revenue stream beyond selling the original device, which its portable media player competitors lacked. That revenue stream, in tandem with iPod sales, was a powerful growth engine for Apple. Revenue from the iPod peaked at around $4 billion for Apple in the first quarter of 2008. Total sales from iPods reached $9.2 billion that same year, while the iTunes store brought approximately $3.3 billion in revenue. For every $3 in revenue from iPods, Apple made an additional $1 in music sales, a revenue stream that no other vendor of MP3 players was obtaining. In less than four years, Apple had successfully shifted a revenue stream from the music industry to add more than $3 billion to its own revenue. Beyond the dual revenue stream, the iTunes store created a unique selling point, a reason for customers to stay on the iPod, and a feature that other vendors couldn't immediately replicate.

While iTunes music sales have peaked, Apple has tapped additional sales in video, applications, and books. In 2016 alone, Apple added an estimated $28 billion in revenue from sales of media, which grew about 40 percent over the previous year, more than four times the peak sales of iPods.

Apple's sales of applications have been incredibly successful as well. In 2019, Apple's App Store sold more than half a trillion dollars in goods, services, and in-app advertising. Apple had more than $20 billion in iOS application revenue in Q4 2020, an amount that grew 300 percent over four years. Because of this, they have managed to create a robust developer ecosystem model that shared revenues of more than $155 billion back to developers.[5] As with the iPod, application sales provided both a robust additional revenue stream for Apple and a selling point for iPhone customers.

Apple's ability to create high value for its customers and uniquely capture new revenue streams represents a pattern and principle that is common across nearly all transformative companies. When there is an innovative shift in the value provided to the customer, there is almost always an accompanying shift in the business model to capture the value that is created.

From Apple to Intel and from Google to Netflix, transformative companies' innovation includes both a method of new value creation and a new, complementary mechanism to capture new value in return. And that ability to change a company's business model sets such companies apart as true business innovators.

Redefining Business Models

At its most fundamental level, the foundation of a business model starts with how your organization makes money through value exchange—including both a mechanism for creating value and another for capturing value.

Business models start with value creation because that ultimately defines how organizations can charge for their products. To understand that, look no further than two very different organizations: Amazon Web Services and Dollar Shave Club. While there are no similarities in providing cloud-based computing and men's razors, both have taken a product that can be bought and paid for one time and turned it into a service that customers are willing to pay for every month.

Value creation includes how a company develops, packages, and delivers value to the customer and over what time period. Understanding and changing the value proposition can radically change how an organization is paid for it in return. Too often, organizations want to jump to value capture—how they get paid—without fully understanding how to improve value creation for the customer.

The second component of the equation, value capture, is still important. It is concerned with who, how, how much, and how often organizations receive value from the customer or other sources in exchange for what they provide. It focuses on targeting a specific customer and identifying the mechanics for receiving value in return.

The third component, delivery, is concerned with how the organization sources its value creation activities and delivers them to the customer in a valuable and profitable way. This can include value creation activities, the resources they use, and the channels and partnerships companies use to get value to the customer.

These three items—value creation, value capture, and delivery—form the basis of any business model, which should result in a profitable and defensible formula for the organization. Business model frameworks such as the Business Model Canvas, developed by Alexander Osterwalder, are more detailed views on these three components. The Business Model Canvas, for example, details nine components of a business model: partners, activities, resources, value proposition, customer relationships, customer segments, channels, cost structure, and revenue streams.

Business Model Canvas is popular because new business models have become an attractive way to lock in the benefits of innovation. Boston Consulting Group recently interviewed 1,500 senior executives at some of the most innovative companies, finding that 94 percent had reported their companies had engaged in some type of business model innovation. Authors Zhenya Lindgardt and Margaret Ayers identified how elusive innovative business models are: only 27 percent of those interviewed reported that their organizations were actively pursuing such a model.[6]

These low implementation rates are not uncommon. In a review of 2,500 top-performing companies, McKinsey found that less than 30 percent of top-quartile performers felt that they were getting their business model right. Only 10 percent of those in the second quartile of performance said they were good at business model innovation.[7] Over the eight innovation areas McKinsey identified as essential to success, organizations consistently scored themselves the lowest at business model innovation.

Low rates of business model innovation are perplexing given that companies that prioritize innovative business models see their profitability grow 5 percent faster than those who were just seeking product or service innovation.[8] This gap between the benefit of business model innovation and the low number of incumbent companies that pursue it has created an opportunity for transformative companies to innovate their business models.

Transformative Value Exchange Models

When discussing business model innovation, subscription might be the first word that comes to mind. Although the subscription model has been around for centuries, covering everything from newspapers and book clubs to the rent on your first apartment, it has exploded in popularity in recent years—and with good reason. Software companies kickstarted the current trend of subscription payments, which can now be found in travel, scuba diving, fashion, music, and even automobiles. Virtually any business that can demonstrate consistent value or regular fulfillment over time can charge a subscription.

Subscription models are popular for their ongoing and predictable revenue stream and low customer churn (turnover). Importantly from a market entry standpoint, subscriptions lower barriers to entry, attract new customers, enable breakout growth, and can disrupt established business models, a path that incumbents find hard to follow because it breaks their current way of capturing value. Business model innovation goes to the heart of the power of transformative change by threatening incumbents and their existing profit models.

There is no better example of this than Netflix 1.0. It was only when Netflix rolled out a subscription model, charging up to $19.95 per month for unlimited rentals, that their offering became genuinely transformative. It not only opened up an entirely new way to consume movies, but it also provided the rapid adoption that quickly got the company to 250,000 subscribers and created a model that Blockbuster, with its addiction to late fees, could not replicate.

Subscription models are an effective way to capture value, but not the only way. It may matter less, in fact, which model you choose, as long as it is profitable, unique, and defensible. What matters more is focusing on how you are creating differentiated value and then how to adequately capture it and use the business model to reinforce your advantage.

For example, take the contrast between two transformative companies, Apple and Dell, which started with two decidedly different business models for the PC market. Steve Jobs once derisively declared the difference between these two successful models: "Pretty much, Apple and Dell are the only ones in this industry making money. They make it by being Wal-Mart. We make it by innovation."

Both companies derived unique customer value and captured it in different ways. Apple was the premium brand that owned everything end to end from hardware to software, had limited distribution, and charged premium pricing. On the other hand, Dell owned almost nothing, not even manufacturing, sold directly to customers, offered extreme levels of customization, and priced toward the lower end of the spectrum. The only commonality between the two companies was that they were both built on models quite different from the business model that every other PC manufacturer followed, one that was difficult for anyone else to copy.

Creating Uniqueness through Business Model Innovation

Understanding that value creation and value capture go hand in hand, the possibilities for creating the right combination for a unique and transformative solution are endless. Three primary considerations that will help organizations find their own unique combination: redefining value, shifting value capture, and optimizing operations.

Redefine Value

First, consider how to redefine value. You can't create a model for capturing value if you haven't figured out how to create it.

For example, three fundamental outcome changes we have previously covered—convenience, friction reduction, and personalization—often drive subscription business models. On-demand access, curation, and flexibility in supply can make ownership less attractive compared to subscription-based access.

Dollar Shave Club showed that organizations can base a new subscription business model on convenience and reinforced it with membership in a community of like-minded individuals.

Curation, the act of becoming an intermediary that adds value, is a powerful way to establish the foundation for a new model, especially when it includes personalization and qualification. Netflix is an example of curation that qualifies a vast amount of content. Customers pay not just for content but also for a curated library tailored to the customer's interests.

The Google Adwords platform provides a form of curation with an auction system that qualifies an audience searching for specific search terms. Google's system enables customers to create ads right where customers would find them on the search results page and allows customers to identify and bid for the search terms by which they could target the right customers. Their auction-based dynamic pricing model made it cost-effective to buy advertising by determining when to display ads based on how much the customer is willing to pay.

On-demand models also enable value capture by providing access to services only when, how, and to the degree to which they are needed. Amazon Web Services changed the value capture model of cloud infrastructure with accessibility to scalable services on demand. Unlike emerging cloud hosting models, AWS created a fluid model that could turn up or down at any time, allowing customers to scale gradually as their needs increased. AWS is frequently more expensive than other cloud infrastructure if you can predict what your demand is, but for the vast majority of organizations, it allows for an exact fit of needs at any time without a requirement to overbuild and pay upfront or scramble when demand dictates it.

Even non-subscription models are improved when value creation is high. Most shoppers hate the idea of paying the full retail price for a pair of shoes, but they do it on Zappos, which rarely discounts prices, in exchange for the convenience of ordering and trying on at home.

Shift Value Capture

An often-overlooked method of creating new value capture models is through value shifting, creating value in one place while capturing it another. This model is especially useful when companies are working with customers on limited budgets.

Ryanair created a profitable air travel model through lower costs of operations. Critically, they also created more value for themselves by capturing a larger slice of the total vacation budget from other services, including hotel reservations and rental cars. The airline reservation is the enabler that allows them to capture additional value that might have been generally gone to an online travel provider or directly to the hotel or rental car company.

Google utilizes a value shifting strategy with its online applications such as Gmail and Google Docs platforms. By trading off Gmail as a free email application in exchange for access to the information that customers are sending and receiving, Google generates ad revenue, shifting the value capture from the customer to its advertising customers.

Craigslist used value shifting by digitizing and aggregating the market for classified ads and creating a high value from the volume of buyers and sellers on the platform. The core platform is made up of free classified ads, which produces high traffic. This high traffic allows Craigslist to capture value from offering a few paid ads for jobs and other services.

Value shifting can be beneficial in enabling a company to compete directly in a market without using the same value capture method as competitors. This second source of revenue gives companies the ability to compete aggressively in the primary market while protecting their profit model.

Optimize Operations

A third way to improve business model effectiveness is in operational optimization. Many transformative companies use optimization to lower operating costs and create more value for the customer. These companies often limit or exclude costly elements to pare down the core service compared to incumbents. Increasingly, companies use digital catalysts to lower costs.

IKEA has become the world's largest furniture provider with revenue of over 41 billion euros in 2019 from the simple premise of selling well-designed furniture at a low cost. Its primary innovation is its business model, which combines good quality, well-designed furniture with low cost, and it attracts more than a billion customer visits per year. IKEA limits labor and warehousing costs by asking customers to participate in the final stages of what would typically be part of the value delivery for other providers: furniture pickup, delivery, and setup. Customers willingly participate in the process in exchange for lower prices. IKEA lowers cost by limiting variety, creating higher economies of scale, lowering labor and shipping costs, and reducing space requirements. This combination has created a profitable model for IKEA, which generates much higher operating margins than competitors.

These three models for value capture are not mutually exclusive and can be reinforcing. Innovators often combine them to maximize value capture and strengthen the uniqueness of their value capture. Organizations such as Dell, Apple, and Dollar Shave Club have integrated multiple value creation and capture strategies into their business models, making them even more valuable and challenging to replicate.

In the next and final chapter of this section, we turn to how organizations can generate more creative approaches to market entry and value creation with two final scale accelerators. The first is rule breaking, how organizations learn to set aside the rules and accepted practices of their industry, and the second is recombining, the art of creatively and proudly borrowing from and building on the ideas from others to create innovation of your own.

From Concept to Action

1. What segments of current consumers does the market address? What are they seeking to accomplish? What benefits do they receive?
2. How would we characterize nonconsumers and under consumers? Are they seeking a different outcome? How could we better address their needs?
3. Will our solution ultimately change what current market customers value?
4. How could we offer a solution to existing customers that would get them to use it in other situations, for example, in different times, locations, or for different outcomes and benefits?
5. In what ways can we change the value for customers from what is currently offered?
6. Can we offer a solution that provides continuous benefit?
7. Can we find overserved customers? How could we offer to unbundle them from broader solutions?
8. What opportunities for shifting value from other revenue streams could we employ?
9. In what ways can we optimize our operational cost structure?

Chapter 9

Recombining and Rule Breaking

Adopting an innovative approach to market entry requires a creative mindset to uniquely generate value. Two key skills are helpful. Recombination is a critical capability to aid companies in creatively borrowing and recombining existing ideas, concepts, features, products, and services and turn them into their own unique innovation. Companies can also master rule breaking, dispelling beliefs, and eschewing accepted practices to improve customer outcomes and create a sustainable advantage.

Recombining

Great poets imitate and improve, whereas small ones steal.
D. H. Davenport

Apple's 1984 launch of the Macintosh computer was by all standards a revolution in personal computing. The Mac was the first affordably priced commercial computer to feature a graphical user interface (UI), movable and adjustable windows, and a mouse. It was a cleaner, more elegant, and better user experience that we take for granted today.

Apple CEO Steve Jobs had developed these and other ideas from a meeting he had arranged with the famous Xerox PARC labs. He and Apple engineers saw at PARC Labs a Xerox prototype computer called the Alto, a computer with a graphical UI. During the meeting, he couldn't contain his excitement, stating to the research team, "Why aren't you doing anything with this? This is the greatest thing. This is revolutionary!"[1]

Jobs paid $1 million in Apple pre-IPO stock to a reluctant Xerox Corporation in exchange for the meeting and access to their ideas. The concepts he saw that day became the foundation of today's Apple, a company currently worth over $2.1 trillion. By any calculation, it was worth it. But Jobs didn't walk away from that meeting with any technology, software code, or intellectual property. What he did come out with were ideas that he could make his own.

As much as those ideas at Xerox helped Jobs and Apple create insanely great computers and many other devices, it was his interpretation and reuse of those ideas that generated the real value. That is the value of recombining, the art of taking both existing and novel elements and reassembling them into new innovations. Recombination is a common trait of transformative companies, contributing to how they rethink and approach existing markets with new and better solutions.

Recombination has been used for as long as ideas have existed. Even Silicon Valley, long viewed as the land of independent innovation, has embraced the idea. Of course, it has put its own spin on it and created an acronym for the art of borrowing and improving, known as PFE: Proudly Found Elsewhere. Many tech companies, including Salesforce, Facebook, and Google have built by borrowing.

They know what great artists have known for years: great art is often derived by borrowing and building from others' work. Hollywood has a long tradition of borrowing to achieve creative genius. The movie *Jaws* very closely resembles Moby Dick on Long Island. *West Side Story* transports Romeo and Juliet (which Shakespeare himself borrowed) to New York in the 1950s. Even the movie *Lion King* features a cute and very likable little lion who bears a strong resemblance to Hamlet, the Prince of Denmark.

The Broadway super-hit musical Hamilton is a fantastic performance that has deservedly won critical praise, eleven Tony Awards, and the Pulitzer Prize for drama. Based on the biography of Alexander Hamilton by Ron Chernow, it's not the first play based on the treasury secretary and founding father. Nor is it the first musical to use hip-hop or black and Hispanic actors to portray white characters. But together, the combination of these elements has created something emotionally satisfying and unusual, and, as sell-out shows and ticket prices indicate, immensely enjoyable.

The Power of Recombination and the Fallacy of Invention

The fact that these and hundreds of others have borrowed to create their work makes them no less creative or entertaining. Recombination looks for opportunities to adapt models, capabilities, and functions and improve them to create extreme value. It's an effective and efficient path to innovation.

A common fallacy of invention and creative genius places a premium on new ideas being created out of nothing. Yet many great ideas are simply borrowed from and built upon from the ideas of others, often even from other fields. There are three distinct methods of recombination organizations use to creatively borrow and adapt concepts from others: point adaptation, analogical mapping, and digital recreation.

Point Adaptation

Point adaptation is the borrowing of features and concepts that have worked in other markets and applying them to a new market to create a unique innovation.

Henry Ford's assembly line adapted a concept that was already being used by slaughterhouses, flour mills, breweries, canneries, and industrial bakeries, thereby lowering the cost of manufacturing the standardized Model T. As I described earlier, while Ford's early competitor, Ransom Olds, had already used the assembly line, Ford made it more efficient, breaking the Model T assembly down to 84 specific steps and creating time and motion studies to improve process efficiency and proficiency. Ford's innovation was to move the car on the assembly line forward in front of the worker, permitting them to perform the same task repeatedly. He had observed the same method used in the local slaughterhouses, where the meat was moved from worker to worker for dressing. His adaptation and unwavering focus on efficiency dropped the time to build a Model T to just 93 minutes.

Point adaptation works particularly well for defining a solution to a specific problem. Because the method is already used elsewhere, adapting it for a specific application lowers risk. The result may already be familiar to customers if they have experienced it elsewhere.

Airbnb's model of matching renters and accommodations was immediately familiar to customers who already used other market-making services, including eBay and Craigslist. In fact, Airbnb's earliest room providers were already offering rooms through Craigslist ads. Airbnb's point adaptation of peer-to-peer reviews (similar to eBay) let users rate each other and an innovation that helped popularize the site and create a more marketable service by building trust. The dynamic pricing models used by Airbnb to regulate supply and demand were later adapted and improved upon by ride-sharing companies Lyft and Uber.

Analogical Mapping

Analogies play an essential part in our understanding and learning, even in business. If someone were to say that Tesla is the Macintosh computers of cars, an observer could immediately see parallels between the two companies. They would recognize the visionary drive of both Tesla CEO Elon Musk and former Apple CEO Steve Jobs. It would be equally evident that both companies' products rely heavily on owning and integrating hardware and software, the essential nature of design simplicity, and reliance on software-based differentiation. Other similarities might include premium pricing and a distinct and recognizable hardware design.

Analogical mapping is a powerful tool because it provides a high-level association that enables interpretation across domains and markets. Associating a company, product, or circumstance with another that has been successful provides innovators an opportunity to think creatively. Analogical mapping solves problems and enables innovative market approaches by borrowing from others and connecting to a philosophy and attitude.

Steve Jobs used this type of analogical reasoning to create a vision for the original Macintosh by borrowing from the concept of small home appliances, resulting in a form factor that hid cables and replaced the metal box with an all-in-one design. Looking for inspiration, he once visited a local Macy's department store in Palo Alto on the weekend to browse appliances and asked his design team to buy a particular Cuisinart appliance as inspiration for the Mac's hardware design.

Analogical mapping is appropriate for creating a bigger picture or helping the organization to build a theme-based view of innovation. It can help draw out new innovative concepts that don't come directly from the original analogy. Startups often use this technique to enable greater creativity.

Salesforce founder Marc Benioff created this type of vision with the analogical question: "Why can't business applications be delivered through a website that was as easy to use as Amazon.com?" In the early day of online computing, Application Service Providers (ASPs) distributed rented applications to users, using the Internet simply for distribution. Benioff, however, saw a powerful new model that had been put in place by Amazon of a single application, the website, which was able to service thousands of people simultaneously. Each user was able to log in and use the same site in a model that formed the foundation of Salesforce, a model which eventually became the basis for delivering tens of thousands of cloud-based applications we run today.

Digital Recreation

The third possibility of recombination is digital recreation, lifting an existing model and creating it in a digital version. Creating a digital version of the current system unlocks new capabilities and features that couldn't be provided in the analog realm.

Examples of this type of recombination are numerous. Craigslist's digital recreation of newspaper classified ads came as founder Craig Newmark started to see individuals posting jobs on the site he created for local San Francisco events. He added a job category and then other categories as requests came in, eventually growing to displace newspaper classifieds.

It appears that these types of opportunities are now less frequent only because they are less obvious to the casual viewer. Digital replication can effectively create effective point solutions, especially in solving current problems, frustrations, and inconveniences. For example, Redbox offers a mobile app that enables customers to reserve a video at a specific location for pickup, increasing convenience, and eliminating uncertainty. Increasingly digital catalysts such as chatbots, AI, machine learning, and virtual and augmented reality will increase the opportunity for digital recreation.

Recombination Method	Definition	Applications
Adaptation	Borrowing features and concepts that have worked in other markets to create a unique innovation.	Creating point solutions to a specific problem.
Analogous Mapping	A high-level association that opens the way to creating interpretation.	Creating a bigger picture vision or requiring a theme-based view that opens up an innovative approach.
Digital Recreation	Creating a digital version of the existing system or process.	Creating compelling digital point solutions.

Figure 9-1: Recombination Types

Making Recombination Unique: Adaptation and Improvement

Recombination involves more than borrowing ideas, creating analogies, or perfecting digital clones. To be impactful, unique, and valuable, transformative companies have an aptitude for improving the functions, models, and analogical mapping they observe by using a formula of adaptation and improvement. Adaptation is the mindful application of the recombined capability to alter and adjust it to your circumstances and needs. Improvement creates new innovations that build on the original concept to create higher value.

The success of Starbucks comes from adaptation and improvement, borrowing heavily from the concept of Italian cafés that former CEO Howard Shultz observed on a trip to Italy as the concept model for its coffeehouses. As Shultz recounts,

> I was sent to Italy on a trip for Starbucks and came back with this feeling that the business Starbucks was in was the wrong business. What I wanted to bring back was the daily ritual and the sense of community and the idea that we could build this third place between home and work in America. It was an epiphany. I was out of my mind. I walked in and saw this symphony of activity, and the romance and the theater of coffee. And coffee being at the center of conversation, creating a sense of community. That is what spoke to me.[2]

The vision Shultz created was heavily adapted from what he observed. An Italian visitor to Starbucks would see very few similarities between today's Starbucks store and the cafés from their home country. Deviating from the small, often cramped Italian counterparts where patrons often sit on tall stools at a bar around the barista area, chatting with the coffee maker or each other, Starbucks created an environment to provide more opportunity for the creation of this "third place." This involved eliminating the bar, opening up floor space, and providing tables and lounge chairs that could provide separation for patrons to relax, hold meetings, or work, creating an environment that drew them in time and again to find their own space.

Modification from the original borrowed concept is the essence of true recombination and adaptation. Figure 9-2 shows how other organizations have adopted and improved on other's original ideas to improve their customer outcomes.

Company	Adaptation and Improvement
Ford	Created a moving assembly line from observation of slaughterhouses and perfected it with time and motion efficiency studies.
Airbnb	Used peer-to-peer model and applied customer and supplier peer-to-peer review concept. Added dynamic pricing to create market supply during peak demand times.
Redbox	Borrowed the concept of kiosk-based selling to deliver DVDs from its precursor, Tik Tok Easy Shop grocery kiosks. Improved the DVD rental model with flexible returns and eventually preordering and pickup.
Zappos	Recreated the brick-and-mortar experience of trying on multiple shoes online. Adapted the extreme customer service model popularized by Nordstrom. Added a consultative online service and turned it into a key element of company marketing.
Salesforce	Used Amazon-like website concept and adapted existing Internet delivery of applications into a multi-tenanted application delivery model.
Dollar Shave Club	Applied a men's club concept of grouping like-minded individuals to personal grooming.
Craigslist	Combined the concept of classified ads and existing peer groups such as Usenet into online classifieds that are simple to set up.
Dell	Applied catalog sales model to computers, creating a unique build-to-order model that appealed to consumer and business customers.
Starbucks	Borrowed concepts from existing coffee houses such as Peet's Coffee and the theatrics of Italian cafés and baristas.
IKEA	Founder Ingvar Kamprad took many of IKEA's concepts from his hometown values in Sweden. The childcare area inside of IKEA stores is even named Småland, an homage to his hometown.

Figure 9-2: Recombination Examples of Adaptation and Improvement

Recombination is a fundamental enabler of transformative thinking, resulting in, creating, or supporting the development of new customer outcomes with unique customer benefits. These new benefits become the category-creating inflection points that move markets.

When taken as part of an approach to a new market, recombination can lower time to market and reduce risk and uncertainty as companies adopt established functions, concepts, and methods proven in other markets. Ultimately, recombination can provide significant differentiation and advantage when applied well and adapted to the company's specific needs.

Rule Breaking: Violating the Inviolable

Hell, there are no rules here—
we're trying to accomplish something.
Thomas A. Edison

Many leaders think of their companies as pioneers. CEOs like to fashion themselves as rebels and rule breakers. Steve Jobs once declared that it's better to be a pirate than to join the navy.[3]

While many companies like to break the rules, transformative companies know how to create an advantage by breaking the right rules. To achieve their objective of category-creating solutions and the right customer outcome, transformative leaders know to put everything on the table, including the traditions, beliefs, accepted practices, and behaviors in the market. And when they break the rules, it shapes their industry and puts them at an advantage.

Ryanair, the European low-cost airline, started with a fundamental challenge to create a low-cost service in a high-cost, highly regulated, and crowded market like Europe. The key to their success was breaking established industry rules.

For example, Ryanair broke the rules by emphasizing quick airport turnaround time, offering no seat assignments to facilitate fast onboarding, charging for in-flight snacks, and avoiding the use of travel agents, which Ryanair CEO Michael O'Leary once described as "a complete waste of time."[4] As I described earlier, the biggest rule they broke was to choose to fly into smaller secondary airports rather than high-traffic primary airports. Many of these airports were developed during World War II near major European cities, offering an attractive alternative to flyers.

When Ryanair flies customers to Stockholm, Sweden, they land at Skavsta, a secondary airport 70 miles away. Instead of flying into Amsterdam, customers fly into Eindhoven; in Rome, they land at Ciampino instead of the primary airport, Leonardo da Vinci. These smaller airports don't have the amenities one would expect at a larger airport. However, they do feature smaller crowds, inexpensive parking, and a shorter time from the parking lot to the boarding gate.

This unique strategy enabled the air carrier to negotiate lower airport fees and pass the savings on to its customers. They also shortened aircraft turn-around time to 25 minutes, compared to 50 minutes for rival British Airways. Ryanair negotiated flight schedules in and out of these airports at hours that were earlier or later than were available at many of the larger airports. With the short flights of many of their European destinations, earlier or later flights meant passengers could arrive at their destination early in the day or return home late in the evening, maximizing their vacation days.

Ryanair's choice to fly to secondary airports broke a cardinal rule of air travel: using busy primary airports. It was a move that no established airline would dare replicate, creating customer inconvenience by making them drive to a more distant airport. But Ryanair's customers were different: they were already underserved by existing airlines and might have opted to drive, take the train or bus, or stay home as their alternative vacation. Customers have been willing to make that value tradeoff for lower cost, propelling Ryanair to become the largest air carrier in Europe.

Like Ryanair, many others have found an advantage in rule breaking, helping them reach underserved and unserved customers, and dramatically expanding their market with a new type of consumption: inexpensive weekend vacation travel. The company found both new markets and created unique advantages with rule breaking.

Rules Definition

Before going further, let's take a moment to define what rules are. As industries mature and their products become more standardized, they tend to establish explicit or implicit rules that can take the form of principles or guidelines that govern companies' conduct and their activities, in other words, how the industry should work. These rules often take form as:

- **Practices**: expected or customary ways of doing something.
- **Axioms**: statements or propositions that are held to be true.
- **Beliefs**: acceptance of something to be true, often without testing.
- **Customs**: shared or widely accepted ways of doing something.
- **Processes**: standard series of steps or actions to accomplish an end.
- **Regulations**: industry or legal rules the company is obliged to follow or maintain.

Thus rules can be any guiding principle or practice that establishes industry practices and guides company behavior. Breaking rules should not be confused with violating government laws and regulations. While some companies have violated industry regulations and laws, I am not encouraging you to do that. Breaking laws is ethically questionable and provides no long-term advantage.

Rules exist for a purpose. As an industry develops, competition leads companies to adopt best practices for operation. Products mature over time, and advantages give way to commoditization. Companies compete along similar parameters, and business models align to the best way to make a profit. Internal processes become more efficient. Thus, companies become nearly identical to each other and start following similar paths and performance trajectories.

Often companies take these standard industry practices and assumptions for granted as requirements even when they are no longer useful. Rule breaking is about spotting opportunities to deviate from industry assumptions and practices that no longer matter or are actual impediments.

Often, opportunities to break the rules are enabled when shifts occur in the broader contextual environment. Advancements in data analytics and the ability to collect customer data, for example, have enabled consumer companies like Dollar Shave Club to sell directly to customers, breaking traditional industry norms and enabling them to better serve their customers. Organizations that continually review changes to the contextual environment in which they operate, for example, understanding the political, economic, social, technological, environmental, and legal context of their industry often find advantages. I described PESTEL analysis in chapter 6.

The Rules of Rule Breaking

Can there possibly be a set of rules about rule breaking? Maybe not, but understanding which rules to break will increase success and reduce wasted effort. In particular, organizations should pay attention to rules that prevent better customer outcomes, create bottlenecks in supply or limit consumption, reduce performance, limit convenience, and are generally limiting broader market adoption. These are the rules to break!

Break rules that aid in improving the customer outcome, give the company a strategic advantage, and are difficult for incumbent competitors to replicate. Those that are foundational to the industry are often the most strategic and beneficial to break. They are often supported at a high cost because they are seen as necessary to the company's current view of customer value. Breaking them when they create an advantage for you creates strategic dissonance with incumbents, making it hard for them to follow.

Focusing on rules that increase friction or are impediments to convenience or personalization consistently pays dividends. IKEA started with the customer outcome in mind: enabling customers to take home their furniture that same day. To achieve it, they had to break a cardinal industry rule and require people to take the kit home and assemble it themselves. No one would even question this as a basic tenet of the furniture industry: customers want their furniture delivered and assembled.

Why would anyone be willing to put together their own furniture? This was contrary to the very concept of convenience. IKEA proved that this rule was not only breakable, but it was also profitable to do so. IKEA found that instant availability equaled convenience and that lower cost is worth the effort of building the furniture yourself. One study identified an additional benefit—

called the "IKEA Effect"—by taking part in building their own furniture, customers actually value IKEA furniture more.

Zappos broke through the most fundamental axiom of online retail—to avoid customer returns—and turned it into virtue and competitive advantage to create the world's largest online shoe store.

Cirque du Soleil transformed the live performance industry and created a thrilling circus-like experience without circuses' fundamental attraction: animals. By combining circus and Broadway-like experiences and centering performances around human physical performances, they have created an equivalent experience without the cultural downside or the high expense of maintaining animals. The cost of maintaining a single elephant for (now defunct) Ringling Brothers was estimated at $65,000 per year.[5] Cirque was able to eliminate this expense and still create a circus-like experience that wins both critical and popular acclaim.

Benefits of Rule Breaking

Urban car-sharing startup Zipcar increased customer convenience by doing away with set locations, parking lots of vehicles, contracts, and waiting. By breaking the industry-wide process, they facilitated access and created a new membership renting model for automobiles. For them, the benefits were obvious: creating a new market opportunity.

A study in the Harvard Business Review of rule-breaking companies found that breaking rules and accepted practices resulted in one of five different types of positive outcomes: updating outdated purchase or usage experiences, removing superfluous major expense categories, reducing significant financial risks for customers, reengaging disengaged or demotivated employees, and removing detrimental side effects of the product or service.[6] The research for this book uncovered many others, including providing new customer benefits, changing consumption models, improving customer loyalty, unlocking supply and availability, knocking down barriers to entry, and creating customer confidence.

Because rules are the basis of industry structure, breaking them is fundamental to creating a new approach to market entry. Rules that create barriers to improved customer outcomes don't always manifest themselves easily, and you can't discover them by talking to customers, who often become accustomed to their own problems. Therefore, it is incumbent on transformational leaders to continually scan for opportunities to break the rules to unlock higher customer value and create competitive advantage.

Leaders enable recombining and rule-breaking opportunities by creating an outsider's viewpoint, that beginner's mind that we discussed in chapter 6, and encouraging a questioning mindset. Hiring from outside the industry and actively studying other markets and companies helps. In the words of author Carla Johnson, "We have to start being able to look at brands and ideas and experiences . . . that have nothing to do with our industry or with marketing."[7] So does learning not to take assumptions as given and questioning what impedes their organization from doing things differently or better. Enabling answers to those questions alone will increase the probability of understanding what rules to break for success.

Unfortunately, we are mostly conformists by nature. Studies show that social and cultural factors constrain us from breaking out of accepted norms even in morally compromising or life-threatening situations.[8] If this is the case, how do organizations develop the capability to break the right rules and look for ways to proudly borrow elsewhere? It starts with building a higher vision of what you are trying to achieve and using intentionality, discussed in the next chapter, to focus on innovating outcomes and aligning your organization.

In the next section and final section, we will explore the cultural elements of innovation and how aspiring transformative organizations create cultures that build intentionality, cultivate a sense of mission, encourage innovative thinking, and focus on identifying and overcoming challenges at an accelerated clock speed.

From Concept to Action

1. What are the biggest challenges our company or industry faces today?
2. What are the biggest impediments to growth?
3. Are there analogous situations or companies that we could learn from to solve these challenges?

4. What company has gone through similar circumstances that we could hire or learn from?

5. If we were to identify the most significant customer pain points to a better customer experience, what would they be?

6. Conversely, if we were to create the worst customer outcome and experience, what would that look like? How could we invert it to become the best outcome?

7. How do we increase exposure to new ideas outside of our industry that we could borrow? Would we benefit from someone with knowledge of a specific industry?

8. What industries have gone through similar issues or solved similar problems as ours?

9. What industry rules stand in the way of a better customer outcome?

10. What is the largest impediment to a broader market?

11. What does everyone in our industry assume or take for granted will always exist?

12. If we could work backward from a specific customer outcome, what would it look like? What rules and accepted practices would need to change to achieve it?

Section IV

Retooling Your Organization for Success

Chapter 10

Defining a Path to Differentiation

As you start your journey, the first thing you should do is throw away that store-bought map and begin to draw your own.
Michael Dell

To be successful, organizations need to create solutions that are differentiated—distinctively valuable to their customers and unique to their organization. Differentiation requires continuous attention and action. It starts by creating intentionality, which defines upfront what winning looks like in the minds of employees and leads the organization to develop deliberate and focused actions that produce winning innovations.

Retooling Your Organization for Differentiation

In this final section, we will explore the key concepts to help you retool your organization for success and set you on the path towards differentiation. We will start by exploring how companies create the momentum that helps them define their innovation goals and create game-changing innovation.

One of the most important things successful organizations accomplish is to distinguish themselves in the minds of their customers. Differentiation is so crucial that companies spend more than half a trillion dollars per year to advertise their claims of why they are different, better, cheaper, or otherwise more appealing. They spend billions more on marketing and branding efforts to support those claims.[1]

So much is invested because so much is at stake. After years of research, product development, commercialization, branding, and developing channels to market, an organization may only have seconds to catch the customer's attention and establish that they are offering something uniquely valuable.

Real and lasting differentiation is more than a simple marketing message. To achieve it, a company must satisfy the four qualifications in the VRIO model, a litmus test of long-term, sustainable advantage:

1. **Valuable**: Is what you are doing valuable? Does it help your customer increase value or defend against value loss?
2. **Rare**: Is it difficult to create? Do only one or a few organizations have it?
3. **Inimitable**: Is it hard to copy, imitate, or substitute?
4. **Organizational**: Can your company effectively organize itself to efficiently create it?

This test distills down into two clear elements of differentiation that need to be satisfied: differentiation happens when something is 1) distinctively valuable to the customer and 2) uniquely done well by your organization. Many organizations fall into the trap of achieving what they do well while failing to do something distinctly valuable. Successful transformative organizations learn how to master both elements.

In chapter 3 we discussed how organizations could use outcome and structural innovation to create transformative change. It may have given you some ideas on how to produce new, category-creating outcomes. But many companies find it challenging even to know how to start. So, in this chapter, we will focus on how organizations start rethinking solutions and maintain the momentum to achieve the differentiated outcomes they seek.

According to Harvard Business School professor and former *Harvard Business Review* editor Theodore Levitt, "Differentiation is one of the most important strategic and tactical activities in which companies must constantly engage."[2]

Levitt highlights two critical factors to achieve and maintain differentiation. The first is that achieving differentiation requires both strategic and tactical activities. That means it starts with a strategic objective and is accompanied by a defined set of choices and actions to achieve it.

The second is that companies must *constantly* engage in the activity of differentiation to maintain it. Differentiation is not a singular state; it is a continuous process. To constantly maintain it, the objective of differentiation must be continuously at the forefront of the organization.

For many organizations, differentiation only becomes a priority when marketing tries to define it at the launch of a product or service. At that point, companies are left to sift through product features and define which are most important to the customer and describe their benefits. But differentiation pursued only as a messaging exercise by the marketing team after the fact is doomed to be tactical and superficial. In the words of David Packard, cofounder of Hewlett Packard, "Marketing is too important to be left to the marketing department." To achieve true differentiation, it needs to be designed at the beginning.

Defining and Maintaining a Path to Differentiation

If differentiation is an ongoing process, and organizations need to constantly engage in finding it, making it relevant, and maintaining it, how is that effort coordinated and channeled? Who is in charge of differentiation?

Innovation is often viewed as analogous to a flywheel. Once a flywheel is in motion, it can maintain its forward momentum with just a relatively small force. And even when there is a lull in the energy applied, for example, lifting up on the accelerator of a car, the flywheel keeps the momentum going. Likewise, an organization's innovation process, once moving forward, tends to gain momentum and builds energy and direction.

If that flywheel of innovation for your organization were literally in the front lobby of your company, you'd ideally like every person in your organization to place their hand on that wheel each day and help move it forward to build momentum and overcome inertia. The more people you invite to drive that motion, the faster innovation moves, and the more differentiated—valuable and unique—your organization has the potential to become.

Your success as an organization is mainly dependent on your ability to pull together a team of individuals and align them to continually engage in the tactical and strategic actions that lead to differentiation.

However, unlike a flywheel, when it comes to innovation, both momentum *and* direction are essential. And since the best path to success is an innovation strategy that changes the rules of the game, it requires an aspirational vision that creates organizational alignment and empowers your entire team to rethink and deliver better customer outcomes. That comes from a leader's ability to create intentionality.

Creating Momentum: The Value of Intentionality

Intentionality is a broad sense of organizational intent that aligns vision and drives momentum. It defines a goal that drives action, but it is loose and aspirational enough to inspire the team to participate in how to achieve it and maintain it.

There is one question that determines an organization's likelihood of achieving differentiated success: "What is the goal of your innovation efforts?" The answer you hear determines intentionality.

Common responses I've heard are "We don't have a goal" or "I don't know," often accompanied by a look of confusion as to why someone would ask such an odd question.

Other responses are entirely product-oriented, such as:

"We are designing the best [product]."

"We are building the next generation [product name]."

"We are creating a product like [competing product] and that does [features]."

There are more ways to answer the question, and the range of answers is likely to come out somewhere along two different perpendicular axes as shown in figure 10-1. The horizontal axis ranges from a product-oriented focus to a customer-oriented focus on the other. The vertical axis ranges from being well-defined on one end to more aspirational on the other end.

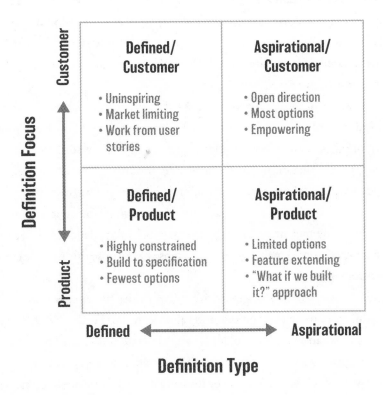

Figure 10-1: Options for Innovation Direction

Empirically, companies seeking opportunities to for greater differentiation set their sights for innovation in terms that are more aspirational and customer-focused, describing the goal of their innovation strategy as an aspirational customer experience. That vision is energizing and empowering, setting intention without rigidly defining it. It leaves open the possibilities of how to innovate. In short, intentionality sets a vision for the outcome, allowing the team to define the journey of how to get there.

It may seem too simplistic to believe that an organization's innovation success can be evaluated by simply asking, "What is the goal of your innovation efforts?" But I wouldn't just ask the CEO or the leadership team. To get a real sense, I would ask the same question to every person in the organization.

As with a flywheel, company innovation works best when the entire team is behind it, putting their hand on the wheel to move it forward. And the more members of your team are on board, the broader your options for achieving truly differentiated innovation. Your ability to set a clear vision for success and communicate it so that the entire organization understands and can help define and deliver it will dramatically increase your chance of success. That is the purpose of intentionality.

In the words of former Amazon CEO Jeff Bezos, it's the difference between building a team of mercenaries to do a job you've defined or developing a group of missionaries whose zeal leads them to the right result. He stated, "I strongly believe that missionaries make better products. They care more. For a missionary, it's not just about the business. There has to be a business, and the business has to make sense, but that's not why you do it. You do it because you have something meaningful that motivates you." That missionary zeal comes from creating intentionality—creating a sense of purpose through the eyes of the customer outcome.

Intentionality is the intangible drive that provides the momentum toward delivering something truly unique and valuable. It starts with a vision of what winning looks and feels like and leads to a deliberate and intentional focus on how the organization will achieve it, along with a rethinking of what it will take to achieve it. While it is unlikely to be formalized and documented, you can hear it throughout the organization. It's often informally codified in a short statement that expresses the vision that drives the organization. It's an expression of intent that is at once both defining and flexible enough to inspire contribution.

Steve Jobs was a master at creating intentionality. He used it to drive Apple to develop a personal computer that would "change the world." That was exhibited in its famous *1984* advertisement that symbolized Apple freeing the world from the oppression of the IBM Personal Computer. Jobs used intentionality again when developing the first iPod, making it clear that the vision was to "Put 1,000 songs in your pocket." When the iPhone was under development, the intentionality was to "Make the phone the killer app."

Other transformative companies similarly demonstrate the ability to create intentionality in terms that are visual and clear. Uber's intention to make "Transportation that is as reliable as running water" is simple and clear but also open to inspired interpretation.

Zappos, which became one of the fastest companies ever to reach $1 billion in revenue, would seem to have a rather ordinary objective of selling shoes, but CEO Tony Hsieh developed intentionality around the aspiration of "delivering happiness," which evokes an emotion around the customer opening that box (or boxes) at home and trying on a pair of shoes or the ease of calling the company's exceptional customer service or returning shoes with no questions asked. Those two words continually inspire Zappos's innovation.

Netflix created intentionality that has powered it through three different iterations of the company with a straightforward question: "How do you transform movie selection so customers *can find a steady stream of movies they love?*" Each time Netflix has addressed that question, it has built a new version of itself to achieve it.

Henry Ford's original objective to "democratize the automobile" led to a vision of delivering a practical and affordable car to every household.

Intentionality is codified as an aspirational customer experience, a definition of what winning looks like from the customer's perspective. This higher aspiration pulls your team up to focusing on achieving more innovative outcomes that transform markets. It is both inspirational and directional, while leaving open the details and method of achieving it that gives the organization an innovative thread to pull on. Ideally, a customer aspiration should create intentionality through the following qualities:

- **Customer-focused.** The higher the focus on the customer, the more latitude you create for innovation.
- **Envision the experience.** You should be able to visualize the customer using what you provide in some way.
- **Evoke a feeling of motivation.** It provides a sense of positivity and energy around the customer achieving his/her goal.
- **Inspire options for innovation.** To be successful, it should continually inspire employees to pull on the thread of innovation, creatively looking for new and better ways to achieve it.

You might rightly ask if intentionality can't be derived from a company's mission or vision statement. Let me provide you with my own experience to illustrate why it is different.

I learned firsthand about the power of intentionality in the first startup I joined. It was a small tech company that built networking hardware to connect computers and networks to the Internet (yes, it was that long ago). We had a mission statement that I don't know if I ever knew, which never changed from the time it was created. But shortly after my arrival, we created an innovation strategy to develop something new, focusing specifically on underserved small- and medium-sized business users.

We had codified our strategy with an aspiration to democratize networking and Internet access for small- and medium-sized businesses. That inspired us to accelerate our understanding of what our customer wanted to achieve and redefine not only the product we delivered but everything that touched the customer. We approached with new eyes the way we thought about and designed the product, how it was set up, how we spoke to the customer, the documentation we provided, how customer service resolved issues, the product's packaging, and even where and how we sold our products. Our goal was to make what we were doing accessible enough that the target customer, a business owner, could set it up and run it themselves.

To get there, we all knew we needed to understand our customers well, so we spent a lot of time interviewing them and visiting them in their offices. Those of us at the forefront of change felt that we understood them, but we didn't feel like our firsthand experience translated well to the rest of the company. So we created our aspirational intent around a hypothetical small business owner we had profiled and named Ben. And although nearly all the entrepreneurs we met at the time were men, we created a Betty persona as well.

We profiled Ben and Betty thoroughly, creating details about their problems and needs. We hired a graphic designer to create life-sized cutouts of our representative customers, which we put up around the company. But the most important thing we did was to establish an aspiration around our customer profiles and what they would accomplish with our products. Our mantra for everything we built was that it needed to be easy enough that Ben or Betty could set it up themselves during their lunch hour.

I learned then a valuable lesson: Few people are inspired to become—in the terminology of most organizations' mission statements—"The dominant provider of [product name here]." However, they are inspired by delivering a valuable and unique outcome to the customer and are more motivated when they are invited to be part of determining how to achieve it.

I knew our little startup would be successful when I was sitting in a meeting reviewing a product specification, and an engineer challenged one of the features my team had outlined, saying, "Ben won't find any use for that feature the way it is." After he expressed his reasoning and proposed an alternative, it was clear that he was right, so we changed it. We brought in the team and actively engaged them in changing the outcome for the customer and once they were on board, everyone was focused on creating the most relevant solution possible.

Eighteen months after we started, just as we were launching our products, we were acquired by Intel Corporation. During the acquisition negotiations, I had lunch with a senior vice-president at Intel who explained why they were acquiring us. "You know, we like your products, but what we like even more is how thoroughly you know your customer and how inspired the organization is to create something valuable for them," he said. "We want your team to help us create that same drive for all of our small business products." The drive that he witnessed and wanted to infuse into their organization was our intentionality.

From Intentionality to a Winning Innovation Strategy

Pithy phrases and buyer personas aside, intentionality needs to do more than energize. It should result in a company-wide focus on how to achieve real transformative change, starting with breakthrough customer outcomes. Intentionality should bring the organization to reexamine and reconstruct the customer outcome in a way that discards current biases, resulting in a unique new set of guiding priorities. To be effective, leaders use intentionality to generate a set of actions that are:

- **Deliberate.** Prioritize actions that will have the highest impact on achieving a unique and defensible outcome. Pursue a deliberate process that challenges existing assumptions and biases.

- **Action-based.** Intentionality compels the organization to act to reach its objectives. In the words of management guru Peter Drucker, "Plans are only good intentions unless they immediately degenerate into hard work."
- **Focused.** Intentionality should generate a small number of impactful initiatives. When directed toward customer outcome and strategic innovation, a few carefully selected actions are enough to create game-changing innovation. Intel CEO Andy Grove stated that "The art of management lies in the capacity to select from the many activities of seemingly comparable significance the one or two or three that provide leverage well beyond the others and concentrate on them."[3]
- **Adaptive.** Intentionality focuses on the end objective, not the means of getting there. Intentionality creates an underlying discontent that accepts that no plan is perfect while avoiding the "set it and forget it" mindset. Instead, it drives the organization to continually review, analyze, and adapt the actions required to achieve its goal.

If these sound like the basis for the choices and actions of strategy, you're right. Examples of intentionality as a driving force for action abound.

Having seen the rapidly growing class of stores called discount retailers setting up in growing urban areas, Sam Walton knew immediately that rural customers would want the same type of merchandise, availability, and lower prices as those in more urban locations.

Walmart's intent was to provide rural customers with better products, wider selection, convenience, and low pricing. It was this customer outcome that drove rapid adoption in nearly every town Walmart chose and created a more significant market opportunity.

As great a customer outcome as it is, this type of vision could not be achieved without turning that intentionality into a focused effort to develop and deliver unique ways of achieving it. Since these stores couldn't be profitable under the same model as large discount retailers like Kmart, which served heavily populated areas, Walton realized that he would need to develop his own unique set of capabilities that would allow the stores to run efficiently. He created advantages that no one else had: better merchandising, computer-based systems to control inventory, real-time inventory systems that tied into his suppliers, and even a fleet of trucks. Because it had captive customers in rural markets, Walmart eventually became a platform of products and services that created high barriers to entry for others. Walmart leveraged both customer outcome and structural innovation to uniquely fulfill a customer outcome that was valuable, rare, inimitable, and organizational. Intentionality resulted in deliberate actions to achieve the desired goal.

Likewise, Dell Computer started in 1984 with the concept that customers would prefer to configure their own build-to-order personal computers to match their specifications—if Dell could deliver them quickly at a low cost. Michael Dell's vision was to eliminate the trade-off of cost and time with the specific needs of the customer. Starting with this envisioned customer outcome, Dell intentionally focused on building the customer and logistics capabilities to deliver a custom solution that was more convenient, personalized, and less expensive than that in a store. The resulting solution shook up the personal computer market; competitors IBM and Compaq couldn't replicate it without alienating their distribution channels. Through its focused actions, Dell became the fastest growing and most profitable vendor in the PC industry and the only major company to remain in the personal computer market 35 years later.

Entertainment company Cirque du Soleil used intentionality to define a circus-like outcome in which people, not animals, are the center of performance. That intentionality propelled the organization to transform the customer outcome, and the result was theme-based experiences that bring customers back again and again for the thrills of a live performance. By focusing on human performers in fixed locations, Cirque eliminating the traditional negative factors associated with the circus: the trouble, expense, cost, smell, and, some would argue, the inhumanity of a traveling, animal-based circus. Cirque has upended the circus industry and, while the former market leader, Ringling Brothers, no longer exists, Cirque du Soleil thrives with more than two dozen shows running concurrently.

The examples of Walmart, Dell, and Cirque du Soleil show that intentionality is valuable when it leads the organization to create and act on a set of deliberate actions that achieves its goal. It's the first step in aligning your organization behind a vision for outcome innovation and engaging your team to create a strategy for achieving game-changing customer outcomes.

An Exercise in Developing Intentionality

Achieving true differentiation is a journey that requires ongoing attention and action. It is a challenge for any organization to create the right intentionality to deliver an aspirational thread for the organization to pull on. It is particularly challenging for companies with established sets of products or services. Whether you are an established organization looking to kickstart innovation or are thinking up your next startup concept, the following exercise will help.

The exercise is to create upfront a product positioning statement, a short declaration that defines the position you wish to establish in the minds of your target customers relative to their needs and competitive alternatives. Near the time of a product launch, marketing teams typically create a product positioning statement that positions the product as an attractive and differentiated relative to the competition by highlighting unique customer benefits. When written at the point when a product is launching, it's a deceptively tricky document to write because it requires sifting through the myriad of features to piece together a coherent statement of differentiation. Although such documents are generally less than a page long, they can take days or weeks for a team to create.

However, when the product positioning statement is written upfront before product development, this same statement becomes a guiding rather than a detailing exercise. Writing the document then becomes a strategic exercise in working backward, described in chapter 4, to create a vision of the target customer, their needs, and why the product is unique and valuable.

Importantly, it trains organizational leaders to identify the few things that matter to significantly differentiate themselves. In short, it builds a sense of intentionality. To focus on intentionality, think about either an upcoming product you are considering or an existing product or service that has potential unserved or underserved customers. Preferably with colleagues, identify how you can reach those customers with a solution by answering the customer outcome-focused questions in figure 10-2. Then, identify which benefits they will receive from that outcome.

Creating Intentionality	
Question	**Explanation**
Who is our target?	Define the target customer and their attributes.
What are they seeking?	Focus on describing customer needs or the problem they are trying to solve at a higher or more basic level than currently solved by solutions today.
What outcome do we aspire to deliver?	Describe what you can provide to the customer that will help achieve their higher-level need or use an adjoining "and" statement to indicate how you will provide what they achieve today "and" something new.
What are the benefits?	Outline the benefits to the customer.
What are the possible statements of intentionality?	Use this to outline statements that describe the solution in terms of customer experience, statements that you can use to create intentionality. These statements should represent the desired customer outcome, create emotion, and infuse a sense of motivation toward creating the solution.

Figure 10-2: Intentionality Statement Exercise

This exercise works well for an existing product as well. In that case, rewrite what you would like to deliver to the customer in terms of their outcome and benefits.

In the next chapter, we'll continue to address how to retool your organization by looking at the role and benefits of a strong organizational culture.

From Concept to Action

1. What is unique and valuable about what we do today?
2. What elements of what we do would pass the VRIO (Valuable, Rare, Inimitable, and Organizational) test?
3. Does our organization work with a sense of intentionality? How is it encapsulated? How broadly is that found in our organization?
4. If we were to better envision new intentionality, what outcomes would we express that best summarize it?

Chapter 11

Building a Culture That Feeds Strategy

The thing I have learned at IBM is that culture is everything.
Louis V. Gerstner Jr., former CEO, IBM

Transformative leaders understand how to use organizational culture to increases the likelihood of success today and anticipate the need to adapt in the future. The right culture feeds strategy in three ways: driving performance, delivering differentiation, and enabling adaptation. Organizations can evaluate and improve their culture by starting with a cultural assessment; creating context, vision, and mission; and creating and living by their values. Organizational culture can change over time, but it requires consistent effort to manage it.

Achieving Transformative Change

There is a management theory you may never have heard of called the theory of the firm. I hadn't come across it until I had started an intensive study of academic literature on management in graduate school. There are multiple versions of the theory that all seek to answer a simple question: why does a firm exist?

Despite working with dozens of companies and looking at hundreds more as an investor, I honestly had never thought about it before. Why does a company exist? Why do we go through the expense and difficulty of creating an organization, hiring and assembling a team, and incurring the administrative overhead to run it? It's a valid question in today's world of consultants and gig employees. There can be many answers to that question, but the most significant is this: you can accomplish more as a team working together for a common purpose. That is the power of organizational culture.

In these final two chapters we will discuss two major components of retooling your organization for innovation success. This chapter starts by covering the importance of organizational culture, and chapter 12 outlines how to create a challenge-setting organization.

Some people might question why a book about innovation includes a section dedicated to culture. The reason is this: at the end of the day, organizations are human enterprises. An organization is a group of people trying to optimize how they work together to achieve a defined outcome at the highest level of performance. Great leaders recognize that a strong and positive organizational culture is one of the best ways to achieve high performance and overcome challenges. Therefore, they focus on the question of how to build a culture that will aid their organization in creating advantages now and adapt in the future.

A review of the history of Netflix gives us a good understanding of how culture can help drive both performance and change. After nearly a decade, Netflix realized its long-held aspiration of evolving from a DVD-by-mail company to a streaming service with its first 1,000 titles, a fledgling offering compared to the more than one million DVDs the company was shipping daily. Netflix began spending tens of millions of dollars on cloud-based infrastructure and developing the capability to create, build, and optimize a cloud-based video streaming service.

Then in 2013, Netflix embarked on creating its own content, one that required new market understanding, creative and production capabilities, and spending billions of dollars per year buying and creating its content.

During this time of the company's transition to streaming and its own original content, the company embarked on a rapid international expansion that took the organization from its single market in 2010 to 190 countries by 2017.

Along the way, the company survived both the dot-com bust in 2000 and the economic downturn recession after 9/11 in the US that contributed to the company's need to lay off one-third of its employees.

Netflix had to recover from several self-inflicted and potentially disastrous issues as well. In an early attempt at the online market, the company spent considerable time developing a Netflix set-top box that would permit movies to be downloaded for later viewing, an idea already prevalent in the market that simply did not work. The company also created an independent film group, Red Envelope Entertainment, which it shut down two years later due to competitive issues with studios.

Then, there was the disastrous transition from the DVD business to streaming in 2011. Netflix raised its pricing by as much as 60 percent and tried to split subscriptions to DVDs to a new brand, Qwikster. Subscribers revolted, and Netflix pulled back on the strategy but not before losing as many as 800,000 subscribers and seeing its stock price drop by 35 percent.

Netflix managed to adapt and reinvent itself enough times that *Forbes* magazine dubbed CEO Reed Hastings the "Master of Adaptation."[1] Why did they succeed? Hastings has had an answer since the beginning: "I would say, on balance, [that] culture will help Netflix prosper through multiple eras." He continues, "We've been able to adapt from DVD-by-mail, taking on Blockbuster, defeating a company that was 100 times larger than us, to then go from DVD-by-mail to streaming of other people's content, to streaming of our own content, from 100 percent domestic to global...we've encountered many challenges, which [my previous company] in the 1990s would not have been able to do...I'm very personally convinced that the culture has been helping on that."[2]

Like other leaders of other transformative organizations, Hastings has focused on developing a culture that drives company performance and provides a clear differentiation that sustains its organization over the long run. The development of a strong organizational culture is a common approach shared by nearly every transformative organization studied in this book, including not just Netflix but Amazon, Apple, Airbnb, Zappos, and Walmart.

The Importance of Culture

Culture is the cornerstone of Netflix's performance and adaptability precisely because of Reed Hasting's experience with his previous startup, Pure Software. Hastings went through a cycle of trying to put more of his own personal effort into the organization then creating a new process or set of rules to compensate for failures in the organization. Hastings learned from that experience that, in his own words, by building too many rules and processes, "The problem was we were trying to dummy-proof the system, and eventually only dummies wanted to work there."[3]

At Pure, Hastings was frustrated with his role as CEO to the point of asking the board to replace him. They refused, and Hastings remained in the position until the company merged with a larger competitor. After leaving the organization, he spent two years thinking of how to avoid the same leadership traps in the future.

Hastings put those ideas into place at Netflix, creating an organization whose policies and processes did not expand with the organization's growth. The result was the creation of an organizational culture that forms the basis of a high-performance organization based on few actual rules and that allows employees to make decisions for themselves by balancing freedom and responsibility.

That approach is encoded in the Netflix Culture Deck, a presentation covering the seven aspects of company culture that includes behaviors Netflix looks for in individual employees, values, and philosophy on processes and policies. Facebook COO Sheryl Sandburg said that the Netflix Culture Deck "may well be the most important document ever to come out of [Silicon] Valley." It has been downloaded more than 15 million times since Netflix posted it on its website and its tenets copied time and again.

The Culture Deck embodies transformative organizations' approach to enabling a vibrant culture that supports leadership priorities and enables organizational adaptation.

Organizational culture is a term that we believe we understand but one that often defies definition. On one side of the interview table or the other, you've likely asked or been asked the question, "So what is the company culture like?" We often find it hard to describe what culture is and to identify the culture of a specific organization.

Although culture has been around for as long as organizations have existed, it was first described by social analyst and management consultant Elliott Jaques in his book *The Changing Culture of the Factory* in 1951. Creating a study of a ball bearing manufacturing company in the UK, Jaques noted that "the culture of the factory is its customary and traditional way of thinking and doing of things, which is shared to a greater or lesser degree by all its members, and which new members must learn, and at least partially accept, in order to be accepted into service in the firm."

More specifically, culture is "a set of shared assumptions that guide action [and] appropriate behavior."[4] As shown in figure 11-1, it is the social construct defined by the shared values, customs, beliefs, and norms of an organization. The characteristics of culture are shared, enduring, pervasive, and implicit. Because of this, our attempts to describe culture may align with the sentiment behind the motto of Texas A&M University, "From the outside looking in, you can't understand it. From the inside looking out, you can't explain it."

Figure 11-1: Organizational Culture Overview

If culture comprises an organization's values, customs, beliefs, and norms, those components are the product of many influencers. Figure 11-1 highlights some of the most powerful elements that impact an organization's culture. Some have a more tangible effect, and their absence is noticeable. Others, such as a shared view of the world or company mission and a set of defined values, are often missing and significantly impact the organization's culture and success. One major determinant, values, always exist in any organization, whether defined or not. Whether they positively contribute is a matter of whether you have defined and are following the right ones.

The Three Advantages of Culture

We've all heard the phrase, frequently attributed to Peter Drucker, that, "Culture eats strategy for breakfast," a saying that denotes how strong an influence culture can be, even to the point of overpowering a company's objectives and plans. It's a decidedly pessimistic view on organizations' ability to effectively change or pursue a course of action without significant, often fatal, subjection to the inertial, momentum-killing attribute of culture. Unfortunately, it's an observation that is widely upheld by empirical observations.

While strategy is set from above and includes one or more goals and conscious decisions of what to focus on, culture—that set of accepted values, customs, beliefs, and norms—is constantly active at the individual level, in hundreds, if not thousands of choices and actions made each day by every employee. If those choices and actions don't support the strategy, it will never be accomplished. In this case, culture trumps strategy, and the strategy will never be enacted.

So while many companies treat culture as a nice-to-have, define it as a good "family atmosphere," or point to a set of perks and benefits that attract talent, transformative organizations approach culture as the underpinning of the organization's performance and the driver of success. In the words of Progressive CEO Tricia Griffith, "With the right people, culture, and values, you can accomplish great things."

While Netflix, for example, broadly acknowledges that "culture is how a firm operates," it emphasizes that it is the key to the company's performance and future, stating that culture is "the best chance of continuous success for many generations of technology and people."[5]

Companies are successful due to various factors, including strategy, capabilities, culture, timing, and some luck. While many of these factors seem manageable, organizations often fail at culture because, while strategy can be documented and capabilities can be built, culture is seemingly less tangible and more challenging to manage.

Let's be clear, when I talk about a strong culture, I mean specifically an organization's ability to use its values, customs, beliefs, norms, and expectations of how to act in a way that unifies the organization to support a common set of strategic goals and actions. A strong culture also aids the organization in anticipating when it needs to adapt and adjust to changing conditions. Without a strong and driving culture, it is impossible to innovate to win.

Organizations that focus on managing culture recognize just how tangible it is. For Walmart, culture is a true differentiator that has brought about most of the elements of their strategy. As the world's largest retailer, it has relied on a few key strategic elements that have made it successful. Store placement, logistics, merchandising, supplier partnerships, and focusing on lowering costs and prices have been the cornerstone of its success. The company built key capabilities, such as extensive logistics, hot docking, and early use of customer analytics.

But much of Walmart's success and growth in its early years resulted from the culture created by its founder, Sam Walton, who believed in giving autonomy to his store managers to develop and test ideas in the individual stores. His goal was to spark innovation, which could then be shared in the company's Saturday meetings between managers. As Sam Walton stated, "I've made it my own personal mission to ensure that constant change is a vital part of the Wal-Mart culture itself. I've forced change...at every turn in our company's development. In fact, I think one of the greatest strengths of Wal-Mart's ingrained culture is its ability to drop everything and turn on a dime."[6]

Culture drove much of Walmart's early innovation. As Harry Cunningham, founder of Kmart, once stated, "Sam's establishment of the Walton culture throughout the company was the key to the whole thing. It's just incomparable."

Despite the obvious benefits, most leaders fail to ask themselves how they can create a culture that feeds their strategy and increases innovation. Recognizing they are inextricably linked is the first step. Reed Hastings admonished, "I encourage people not to believe...that 'Culture eats strategy for lunch.' Both are really important. We spend a lot of time on strategy, and why not do both well? Why do you have to rank them? Let's try to do culture well, let's try to do strategy well."[7]

From my personal experience, there are three ways in which culture feeds strategy. First, culture drives performance. Second, culture delivers differentiation. Third, culture enables adaptation and change.

Culture Drives Performance

When founded in a shared vision and mission, culture drives performance and facilitates management. A study by John Kotter and James Heskett found that organizations with strong cultures outperform others by a significant margin in overall performance, growth, shareholder value, and profitability.[8] And a study of culture in Fortune 100 companies showed that those that espouse unique company values consistently outperformed their peers.[9]

Research into culture and innovation by Rajesh Chandy of the London Business School, Gerard Tellis of USC, and Jaideep Prabhu of Cambridge University found that "Corporate culture is, above all, the most important factor in driving innovation." The group concluded their study of over 750 companies with the admonition that "Managers have control over the fates of their firms in that they can help build the culture of innovation. A sharp manager would look across industries and countries to spot innovative traits and strategies."[10]

Strong, positive cultures reinforce a performance orientation and attract and keep individuals who pursue quality work in themselves and hold others to the same standard. In the words of former Amazon CEO Jeff Bezos, "A culture of high standards is protective of all the 'invisible' but crucial work that goes on in every company. I'm talking about the work that no one sees. The work that gets done when no one is watching. In a high standards culture, doing that work well is its own reward—it's part of what it means to be a professional."[11]

One of the ways strong cultures drive performance is by increasing employee engagement, a major challenge for most companies. According to a recent

Gallup poll, only 32 percent of employees characterize themselves as actively engaged in their role. Another 67 percent of employees say they are "not engaged" in their workplace while an astounding 16 percent are actively disengaged in their work and workplace. This is disturbing given that organizations with high engagement were, on average, 21 percent more profitable than those with bottom quartile engagement levels. A Gallup study estimated that negative economic impact of low engagement is $7 trillion per year.[12]

A recent, massive survey of over 28,000 employees in 15 different countries unveiled the secret to higher engagement: the level to which employees made a personal connection to the company's core values—a component of culture— was the best indicator that they are engaged in their work.[13] Former Zappos CEO Tony Hsieh, who hosted thousands of corporate visitors who came to study his organization's success, said it plainly: "If your culture isn't engaging and empowering your team, you're losing money."[14]

Culture also aids performance by reinforcing good (or bad) behavior in an organization, thereby making management's role easier or harder. Good cultures created by organizations with defined values develop a practice of adhering to those values, facilitating management's job.

Not long ago, I had lunch with the CEO of a Fortune 500 financial services company who lamented that in his current role he spent more than half his time on personnel-related issues and wished that he spent more time paying attention to his organizational behavior classes from his MBA program.

As our conversation went a few questions deeper, I realized that what he viewed as a deficiency in his education in dealing with performance issues was actually a problem with the company's culture. While the company had a mission, vision, and set of published values, management rarely spoke of them, and no one managed to their values. What he saw as HR issues stemmed from misalignment of the organization to the stated mission or individual performance issues that would have been mitigated through an emphasis on and reinforcement of company values.

He failed to realize that strong cultures are the guardrails of performance and behavior, facilitating the leader's role in managing and reducing energy spent on dealing with exceptions and problems.

Culture Delivers Differentiation

The second way that culture drives strategy is that culture can be a true differentiator in organizations, a quality of those organizations that is difficult, if not impossible, to copy. This is why Kmart, recognizing culture was Walmart's differentiator, was never able to replicate it.

It's not that organizations don't try. But when people talk about copying culture, they miss the critical elements that are most difficult to see and understand and that form the foundation of culture. Instead, they focus on the superficial policies, practices, and rules of engagement that are the most obvious manifestations of an organization's culture. However much we try, recreating Netflix's policy of no set vacation time or Google's free lunches serves only to get you people who are attracted to unlimited vacation time or free lunches.

As former Zappos CEO Tony Hsieh stated, "Our belief is that our Brand, our Culture, and our Pipeline (which we internally refer to as "BCP") are the only competitive advantages that we will have in the long run. Everything else can and will eventually be copied."[15]

One of the essential reasons why culture is so difficult to copy is that the leaders who try to do so have not previously committed to building a strong organizational culture and are looking to shortcut the process. We see it play out often when companies poach employees from another company, hoping to gain their leadership skills. However, these transplants often find the culture of the new company too challenging to navigate and a leadership team unwilling to commit to long-term change. This is especially true when trying to copy leadership types or hire employees from mission-driven transformative organizations.

Culture is also a differentiator in its ability to attract talent. Increasingly, organizations are facing a global talent war for qualified candidates with the right skills. A recent PWC survey showed that nearly a third of CEOs worry about the availability of key skills, an increase of nearly three times from just five years ago.[16] More importantly, many are finding that the important skills that facilitate the growth and transformation of their organizations are simply lacking.

Moreover, increasingly employees are driven by an interest in working for organizations that have meaning and mission. Culture attracts the right talent. And if your organization doesn't have a strong and positive culture, you will increasingly lose out on the best talent.

No other company better exemplifies the advantage of culture in attracting talent and creating a robust talent pipeline than Zappos. Tony Hsieh saw culture as the key to the company's recruiting process. In his opinion, the company's culture and brand are inextricably linked.

Much of the attraction of working at Zappos is the sense of purpose Hsieh created for the organization. While honorable, selling shoes may not be the loftiest of missions. But Zappos isn't in the business of selling shoes online; according to Hsieh, their mission is to deliver happiness. For Hsieh and the entire Zappos organization, delivering happiness provides a shared sense of purpose and defines it in a real and tactile sense. That purpose of delivering "Wow!" to the customer supersedes the product and goes to the experience they want to have when someone receives that package from Zappos.

It's no coincidence that many companies in the technology industry, where it is difficult to hire, focus on strong cultures to attract talent. Others, such as sharing economy companies Lyft and Airbnb that rely on nonemployee contractors or homeowners, also rely heavily on a vibrant culture to transmit their mission and values. Lyft's VP of People, Ron Storn, says, "At Lyft, our product is really people, and we build a platform that connects communities, so we try to find talent that aligns to that...We try at Lyft to live by the brand—we treat people better. That is in our external community with drivers and passengers, but also internally in how we support and develop our team members."[17]

Culture Enables Adaptation and Change

The third area in which culture feeds strategy is in its ability to enable adaptation and change. While strategy is necessarily a set of defined objectives and decisions that clearly focus on how the organization will accomplish them, it's often wrong. Even the very best strategies need adjustment and change over time. Culture helps in adapting and changing that strategy in several ways.

First, the strong cultures of transformative organizations build adaptability and resilience when issues arise and failures occur. Common across the transformative companies in this book is a shared history of failure, and the resilience to overcome it. Nearly all have had to overcome a near fatal issue. As former Starbucks CEO Harold Schultz observed, "To be an enduring, great company, you have to build a mechanism for preventing or solving problems that will long outlast any one individual leader."[18]

Why does culture help so much in building resilience? Cultures that lock employees into a vision, a mission, a common set of values, and a set of accepted practices and behaviors that allow them to process the failure are more likely to be resilient and learn from their failures. As Andy Jassy, CEO of Amazon, explains, "We accept if you're trying to innovate, sometimes you're going to fail. It has to be a culture that takes risks even if the output doesn't end up being a big success, accepts you may fail sometimes—and tries to learn from it and move on."[19]

One of the most apparent signs of a non-adaptive culture is how its historic failures impact its culture today. I have witnessed this firsthand in organizations that have borne the scars of a previous catastrophe, limiting their ability to move forward and try something again or try something new. What they failed at previously becomes a taboo topic, even when the idea may finally have merit.

The ability to show resilience in the face of failure has been critical for Amazon, whose failures have been wide-ranging, including attempts to go into auctions (Amazon Auctions), travel planning (Amazon Destinations), mobile phones (Fire Phone), local services (Amazon Local), and electronic payments (WePay). However, Amazon's failure in auctions resulted in the organization developing the foundation for Amazon Marketplace, which enables third parties to sell on the Amazon website and now represents more than half of Amazon's online sales.

Apple has been exemplary in its ability to transform industries and much of that comes from a culture that could adapt as needed. In the last 20 years it has focused on four different primary markets: personal laptop computers (MacBooks), music (iPods and iTunes), mobile devices (iPhones and iPads), and now services. Throughout these transformative moves in different markets, each of which required new technological innovation and different strategies, Apple has maintained a consistency in its ability to change and dominate. The consistent source of this dominance has been Apple's cultural differentiation of attention to design, customer experience, hardware and software integration, and innovation. As Steve Jobs puts it, "What is Apple, after all? Apple is about people who think outside the box."

One of the ways Apple supported their ability to change and address new markets is an organizational norm of hiring people with diverse backgrounds, taking advantage of combining engineering and the arts. Steve Jobs, as previously noted, emphasized hiring individuals with a "broad understanding of the human experience," that he believed would ultimately deliver a better designed solution.[20]

Cultural Transformation: Strengthening Your Culture

Because of these advantages, C-suite leaders and boards increasingly understand why culture should be an area of focus. A 2018 study by Katzenbach found that 71 percent of company leaders stated that culture is important, up from 64 percent in 2013. In addition, 65 percent indicated that culture is more important to performance than strategy or their operating model.[21]

Yet despite all the benefits, most leaders find it challenging to manage their organization's culture. A survey by Mazars and Insead found that, despite culture being in the top three priorities for company boards, only 20 percent of 450 London-based directors and board members reported spending adequate time to manage and improve it.[22]

While prioritization is an issue for many, some leaders simply lack the understanding of how to create lasting cultural change. Almost two-thirds of CEOs feel that they are primarily responsible for setting the culture of the organization. However, more than 50 percent of those CEOs have expressed that driving culture change was harder than anticipated.[23]

Most of the companies I describe in this book were conceived by leaders who understood the importance of culture. So the question may be, how difficult it is for existing companies to change their culture?

As more than 80 percent of leaders stated that their organization's culture must evolve in the next five years for their company to succeed, grow, and retain talent, the question is not whether existing organizations can change but how they can change.[24] Although the transformative companies I've described were founded by leaders who understood the importance of culture, organizations such as Apple demonstrate clearly that culture can be changed. Apple's move from its once-moribund state in the 1990s to be the most valuable and most prolifically transformative company for the last 20 years demonstrates that culture can be changed.

Cultural awareness and focus on change are reflected in the theme of "culture hacking"—making tweaks to culture to improve it and change company performance—that has become pervasive, including in Silicon Valley. While the software-oriented term "hacking" may not resonate with everyone, it drives home the point that culture is a dynamic entity. No matter what its status, it can be improved and strengthened with some concerted effort.

My personal experience with multiple organizations has been that culture change is difficult, but it can be accomplished relatively quickly with leadership buy-in. Commitment is vital because your company culture is a result of years of practice, reinforcement, and reward. Leadership is largely in place due to their use of and adaptation to the existing organizational culture.

Recognize as you enter any change process that there is no single culture that just works for all companies. Copying another company's culture is a waste of effort.

While the steps of cultural transformation can be extensive, the seven-step process for cultural change below is an excellent way to think about the process of change. I have created a more in-depth overview of the steps for change on my website (www.williamkilmer.com). This process will help you assess and identify the steps for change. Underlying this effort is the assumption that the senior leadership of the organization is aligned behind the need for change. In this process, the first two steps focus on laying the foundation, steps three through five help assess, identify, establish your target culture, and steps six and seven concentrate on implementing cultural change.

Start at the Beginning: Create Context and Urgency

The first step to developing a strong culture for any organization is to set the context for the organization. Context identifies what's happening in the world around you and trends affecting your industry. It involves telling the story behind your story. It's not the reason why you exist; it's the reason why you *should* exist. Often described as the company's worldview, it tells the background of what is happening in the market and the trends and changes that help your team understand why you are doing what you are doing. Great companies set this context to align the organization before setting its vision and mission. I will discuss this further in the next chapter.

Set Vision and Mission

Without unity of purpose, culture and is ineffective and chaotic. Your vision and mission form the guiding elements of what you are trying to accomplish. Too many companies think these elements are implicit, but this attitude discounts the benefit of the mental exercise required to create them and the unifying value of publishing them. Creating and documenting a vision and mission forces you to drop the irrelevant and focus on what's important. Then, once they are created, your organization's leaders must communicate them by a factor of ten times more than you think is necessary. If you do not, your communication about the vision and mission will be drowned out by every other message your employees hear.

Observe and Audit

Spend the time and effort discovering what your existing culture is before making changes. Much of your understanding can come from simple observation. How well do employees know the mission and vision of the company? Do they know and broadly follow the company's values? Are there historical factors that have influenced the company extensively? Questionnaires are helpful, but so are smaller group settings and one-on-one meetings to understand how others would describe the culture.

Identify Your Target Culture

Identify the type of culture you believe the organization needs and look for gaps between the current culture and that target. Achieving an aspirational culture requires discussion at all levels around what the organization needs. One of the best ways to approach this is to hold open discussion forums to collect ideas at various levels of the organization. Taking a page from the Netflix Culture Deck, repeatedly ask the question, "What values, beliefs, practices, and norms will allow us to succeed now and in the future?"

Establish and Center on Values

Of the components of culture described earlier in figure 11-1, values—agreed-upon beliefs and guiding principles—are essential because they heavily influence the other three. If you already have a set of values and they are not working, don't hesitate to throw them out and start again. If you haven't been espousing them, your true values likely differ from the company's written values. Without exception, I have found that if you ask employees to participate, they are energized to restate and reinvent old, unfollowed values. (You will find a separate process for setting or resetting values on my website, www.williamkilmer.com.)

After your company worldview, vision, and mission, values are the most powerful tool you have in recasting culture because they represent a shared understanding of what the company requires to be successful. Zappos CEO Tony Hsieh, whose 10 company values have become a benchmark for other organizations, once reflected, "If I could go back and do Zappos all over again, I would actually come up with our values from day one."

You don't need to create a long list of values to make them effective. While many organizations have up to 10 or more, Lyft has found success with just three:

- Be Yourself. Live authentically and trust your voice. You belong here.
- Uplift Others. Take care of each other—no matter which seat you're sitting in.
- Make It Happen. Own the work. Focus on impact. Reimagine what's possible.

It is essential that the process for creating company values involves employee input and feedback. Without it, you risk creating a list that is meaningless and feels forced on the organization.

Create Anchors

With a target culture and values in place, it is time to create anchors within your team to start to influence, encourage, and reinforce the practice of following them. The best way to do this is by starting with two groups who will most immediately start modeling and reinforcing the new culture, influencing others to follow.

First, focus on new hires. To accomplish that, become rigorous in your hiring process and place more emphasis on hiring for culture and aptitude and less on skills and experience. No one has refined the hiring process for culture better than Zappos, which not only hires for cultural fit but continually reinforces values and culture post-hire. New employees spend their first two weeks in customer service. They then spend another two weeks in the warehouse shipping shoes to customers. At the end of that time, they are given the opportunity to accept a generous separation payment (around $2,500 when I last checked) if they don't wish to stay with the company.

The simplest and most effective way to accomplish this is to develop a cultural screen as part of your hiring process. Do so by using the cultural attributes and values in your interviewing process. Each interviewer should have the screening criteria in front of them during an interview. Encourage managers to discuss culture in the interview, rate each interviewee on how that individual would uphold or detract from your target culture, and discuss their assessment with others participating in the interview process. Culture should become part of the criteria for hiring or not hiring every individual in the company. Deciding not to hire someone because of cultural fit is an essential tool in creating cultural change and sends a strong message to the team.

A focus on new hires should include creating a culture training program as part of your employee induction program. Training should consist of a review of the values, discussion of the elements of company culture, and ways that individuals can reinforce and reward behavior that strengthens company culture.

Second, create cultural champions. Find and recruit key people in the organization to help. While new employees are a great place to start, you can't ignore the task of creating a sense of the new culture with existing employees. This type of change is often met with skepticism and even resistance. That resistance can come from a general disinterest in change or a feeling that this is only a passing phase that is not worth the time and effort. One of the critical ways to counter this is to create anchors in the effort toward organizational change with a group of cultural champions at the right levels in the organization to assist.

Select individuals for their enthusiasm for the cause, their roles as natural or organizational leaders, and their ability to communicate and model behavior that exemplifies the cultural change you are looking for. Focus on training these employees, meeting with them regularly, and using them as examples and catalysts in your cultural transformation.

Start by training them as you would other employees. Then, consider how to include them in a cultural advisory group that occasionally meets to discuss how the organization is progressing and what initiatives would help to extend the culture change to others in the organization.

Reinforce, Recognize, and Reward

Once you have established a target culture, including context, a clear vision, mission, and values, the next step is to communicate it frequently, recognize positive change toward that culture, and reward it.

Change management guru John Kotter estimated that sharing information on a company's vision and mission represents just 0.0005 percent of all information employees receive.[25] Even modest amounts of communicating the importance of culture and reinforcing company values are lost in the massive information deluge we experience each day.

It is not an exaggeration to say leadership should communicate the new elements of your culture and especially the company values 10 times more frequently than you believe you should. Beyond communication, leaders can reinforce their target culture and values when they recognize and reward positive cultural behavior. This can happen on several levels, including peer-to-peer recognitions, manager to employee discussions, and company-wide forums and communications. It is especially helpful to focus on highlighting individual values and recognizing and rewarding positive role models.

Remember that these steps are just the beginning of creating and reinforcing the type of culture that will help deliver the performance, differentiation, and strategic flexibility your organization seeks. Organizational culture is built and reinforced in small increments, so it should be a continual topic of discussion among senior managers to review how the organization is progressing and how you can better shift the organization toward your target culture. Don't be shy in reinforcing and finding creative ways to recognize and reward the small steps toward success.

Final Thoughts on Culture Transformation

Culture is another hand on the flywheel, the invisible force which enables organizations to build and sustain momentum. However, culture requires attention to maintain and improve. Organizations that are good at it find ways to make it better. As Reed Hastings stated, "We encourage employees to figure out how to improve the culture, not how to preserve it."

Surveys consistently show that a good culture is more important to employees than their compensation level. As organizations seek to differentiate themselves in seeking highly skilled employees, culture will become an increasingly important factor in attracting them.

Retooling your organization requires a strong culture. Fortunately, culture is learned and can be changed. Organizations can adopt new cultural practices and replace old ones. While change takes time, daily practice either reinforces or modifies your current culture. As you make the effort to evaluate and change your culture, you will create the opportunity for sustainable success.

Concept to Action

1. How would we assess our culture currently? What words would we use to describe it?
2. Do our values serve us? Are our employees familiar with them? What values do we model and uphold?
3. What values, practices, and beliefs would best help us to succeed now and in the future?
4. How do we improve the way we recognize and reward our employees for upholding and improving our culture?

Chapter 12

Developing a Challenge-Setting Organization

We always plan too much and always think too little. We resent
a call to thinking and hate unfamiliar argument that does not
tally with what we already believe or would like to believe.
Joseph Schumpeter

Great organizations stay in "Day 1" mode, continually evaluating and creating priorities that sustain their growth and performance. The OODA Loop serves as a model for organizations to observe, orient, decide, and act to improve their position at a high clock speed. A challenge-setting organization creates a worldview, regularly orients itself, and uses first-principles thinking to define current priorities.

Operating a Dynamic Environment

Twenty-five years ago, Andy Grove, then CEO of Intel Corporation, published the management classic *Only the Paranoid Survive*. In it, Grove argued that organizations thrive when they can see upcoming significant potential changes, what he called strategic inflection points, and exploit them to their advantage. His warning was that these inflection points were mainly shifts in the technology landscape that, like "deadly and turbulent rapids" on a river, awaited even the most experienced leaders, ready to tear apart their businesses. Grove warned that in the face of these "'10x forces, you can lose control of your destiny." Conversely, if you can react quickly enough, "opportunity knocks when a technology break or other fundamental change comes your way."[1]

The combination of rapid technological innovation and accelerating customer adoption trends have created a world that is moving faster than ever. Academic, futurist, and entrepreneur Ray Kurzweil rightly observed that we are now in a period of *accelerating* change, stating, "Today it's an axiom that life is changing and that technology is affecting the nature of society. But what's not fully understood is that the pace of change is itself accelerating, and the last 20 years are not a good guide to the next 20 years. We're doubling the paradigm shift rate, the rate of progress, every decade."[2]

According to Kurzweil, because we are now building technology that helps us create new technology, change is moving from a linear to an exponential growth rate. New technology such as data analytics, customer targeting software, social media, and digital delivery now also drives faster customer adoption rates. Growth hacking, the ability to scale customers as quickly and efficiently as possible, has now become a profession in its own right, shifting markets faster than ever.

However, Andy Grove's warning that we need to be paranoid about the next technology disruption only tells part of the story. His viewpoint, primarily shaped by his own experience and the few near misses that Intel experienced, leaves out the more optimistic view. Sometimes an accelerating world is not just one that presents problems; it also frequently offers new opportunities that, if you aren't observing, you simply may miss.

In the introduction to this book, I stated that the greatest challenge organizations face is to develop the momentum to seek change, even when the need to change isn't apparent. A fundamental component of that challenge is the third element of retooling your organization: the drive to create change at a faster tempo than competitors. Clock speed—the pace and cadence of execution, and the ability to recognize the need for adaptation—is critical.

The answer to the call of innovating to win isn't solely based on the next giant leap in technological innovation. Many of the companies I've researched have taken advantage of significant advancements in enabling technology: Internet infrastructure, software, data analytics, cloud computing architectures, and mobile devices, for example. Some, like Intel and Salesforce, are technical pioneers in hardware, software, and cloud infrastructure. But their real breakthrough came from seeking to fulfill higher-level needs and envisioning and creating better outcomes, sometimes before the customers themselves understood them. The best prospects for change come from setting up your organization to look for new opportunities deeply and constantly.

The essence of the transformative framework outlined in this book is that organizations can use a set of principles and accompanying actions to find and create opportunities for themselves in shifting markets, based on new customer outcomes that they create. It's an acknowledgment that innovation is more than just a game of chance or waiting for that next strategic inflection point. True game-changing innovation is broader and starts with a vision to create something unique and valuable.

The Transformative Framework		
	Principles	**Key Transformative Actions**
Principle One	Game-changing innovation is founded on building different and better customer outcomes.	Uplevel focus to the customer's objective and seek to deliver new and differentiated outcomes.
Principle Two	Structural innovation improves outcome innovation and delivers distinct strategic advantages.	Deliver critical strategic capabilities to support unique customer outcomes.
		Create market asymmetries by rethinking and reframing industry structure.
Principle Three	Markets that are expanding and transitioning are the easiest to enter and lead.	Take a market-expansion orientation and develop scale accelerators.
Principle Four	Organizational culture sustains ongoing innovation and adaptation.	Actively engage in developing intentionality, a strong organizational culture, and a challenge-setting clock speed.

Figure 12-1: The Transformative Framework

The transformative framework is the product of years of research into why some companies innovate to win while others don't. It defines a set of principles and actions to help organizations find and develop opportunities that lead to broad-based and game-changing innovation that reshuffles the market in their favor. Those principles are outlined in figure 12-1.

Your ability to reach your objective as an organization depends less on getting the answers to these questions perfectly right the first time than it does on your persistence in trying to answer them and your resilience in overcoming mistakes to find the right path forward.

The question for most leaders is how to get on that path. And, once you are on the path, how do you sustain your momentum forward at the right tempo and pace? With that in mind, this chapter is devoted to how organizations can challenge themselves to set a course and clock speed to continually evaluate where they are and adjust as needed.

Transformative leaders encourage and sustain a pattern of becoming a challenge-setting organization—one that moves forward quickly by continually defining a set of challenges to accomplish. For Jeff Bezos, this is the essence of always staying in "Day 1" mode. Day 1 is a reference to Bezos's first letter to shareholders in 1997 when the Internet was new, and Amazon, with $15 million in revenue the year before, had determined how it would use the Internet "to create real value for its customers and, by doing so, hopes to create an enduring franchise, even in established and large markets." In Day 1, Amazon understood the landscape in front of them, created a massively intentional goal, and started to build what they saw was needed to achieve it.

Nearly 20 years later, in 2016, Bezos was still talking about being in Day 1 mode to his shareholders, offering up their secret to staying in it. "Here's a starter pack of essentials for Day 1 defense," he declared, "customer obsession, a skeptical view of proxies, the eager adoption of external trends, and high-velocity decision-making."

The alternative, he offered, is Day 2: eventual decline. "Day 2 is stasis. Followed by irrelevance. Followed by excruciating, painful decline. Followed by death. And that is why it is always Day 1. To be sure, this kind of decline would happen in extreme slow motion. An established company might harvest Day 2 for decades, but the final result would still come."[3]

Whether you are looking to get into Day 1 or to stay in Day 1 mode, the essence of becoming a challenge-setting organization is constantly observing and understanding your environment and setting those priorities the company needs to get to the next level. It results in asking the questions "Where do we need to go?" and "What actions do we need to take, and capabilities do we need to build to get there?"

Back in chapter 5, I noted that we often admire companies for their capabilities, the skills, processes, know-how, and unique ways of using assets and resources to deliver meaningful results. One of the most critical capabilities that distinguishes transformative organizations is their ability to observe, learn, and adjust their actions to match the current set of challenges they define to move them forward. This takes more than an element of constructive discontent; it is an ability to adjust ingrained in their DNA. To understand it, I turn to a dynamic model that represents the type of thinking needed to become a challenge-setting organization.

Leadership in Dynamic Environments: The OODA Loop

The OODA Loop model was created more than 50 years ago for a real and rapidly changing environment in an era of incredibly rapid change: aerial combat.

The 1950s and 1960s were a time of rapid technological advances for military combat aircraft, which, in turn, had a profound effect on pilots and their air combat tactics. At the end of World War II, the average propeller-driven fighter plane traveled at a top speed of just over 400 miles per hour (644 kilometers per hour). Only seven years later, during the Korean War, the average speed surpassed 600 miles per hour (966 kilometers per hour).

In the following 10 years, new jet aircraft started reaching top speeds of 1,600 miles per hour (2,600 kilometers per hour), four times the speed just 15 years earlier. United States Air Force Colonel and former fighter pilot John Boyd had observed these changes firsthand, noting that the rapid increases in speed were stretching the pilots' ability to react in such fast and highly dynamic environments.

In 1961, Colonel Boyd published his model, known as the OODA Loop, in his book *Aerial Attack Study*, the bible of aerial combat techniques. OODA is an acronym that breaks down the ability to go from understanding new information to taking action based on four key elements:

- **Observation**: the collection of data and information of the current situation
- **Orientation**: the ability to analyze and synthesize data, define a relative position, and form options
- **Decision**: the resolve to define and follow a course of action
- **Action**: the execution of that course of action

In great contrast to the overplanning orientation of the military, the OODA Loop was designed to aid pilots while in the air to continuously observe, adjust analysis and understanding, decide on adjustments, and act in the moment. Boyd's model received widespread interest and adoption in the military and eventually it was applied to other settings as well.

Importantly, Boyd observed that reaction speed was the primary determinant of success in aerial encounters. Specifically, he noted that the faster the tempo at which a pilot could observe the situation, analyze and understand it, make a decision, and act on it, the better their advantage. A master of putting it into practice, he was known as "Forty Second Boyd" for his ability to take any aerial circumstance where he was at a disadvantage and turning it into his advantage in 40 seconds or less.

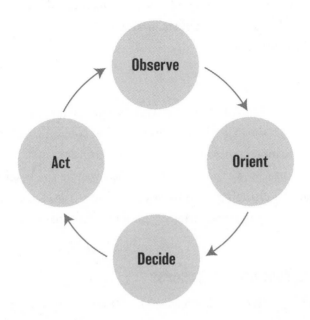

Figure 12-2: The OODA Loop

The basis of Colonel Boyd's model is an acceptance that our understanding of any situation is fundamentally incomplete, or at least constantly changing. Therefore, it requires that we continuously refine and adapt our observed model to identify and understand new observations and adjust accordingly. As shown in figure 12-2, it takes its foundation from a single loop learning system.

Importantly, Boyd's findings recognized the advantage of creating a pattern of immediate understanding followed by action to create change. He identified that the pilot's role was to act on their situation to improve their position once they had partially developed their understanding. Specifically, Boyd's work reached two critical conclusions:

First, the most critical factor for winning was to put the pilot in control as quickly as possible so that they were acting based on their observations.

Second, the greater the speed at which a pilot could observe the situation, analyze and understand it, make a decision, and act on it, the more effective their advantage.

In fact, Boyd found that even in situations when pilots made wrong decisions, they were ultimately better off because of the speed at which they could reassess the situation, understand the error, and correct it.

Boyd's conclusion was that pilots needed to "operate at a faster tempo to generate rapidly changing conditions that inhibit [their] opponent from adapting or reacting to those changes."[4] Simply put, clock speed wins.

Increasing Your Odds of Success

Despite our best efforts in planning and sometimes overplanning, the world doesn't stand still long enough for our plans to last. Facebook's Sheryl Sandberg sums it up well: "Life is never perfect. We all live some form of Option B."[5] While there are no perfect plans and set answers in innovation and strategy, and no single way to achieve game-changing outcomes, there are ways to improve the likelihood of success.

For the very same reasons the OODA Loop was successful in improving aerial combat outcomes, using it can improve your chance of success by increasing the clock speed of getting from observation to decision and to action. You can set the pace of identifying what your organization's most immediate challenges are and prioritizing resolving them. In effect, by becoming a challenge-setting organization, you put yourself in the position to act and set the pace of change.

Let's look at how you can apply the OODA Loop to becoming a challenge-setting organization through four specific steps.

Observe: Creating a Worldview

The first is to start with a worldview by creating and publishing a collective set of observations for your organization. This worldview is simply your organization's unbiased description of the external business environment you work in and what you accept as the observed truth. It includes understanding the trends, problems faced by your customers and their needs, the opportunities available, and specific challenges to your organization. Understanding where you are and what is available to you starts with understanding the context of the world around your organization. It is essential for your organization to collectively understand and share that worldview as the "Why now?" behind what you are doing, as well as be prepared to challenge it when it needs to change.

Great leaders start with a worldview because it grounds the entire organization on how you look at the world. I think the result is something similar to the overview effect felt by astronauts when they see the planet from space for the first time. Looking back at the Earth from space, they often express a new understanding of how important and fragile it is. They gain a renewed sense of purpose.[6] They get the big picture, which helps them understand how to place themselves in it when they return to Earth.

A worldview also gives your team the opportunity to contribute to it and provides the why to your story. Microsoft CEO Satya Nadella, who has presided over one of the most historic company transformations, recognized the fundamental importance of this. Nadella advocated that his teams should "know where the world is going"[7] and has focused on creating a profound sense of Microsoft's ability to intersect the world around them to develop solutions that customers are looking for. In Nadella's own words, "We must always ground our mission in both the world in which we live and the future we strive to create."

Setting your worldview collaboratively with your team and documenting it is fundamental to aligning your organization with an understanding of customer problems, opportunities, and challenges. Without it, many organizations believe they are on the same page as to what is happening in the world around them when they are, in fact, working under different assumptions.

Start by challenging your organization to build a concise worldview for your organization. It can be as short as three to five bullet points or a full document of several pages. To build it, ask your team members to write out what they would include and have them each present their views to your team. The PESTEL analysis discussed in chapter 6 is an excellent place to start.

Orient: Guiding by Questioning

The second takeaway is that leaders use their worldview to orient themselves and establish direction. They use orientation to build on their observations and start to identify options for action.

Leaders encourage orientation by questioning, not by directives. The orderly progression of the transformative questions in figure 3-5 on page 54 is a good place to start and used time and again to reorient themselves. In addition, leaders should ask other higher-level questions. What opportunities should we pursue? What trends can we take advantage of? What incredible benefits can we provide the customer? What are the challenges we face? What are the most impactful actions we can take?

Captain Boyd stated, "Orientation is the *Schwerpunkt* [German word for main focus]. It shapes the way we interact with the environment—hence orientation shapes the way we observe, the way we decide, the way we act."[8] It is designed to give you alternatives for closing the gap between where you are today and where you need to be to win.

Critically, there is a second element of orientation present in transformative leaders which causes them to question their own biases. While in its simplest form, the OODA Loop is a single loop learning model; the best leaders create a double loop model, as shown in figure 12-3. The second loop focuses on questioning your orientation viewpoint, cognitive biases, filters, decision-making models, historical observations, and cultural traditions.

Creating a second loop requires focused effort. As professor Herminia Ibarra of the London Business School stresses: "The paradox of change is that the only way to alter the way we think is by doing the very things our habitual thinking keeps us from doing."[9]

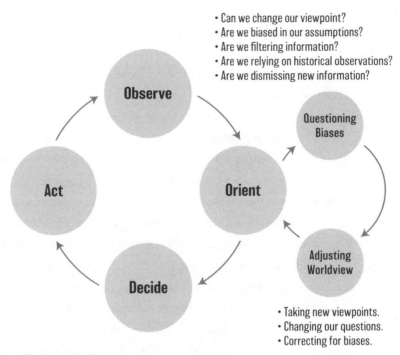

Figure 12-3: Double-Loop Model

This second loop signals us to question whether what we have believed before still applies, putting a check on confirmation bias, which is the tendency to search for, interpret, and focus on information to confirms one's preconceptions. This second loop of questioning our viewpoint is critical for us to process or accept change and overcome a desire to maintain status quo.

It's no coincidence that of the 22 companies that form the research core of this book, 16 were founded by someone who had no prior experience in the industry they entered. The lack of experience and open-mindedness contributed to them thinking outside of the existing industry framework, exhibiting a clear "beginner's mind."

However, this beginner's mind is not limited to outsiders only. Even those leaders with prior industry experience demonstrate high levels of curiosity and the ability to change their perspective.

In his study of superforecasters, Philip Tetlock, author and founder of the Good Judgment Project, found that the best forecasters were open-minded, curious, and, maybe most importantly, willing to update their beliefs and models frequently than others.[10]

Marc Benioff left Oracle to form Salesforce, fundamentally transforming the software industry by moving his solution to cloud-based delivery. Even now, as an insider, Benioff tries to maintain that same attitude, stating, "I try to cultivate the beginner's mind...I kind of try to let go of all the things that have ever happened so far in our industry, which is a lot of stuff, and just go, OK, what's going to happen right now?"[11]

Walmart founder Sam Walton was an industry insider who ran his own Ben Franklin stores but demonstrated a high level of curiosity, open-mindedness, and risk-taking. Walton demonstrated a clear propensity for experimentation and challenged convention. He told his employees and shareholders, "You can't just keep doing what works one time, everything around you is changing. To succeed, stay out in front of change."[12] He encouraged managers to test ideas locally in their stores and share their results in his regular Saturday morning meetings to decide if they should be implemented across the company.

Good orientation often comes from letting ideas bubble up from the team and experimenting with them, which is a benefit of identifying and agreeing upon a shared set of observations. Steve Jobs often brutally killed bad or even good ideas, sometimes to the embarrassment of the champion. But he also realized his role in cultivating good ones around the organization, saying, "When a good idea comes, part of my job is to move it around, just see what different people think, get people talking about it, argue with people about it, get ideas moving...get different people together to explore different aspects of it quietly, and, you know—just explore things."

Decide: Setting Clear Challenges

The third essential element is the ability to translate orientation to action by closing the gap between where you are and where you need to be. This is best done by periodically identifying and setting a small number of well-defined challenges for the organization to complete.

For most organizations, this is hard to do, primarily because they have developed processes, invested in assets, and accumulated knowledge to get good at what they do. Their focus is to improve on them. This is the classic dilemma of organizations: the allocation and time and effort between doing what you do better and learning new capabilities.

Andy Grove was a proponent of limited priorities that stood above the day-to-day of running the business, stating, "The art of management lies in the capacity to select from the many activities of seemingly comparable significance the one or two or three that provide leverage well beyond the others and concentrate on them."[13]

Setting the right priorities comes from first-principles thinking, an Aristotelian concept that seeks to break down a problem into its simplest elements to find a solution. Starting with a set of first principles, "a basic, foundational proposition or assumption that cannot be deduced from any other proposition or assumption," it involves breaking down the current situation to its most fundamental level and then rebuilding those principles back into something new. This thought process directs you to a set of basic assumptions that cannot be reduced any further and results in a set of the right actions to take.

Act: Creating a Sense of Urgency

Finally, the fourth element is to develop a clear sense of urgency that leads to action. This is the essence of creating a challenge-setting organization: creating a tempo of urgency. In the words of Jeff Bezos, it means cultivating the trait of high-velocity decision-making.

In a recent survey, 44 percent of CEOs surveyed expressed that they were concerned about the speed that technology was affecting their industry. Yet decision-making is often slow, waiting for the right data to make sure we get it right. On the other hand, the ethos of Amazon is not to wait, making a decision based on "70 percent of the information you wish you had."[14]

This type of decision-making is supported by a high tolerance for failure and a rapid return to observation mode to quickly assess and adjust when needed. "Staying in Day 1 requires you to experiment patiently, accept failures, plant seeds, protect saplings, and double down when you see customer delight...A customer-obsessed culture best creates the conditions where all of that can happen."[15]

Amazon reinforces a culture built around resilience and learning based on Bezos's delineation of type one and type two decisions. Type one decisions are significant and irreversible, deserving the time to methodically gather information and deserving deliberate study and consultation. In Bezos's words, they are one-way doors where "If you walk through and don't like what you see on the other side, you can't get back to where you were before." They take more time and consideration.

Type two decisions, on the other hand, are two-way doors that can be reversed. These types of decisions can and should be made by high-judgment individuals or small groups. Without this type of decision-making, according to Bezos, companies won't continue to succeed. Without this delineation and an acceptance that failures will occur, in his words, the result is "slowness, unthoughtful risk aversion, failure to experiment sufficiently, and consequently diminished invention."[16]

The Transformative Mindset: Creating and Sustaining an Innovative Organization

Ultimately, innovating to win is not about a single technology, product, or set of decisions. It is a continual process of observing, understanding and orienting to those observations, and prioritizing the right set of actions to achieve your goal. Creating a challenge-setting organization sets the tone and the pace for moving faster in the right direction and adapting when needed.

As we conclude, I am reminded of the words of researcher and author Jim Collins who said, "I believe that it is no harder to build something great than to build something good." Those words have stayed with me since I first read them and, from my own experience, I have found them to be true. I have seen companies take the thoughtful leadership path in which they find an opportunity for game-changing solutions and initiating transformative change. It's a difficult and challenging path, one that takes effort to lead and maintain. The alternative is to follow the same path as others, constrained by the same rules, and create similar products with maybe some minor advantages. That path is easier to tread, but much harder to successfully sustain once you are on it.

The vital truth is that transformative leadership, that focus on innovating to win, is about being on a path of discovery. It's not about knowing the answers but knowing to ask the right questions. It's not about getting it right the first time but enabling the process of experimentation and assessment. That opportunity is within reach of any leader in any organization who is willing to walk back through the door.

Concept to Action

1. What is our company's worldview?
2. Where are the greatest opportunities and challenges we face?
3. What priorities would we set to challenge our organization to move forward?
4. How can we increase the tempo of continuously challenging ourselves to action?

Acknowledgments

The central idea of *Transformative* was shaped by hundreds of conversations around boardroom tables, in conference rooms, and inside offices and offsites while formulating strategies and innovation plans in real organizations. It was forged in collaboration with many executives, leaders, and innovators whose insight and creativity have helped me think through the concepts as we collaborated to answer some form of the same basic question, "How do we win?" These concepts were often polished in deep discussions and admiring review of the companies that accomplished something truly special. Those individuals are too numerous to count, but without them, these thoughts wouldn't have come together in a logical form.

Many thanks to those who provided input and feedback along the way, including Josh Bernoff, whose uncompromising editing and feedback, along with steady encouragement made this a better book. This book also would not have been completed without the help of Naren Aryal, Nina Spahn, and Kristin Perry of Amplify Publishing. Thank you for believing in the topic and for your coaching and insight.

I want to express my appreciation to my friend and former academic advisor Stephen Roper at Warwick University who planted the seed for me to write this book many years ago. I also offer a special thanks to Greg Warnock whose detailed chapter-by-chapter review via voice messages was extraordinarily helpful. I would also like to acknowledge my gratitude to those I have learned from firsthand including the late Dr. Clayton Christensen, whose personal example was as significant as his thinking as well as Dr. Robert Burgleman of Stanford University and Jim Collins for their inspiration and guidance. I also express appreciation to author Whitney Johnson, whose support of diversity and inclusion immensely helped influence my perspective and the quality of the book.

Many thanks also to the many who provided input and feedback along the way, including Andrew Gaule, Rudy Parker, Kevin Suitor, Eric Perkins, Martin Sajon, Niall Anderson, Sean Housel, Kerry Faughnan, Sam Barnes, Mike Ray, Kelly Herrell, Lynn Deppe, Jamie Sumner, Uday Kumar, Chris Schoebinger, Nigel Harding, Tom Hogan, Bira De Lima, Laura Juanes, Andy Wilke, Glenn Fitton, Antony Warren, Eric Lundbohm, Terry Wetterman, Mel Shakir, Aaron Lapat, Nico Bolzan, Bryson Bort, Frederic Hanika, Yelibeth Méndez Pérez, Mandy Logan, Brad Rutledge, Janna Ayoub, Greg Grylis, Zulfe Ali, Andrew Miller, Miriam Leenane, Kurt Scherer, Sir Graeme Lamb, John Crown, Drew Podgorski, James Coats, Sir Iain Lobban, Mike Garland, Charlie McGarry, Jamie Lowther-Pinkerton, Allison McDaniel, Alessandro Tome, Paddy McGuiness, Oliver Graham-Yooli, Ken Leung, Kabir Merchant, Time Moss, Karl Sharman, Sandy O'Gorman, Musstanser Tinaulit, Tanveer Kathawalla, Justin James, Robert Galway, Sandeep Singh, Joanna Whittington, Janice Jafari, Greg Trimble, Edward David, Ryan Sanders, Kelly Budd, Lavanya Mahate, and Russel Smith. It's humbling to think that this work is better than I could have originally conceived because of all of you.

Endnotes

Chapter One: Walking Back through the Door

1   Gordon Moore, "Cramming more components onto integrated circuits," *Electronics*, Volume 38, Number 8, April 19, 1965. https://newsroom.intel.com/wp-content/uploads/sites/11/2018/05/moores-law-electronics.pdf

2   Andrew S. Grove, *Only the Paranoid Survive*, 89.

3   "Choreographing a Full Potential Transformation," *Bain Brief*, April 9, 2014. https://www.bain.com/insights/choreographing-a-full-potential-transformation/

4   T. K. Das and Bing-Sheng Teng, "Organizational Bias and Strategic Decision Processes: An Integrative Perspective," *Journal of Management Studies* (November 1999).

5   2015 Fortune 500 CEO Survey, June 2015.

Chapter Two: A Framework for Transformative Change

1   Jeffrey Immelt, "How I Remade GE," *Harvard Business Review* (September–October 2017). https://hbr.org/2017/09/how-i-remade-ge

2   Steve Blank, "Why GE's Jeff Immelt Lost His Job: Disruption and Activist Investors," *Harvard Business Review*, October 30, 2017. https://hbr.org/2017/10/why-ges-jeff-immelt-lost-his-job-disruption-and-activist-investors

3   Geoff Colvin, "What the Hell Happened at GE?" *Fortune Magazine*, May 24, 2018.

4   Alex Moazed, "Why GE Digital Failed," *Inc. Magazine*. https://www.inc.com/alex-moazed/why-ge-digital-didnt-make-it-big.html

5   Scott D. Anthony et. al, "Breaking Down the Barriers to Innovation," *Harvard Business Review*, November–December 2019.

6   "Disrupt and Grow," KPMG U.S. CEO Survey, 2017.

7   22nd Annual CEO Survey, Price Waterhouse Coopers, 2019.

8   "Jeremy Corbyn, Entrepreneur," *The Economist*, June 15, 2017. https://www.economist.com/britain/2017/06/15/jeremy-corbyn-entrepreneur

9   Michael DeGusta, "Are Smart Phones Spreading Faster than Any Technology in Human History?" *MIT Technology Review*, May 9, 2012. https://www.technologyreview.com/2012/05/09/186160/are-smart-phones-spreading-faster-than-any-technology-in-human-history/

10   Richard Foster and Sarah Kaplan, *Creative Destruction: Why Companies That Are Built to Last Underperform the Market—And How to Successfully Transform Them* (Crown Publishing, 2001).

11   Paul Leinwand and Cesare Mainardi, "The Fear of Disruption Can Be More Damaging than Actual Disruption," *Strategy + Business*, September 27, 2017. https://www.strategy-business.com/article/The-Fear-of-Disruption-Can-Be-More-Damaging-than-Actual-Disruption?

12   "Agile or Irrelevant, Redefining Resilience: 2019 Global CEO Outlook," KPMG.

13   "Worldwide Semi-annual Digital Transformation Spending Guide," *International Data Corp (IDC)*, December 15, 2017.

14   "Digital Transformation Initiative," *World Economic Forum*, January 2017.

15   IDC FutureScape: Worldwide Digital Transformation 2018 Predictions.

16   "Leading from the Front, CEO Perspectives on Business Transformation in the Digital Age," *The Economist Intelligence Unit*, September 2017. https://www.globalservices.bt.com/en/aboutus/news-press/digital-transformation-top-priority-for-ceos

17   Ibid.

18   Mark Raskino, "2018 CEO Survey: CIOs Should Guide Business Leaders Toward Deep-Discipline Digital Business," Gartner Research, April 6, 2018.

19   Brent B. Clark, Christopher Robert, and Steven A. Hampton, "The Technology Effect: How Perceptions of Technology Drive Excessive Optimism," *Journal of Business and Psychology* 31, no. 1 (2016), 87–102.

20   Michael Bucy, Stephen Hall, and Doug Yakola, "Transformation with a Capital T," *McKinsey Quarterly*, November 2016. https://www.mckinsey.com/business-functions/rts/our-insights/transformation-with-a-capital-t

21   Laurent-Pierre Baculard, Laurent Colombani, Virginie Flam, Ouriel Lancry and Elizabeth Spaulding, "Orchestrating a Successful Digital Transformation," *Bain Briefing,* November 22, 2017. https://www.bain.com/insights/orchestrating-a-successful-digital-transformation/

22   Ibid.

23   "The State of Digital Business Transformation," IDC 2018 Digital Business Survey.

24   "Leading from the Front: CEO Perspectives on Business Transformation in the Digital Age," British Telecom Report, 2017.

25   "Are Business Leaders Caught in a Confidence Bubble?" Innosight Survey, June 2017.

26   "Plotting the Platform," IBM Global C-Suite Study, 19th Edition, 2019.

27   "Are Business Leaders Caught in a Confidence Bubble?" Innosight Survey, June 2017.

28	Jacques Bughin and Nicolas van Zeebroeck, "The Best Response to Digital Disruption," *MIT Sloan Management Review* 9 (May 2017). https://sloanreview.mit.edu/article/the-right-response-to-digital-disruption/

29	"Competing in 2020: Winners and Losers in the Digital Economy," *Harvard Business Review and Microsoft*, 2017. https://hbr.org/sponsored/2017/04/competing-in-2020-winners-and-losers-in-the-digital-economy

30	PWC 23rd Annual Global CEO Survey, 2020.

31	John Lewis Gaddis, *On Grand Strategy* (Penguin Press, 2018).

32	Jacques Bughin, Laura LaBerge, and Anette Mellbye, "The Case for Digital Reinvention," *McKinsey Quarter*, February 2017. https://www.mckinsey.com/business-functions/mckinsey-digital/our-insights/the-case-for-digital-reinvention

33	Patrick Viguerie and Caroline Thompson, "The Faster They Fall," *Harvard Business Review*, March 2005. https://hbr.org/2005/03/the-faster-they-fall

Chapter Three: Building Category-Creating Solutions

1	Marvin B. Lieberman and David B. Montgomery, "First-Mover Advantages," *Strategic Management Journal* (Summer 1988): 48–51.

2	Peter Golder and Gerard Tellis, "Pioneer Advantage: Marketing Logic or Marketing Legend?" *Journal of Marketing Research*, 30, no. 2 (1993): 158–170.

3	Joseph Schumpeter, *Capitalism, Socialism, and Democracy* (Harper and Brothers, 1942): 42.

4	Eddie Yoon, and Linda Deeken, "Why It Pays to Be a Category Creator," *Harvard Business Review*, March 2013. https://hbr.org/2013/03/why-it-pays-to-be-a-category-creator

5	Tim Harford, "Why Big Companies Squander Good Ideas," *FT Undercover Economist*, September 6, 2018. https://www.ft.com/content/3c1ab748-b09b-11e8-8d14-6f049d06439c

6	Claire Linnane, MarketWatch, "Procter & Gamble's Gillette razor business dinged by online shave clubs," April 27, 2017. https://www.marketwatch.com/story/procter-gambles-gillette-razor-business-dinged-by-online-shave-clubs-2017-04-26

7	"Gillette Spends $750 Million to Make Mach 3 Huge Covert Operation for New Production Line of Three-Blade Razor," *The Boston Globe*, August 17, 1998.

8	Tomio Geron and Rolfe Winkler, "After Early Skepticism, Dollar Shave Club's Investors Generate Big Returns," *Wall Street Journal*, July 20, 2016.

9	Jack Neff, "Dollar Shave Club Claims to Top Schick as No. 2 Razor Cartridge," *Ad Age*, September 8, 2015.

10	Geoff Colvin and Ryan Derousseau, "Power Sheet: How P&G Missed Out on Dollar Shave Club's Rise," *Fortune Magazine*, July 21, 2016.

11	Rashmi Bansal, *Arvind Kejriwal: Into that Heaven of Freedom* (Westland Press, 2013).

12	"A Marketplace Without Boundaries? Responding to Disruption," 18th Annual PWC CEO Survey, 2015.

Chapter Four: Generating Unique Customer Outcomes

1   Apple 1997 Worldwide Developers Conference.

2   Ibid.

3   See Amazon's Leadership Principles.

4   Jeff Bezos, Letter to Amazon shareholders, 2016. https://www.aboutamazon.com/news/company-news/2016-letter-to-shareholders

5   Manmohan Gupta, "Nokia CEO Ended his Speech Saying We didn't do Anything Wrong." https://www.linkedin.com/pulse/nokia-ceo-ended-his-speech-saying-we-didnt-do-anything-manmohan-gupta/

6   Ellis Hamburger, Bloomberg, "The iPhone's impact will be minimal. It will only appeal to 'a few gadget freaks.' Nokia and Motorola haven't a care in the world." https://www.businessinsider.com/iphone-predictions-from-2007-2012-6#bloomberg-the-iphones-impact-will-be-minimal-it-will-only-appeal-to-a-few-gadget-freaks-nokia-and-motorola-havent-a-care-in-the-world-1

7   Charlie Sorel, "More Ballmer Madness: 'There's No Chance that the iPhone is Going to Get any Significant Market Share.'" May 1, 2007. https://www.wired.com/2007/05/more-ballmer-ma/

8   Dan Farber, "We Want to Reinvent the Phone. What's the Killer App?" *Between the Lines, ZD Net*, January 9, 2007.

9   Search Engine Market Share Worldwide, April 2020-April 2021. https://gs.statcounter.com/search-engine-market-share

10 William C. Taylor, *Practically Radical* (Harper Collins, 2011).

11 Daniel G. Goldstein and Dominique C. Goldstein, "Profiting from the Long Tail," *Harvard Business Review*, June 2006.

12 "Convenience Stores Sales, Profits Edged Higher in 2017," National Association of Convenience Stores report, April 11, 2018.

Chapter Five: Aligning and Investing in Capabilities

1   "Building Organizational Capabilities: McKinsey Global Survey Results," *McKinsey and Company*, March 2010.

2   Ibid.

3   "Building Organizational Capabilities: McKinsey Global Survey Results," March 2010.

4   Alexis C. Madrigal, "Hastings's Hasty Move: Netflix Splits in Two, Renames DVD Business," *The Atlantic*, September 9, 2011.

5   Erik Gruenwedel, "Morgan Stanley: Netflix Tops in Original Programming," *Media Play News*, May 23, 2018.

6   "Competing on Capabilities: The New Rules of Corporate Strategy," *Harvard Business Review*, March–April 1992.

Chapter Six: Rethinking and Reframing Your Industry

1   Many thanks to Malcolm Gladwell, whose book *David and Goliath* inspired the reexamination of this ageless story.

2   Anders Pehrsson, "Barriers to Entry and Market Strategy: A Literature Review and a Proposed Model," *European Business Review,* January 16, 2019.

3   Nicolas Evans, "Digital business ecosystems and platforms: 5 new rules for innovators," CIO Magazine, March 21, 2016. https://www.cio.com/article/3045385/digital-business-ecosystems-and-platforms-5-new-rules-for-innovators.html

4   Gary Wolf, "Steve Jobs: The Next Insanely Great Thing," *Wired Magazine*, February 1, 1996.

Section III: Innovating to Win: Scaling to Market Leadership

1   "Beating the Odds in Market Entry," *McKinsey Quarterly*, November 2005.

2   Helen Salavou et al., "Organisational Innovation in SMEs: The Importance of Strategic Orientation and Competitive Structure," *European Journal of Marketing* (September 2004). Vol. 38 No. 9/10, 1091-1112.

Chapter Seven: Democratizing and Simplifying

1   Oxford English Dictionary.

2   Henry Ford, *My Life and Work*, (Doubleday, Page, & Company, 1923): 73.

3   "Ryanair heads Europe's top 20 airline groups by pax 2019," CAPA Centre for Aviation, January 22, 2020. https://centreforaviation.com/analysis/reports/ryanair-heads-europes-top-20-airline-groups-by-pax-2019-510111

4   Farhad Manjoo, "Little-Known Redbox Proves the Power of In-Between Technology," *Fast Company*, July 1, 2009. https://www.fastcompany.com/1297927/little-known-redbox-proves-power-between-technology

5   "Moore's Law: Fun Facts," *Intel*. https://www.intel.com/content/www/us/en/history/history-moores-law-fun-facts-factsheet.html

6   "Amazon's Audible.com Sees Ten-Fold Increase in Audiobook Production," *Daily News*, January 31, 2013.

7   Democratic Design. https://www.ikea.com.hk/en/about/democratic-design/https//www.ikea.com.hkabout/democratic-design/undefined

8   Walter Isaacson, "How Steve Jobs' Love of Simplicity Fueled a Design Revolution." *Smithsonian Magazine*, September 2012. https://www.smithsonianmag.com/arts-culture/how-steve-jobs-love-of-simplicity-fueled-a-design-revolution-23868877/

9   Ibid.

10 "Amazon Web Services Launches," Press Release, March 14, 2006. https://press.aboutamazon.com/news-releases/news-release-details/amazon-web-services-launches-amazon-s3-simple-storage-service

11 "FACT: There Are 80,000 Ways to Drink a Starbucks Beverage," Huffington Post, April 3, 2014.

12 Many thanks to Sean Durham, who explains this language framework so well at www.dubberly.com/articles/starbucks-drink-platform.html.

13 "50+ Netflix statistics & Facts that Define the Company's Dominance in 2020," *Comparitech.com*, November 10, 2020.

14 Carlos A. Gomez-Uribe and Neil Hunt, "The Netflix Recommender System: Algorithms, Business Value, and Innovation," *ACM Transactions on Management Information Systems*, December 2015.

15 Janko Roettgers, "Netflix Spends $150 million on Content Recommendations Every Year, *Gigaom*, October 9, 2014.

16 Carlos A. Gomez-Uribe and Neil Hunt, "The Netflix Recommender System: Algorithms, Business Value, and Innovation," *ACM Transactions on Management Information Systems*, December 2015.

Chapter Eight: New-Customer Focusing and Model Building

1 "The Top 20 Reasons Startups Fail," *CB Insights*, February 2, 2018.

2 Sam Walton with John Huey, *Sam Walton: Made in America* (Bantam Books, 1993): 249.

3 John Furrier, "Andy Jassy of Amazon Web Service (AWS) and His Trillion Dollar Cloud Ambition," *Forbes Magazine*, January 28, 2015. https://www.forbes.com/sites/siliconangle/2015/01/28/andy-jassy-aws-trillion-dollar-cloud-ambition/?sh=36c79b32321e

4 Eddie Yoon, Christopher Lochhead, and Nicolas Cole, "The Difference Between a First Mover and a Category Creator," *Harvard Business School*, November 21, 2019.

5 "Cumulative Apple App Store Earnings of Mobile App Developers as of January 2020," www.statistica.com

6 Zhenya Lindgardt and Margaret Ayers, "Driving Growth with Business Model Innovation," *Boston Consulting Group*, October 8, 2014.

7 "The Eight Essentials of Innovation," *McKinsey Quarterly*, April 2015.

8 "Expanding the Innovation Horizon," the Global CEO Survey, IBM Global Services, 2006.

Chapter Nine: Recombining and Rule Breaking

1 Philip Elmer-Dewitt, "Raw Footage: Larry Tesler on Steve Jobs' Visit to Xerox PARC," *Fortune Magazine*, August 24, 2014.

2 Carmine Gallo, "How Starbucks CEO Howard Schultz Inspired Us to Dream Bigger," *Fortune Magazine*, December 2, 2016.

3 Sarah Todd, "The Steve Jobs Speech that Made Silicon Valley Obsessed with Pirates," *Quartz*, October 22, 2019.

4 Laura Roberts, "Ryanair: How Michael O'Leary Perfected Budget Flying," *The Telegraph*, July 2, 2010.

5 Susan Ager, "As Ringling Ends Circus, See Where Its Elephants Retired," *National Geographic*, September 17, 2017.

6 Barrett Ersek, Eileen Weisenbach Keller, and John Mullins, "Break Your Industry's Bottlenecks," *Harvard Business Review*, June–July 2015.

7 Carla Johnson, *RE:Think Innovation* (Morgan James Publishing, 2021).

8 Search for the "Stanford Prison Experiment" and research Korean Air pilots as examples.

Chapter Ten: Defining a Path to Differentiation

1 GroupM Worldwide Media Forecast, June 13, 2019.

2 Theodore Levitt, *The Marketing Imagination* (New York: Free Press, 1986).

3 Andrew S. Grove, *High Output Management* (Vintage Press, 1995).

Chapter Eleven: Building a Culture That Feeds Strategy

1 Peter Cohan, "Netflix's Reed Hastings Is the Master Of Adaptation," *Forbes Magazine*, October 22, 2013.

2 Reid Hoffman, "Culture Shock: Interview with Reed Hastings," Masters of Scale podcast, 2018.

3 Anne Quito, "Netflix's CEO says there are months when he doesn't have to make a single decision," *Quartz*, April 19, 2018.

4 D. Ravasi and M. Schultz, "Responding to Organizational Identity Threats: Exploring the Role of Organizational Culture," *Academy of Management Journal* (2006), Vol. 49, No. 3, 433–458.

5 Netflix Culture Deck. https://jobs.netflix.com/culture

6 Sam Walton and John Huey, *Sam Walton: Made in America* (Bantam Books): 216.

7 "Culture Shock," Masters of Scale Interview with Reed Hastings, https://mastersofscale.com/reed-hastings-culture-shock/

8 John P. Kotter and James L. Heskett, *Corporate Culture and Performance* (New York: The Free Press, 1992).

9 Karsten Jonsen, Charles Galunic, John Weeks and Tania Braga, "Evaluating Espoused Values: Does Articulating Values Pay Off?" *European Management Journal* (October 2015).

10 Rajesh Chandy, Gerard Tellis, and Jaideep Prabhu, "Corporate Culture Is Most Important Factor in Driving Innovation," *University of Minnesota, Science News, ScienceDaily*, November 18, 2008.

11 Jeff Bezos, Letter to Amazon Shareholders, 2017.

12 Jim Harter, "Dismal Employee Engagement Is a Sign of Global Mismanagement," Gallup Blog. https://www.gallup.com/workplace/231668/dismal-employee-engagement-sign-global-mismanagement.aspx

13 Right Management Global Survey, 2009.

14 Luciana Paulise, "This Is How Tony Hsieh Built an Empire Driven by Company Culture," *Fortune Magazine*, November 30, 2020.

15 Tony Hsieh, *Delivering Happiness: A Path to Profits, Passion, and Purpose.* (Grand Central Publishing, 2010): 137.

16 "PwC's 21st CEO Survey," Price Waterhouse Coopers, 2018.

17 Megan Oliver, "Culture and Hyper Growth: Ron Storn on Keeping Lyft's Values Alive," *Human Synergistics*, July 18, 2017.

18 Howard Schultz, *Pour Your Heart Into It: How Starbucks Built a Company One Cup at a Time* (Hachette Press, 1999).

19 "How Andy Jassy Plans to Keep Amazon Web Services on Top of the Cloud," *Forbes Magazine*, November 27, 2017.

20 Gary Wolf, "Steve Jobs: The Next Insanely Great Thing," *Wired Magazine*, February 1, 1996.

21 Katzenbach Center Global Cultural Study, 2018. https://www.strategyand.pwc.com/gx/en/insights/2018/global-culture-survey.html

22 "Board Leadership in Corporate Culture: European Report 2017," *Mazars*.

23 "Survey: 68 percent of CEOs Admit They Weren't Fully Prepared for the Job," Egon Zehnder Survey, July 20, 2018.

24 Katzenbach Center Global Cultural Study, 2018. https://www.strategyand.pwc.com/gx/en/insights/2018/global-culture-survey.html

25 John Kotter, *Leading Change* (Harvard Business Review Press, 1996): 90–91.

Chapter Twelve: Developing a Challenge-Setting Organization

1 Andrew S. Grove, *Only the Paranoid Survive* (Profile Books, 1988): 51.

2 Ray Kurzweil, "After the Singularity: A Talk with Ray Kurzweil," March 27, 2002. https://www.kurzweilai.net/after-the-singularity-a-talk-with-ray-kurzweil

3 Amazon Shareholder Letter, 2016.

4 Harry Hillaker, "John Boyd, USAF Retired, Father of the F16," *Code One*, July 1997.

5 Sheryl Sandberg and Adam Grant, *Option B* (Random House, 2019).

6 David Yaden et al., "The Overview Effect: Awe and Self-Transcendent Experience in Space Flight," *Psychology of Consciousness: Theory, Research, and Practice*, 2016.

7 Interview with Adobe CEO Shantanu Narayen, Adobe Summit, March 2019.

8 John Boyd, Organic Design for Command and Control, https://static1.squarespace.com/static/58a3add7e3df28d9fbff4501/t/58a4a2c4ff7c504b72043691/1487184582151/Organic+Design+for+C2_May+1987.pdf

9   Herminia Ibarra, *Act Like a Leader, Think Like a Leader* (Harvard Business Review Press, 2015).

10 Philip E. Tetlock and Dan Gardner, *Superforecasting: The Art and Science of Prediction* (Crown, 2015).

11 "How Salesforce CEO Marc Benioff Innovates," *Wall Street Journal* Video, April 20, 2016. https://www.wsj.com/video/how-salesforce-ceo-marc-benioff-innovates/CC82DC0F-3A6A-46F8-B341-93A09D6BB876.html

12 "Walmart Out Front," Walmart Shareholders' Meeting 2006, https://corporate.walmart.com/_news_/executive-viewpoints/walmart-out-in-front

13 Andrew S. Grove, *High-Output Management* (Vintage Press, 1995): 58.

14 Jeff Bezos, Amazon Shareholder Letter, 2016.

15 Ibid.

16 Ibid.